NAZANIN AFSHIN-JAM is an award-winning international human rights and democracy activist, a public speaker and the co-founder and president of the organization Stop Child Executions. She is a former Miss World Canada, singer/songwriter and director on the board of the Canadian Race Relations Foundation. Born in Iran and raised in Vancouver, Nazanin holds a bachelor's degree in international relations and political science, and a master's degree in diplomacy with a concentration in international conflict management. She splits her time between Ottawa, New Glasgow and Paris. Visit her online at Nazanin.ca.

SUSAN McCLELLAND is a feature writer, an investigative journalist and the author of *The Bite of the Mango*, which was published to both literary and popular acclaim in more than twenty-five countries. McClelland has won numerous national and international awards for her work, including two Amnesty International Media Awards for excellence in human rights reporting. Her writing has appeared in such publications as *The Globe and Mail*, *The Guardian*, *Maclean's*, *Chatelaine* and *The Walrus*. McClelland is based in Toronto and Scotland. Visit her online at www.susanmcclelland.com.

THE TALE OF TWO NAZANINS

The TALE *of*
TWO NAZANINS

A Teenager on Death Row in Iran and the Canadian Who Vowed to Save Her

Nazanin Afshin-Jam
and Susan McClelland

HarperCollins*PublishersLtd*

The Tale of Two Nazanins
Copyright © 2012 by Nazanin Afshin-Jam
and Susan McClelland. All rights reserved.

Published by HarperCollins Publishers Ltd

First edition

This book is largely based on interviews with Nazanin Fatehi, as well as information
from those who knew her or from the Iranian Kurdish community, to which she belonged.
In some cases, scenes, traits and events, particularly those dealing with Nazanin Fatehi's
early life, have been created to help tell the story.

HarperCollins books may be purchased for educational, business, or sales
promotional use through our Special Markets Department.

HarperCollins Publishers Ltd
2 Bloor Street East, 20th Floor
Toronto, Ontario, Canada
M4W 1A8

www.harpercollins.ca

Library and Archives Canada Cataloguing in Publication
information is available upon request

ISBN 978-1-55468-972-9

Photo of Nazanin Afshin-Jam on jacket and page i by Chris Haylett
Jacket photo of Nazanin Fatehi courtesy Nazanin Afshin-Jam
Photo of Susan McClelland on page i by Simon Tanenbaum

Printed and bound in the United States
RRD 9 8 7 6 5 4 3 2 1

Little children, let us not love in word or talk
but in deed and in truth.
JOHN 3:18

Save those who persevere and do good works.
For them is forgiveness and a great reward.
QUR'AN 11:11

Turn yourself not away from three best things:
Good Thoughts, Good Words and Good Deeds.
ZOROASTER

If I am not for myself, who will be for me?
But if I am only for myself, who am I? If not now, when?
HILLEL THE ELDER, PIRKE AVOT 1:14

NAZANIN AFSHIN-JAM

February 2006, Vancouver

=====

I was sitting at the computer desk, wedged in between the kitchen and the dining room in the downtown Vancouver condominium belonging to my sister and her husband. The aromas of oregano and basil from the bolognese sauce simmering on the stove drifted through the rooms, with their high ceilings, hardwood floors and modern furniture.

While the garlic bread was baking and they were chopping vegetables for the Greek salad, I checked my emails for the first time in two days. I scrolled down the messages in my inbox. I was receiving more than a hundred messages a day from people I had met when travelling as part of my duties for Miss World, as well as from complete strangers who had heard about me. Many of these emails were from people in Iran or Iranians in exile congratulating me on my pageant success and philanthropy; many others sought my help with one charity or another or endorsements for their products.

Normally I enjoyed reading these emails and helping connect people who could help each other. But over the past month, I had been feeling more and more fatigued. "There are so many emails and so many people wanting things, I don't know where to start," I mumbled.

"What's that?" my sister, Naz, called from the kitchen. (Our similar names had often led to confusion.)

"I don't know how to reply to all these people," I answered. "A student in Iran wants money for his university books; a German cosmetic company wants me to be the face of their products; a young woman wants tips on how to model and win a teen pageant; and a man in Iran wants help in assisting children burned during a school fire."

The truth was, I had no hours left in my days. I tried to concentrate my time on the emails that were most urgent and reply to the rest, as best I could, with lines such as "While I understand your plight, I just do not have the time to fully dedicate to helping you properly." I would then connect them with people I knew who might be able to help them. But now I was feeling so overwhelmed that I couldn't keep up with the pace of emails, what with my already jam-packed schedule and trying to write songs for the album I was making with my brother-in-law Peter.

"Don't be so frustrated, Nini," my sister replied from the kitchen, using the Persian word for "baby," which is the nickname my entire family uses for me. "Stop doing that for a while and relax. Dinner will be ready soon."

I started to pull myself away from the computer, but just then my email dinged, indicating a new message.

The subject line said: YOUR HELP URGENTLY NEEDED.

As I read the email, I found myself entirely present in the moment, fully aware of the sounds coming from the kitchen—the dripping of the tap and the ticking of the clock on the wall above the stove. I could feel, and hear, my inhalations and exhalations.

"What?" I whispered as I leaned into the computer and read the email a second time.

"What is it, another stalker?" Naz asked, pulling up a chair to sit beside me. She was referring to some of the men who had been writing me since I had been named first runner-up at Miss World. Men of all ages, shapes and sizes sent their photos and resumés to me, as if through a dating service. Some had mailed me gifts, paintings and poems. I knew these men were harmless, but part of me was afraid that one might come along who wasn't.

One of these men, for example, had sent me more than a thousand emails about his personal life, which was in disarray, and pleaded with me to be with him as the solution to his troubles. He threatened that if I didn't give in to his demands, he would hurt me. I reported him to the police after he had cc'd me on emails he had sent applying for jobs in Vancouver. Since he lived in California, the police issued a notice to the Canada Border Services Agency, so that if he ever tried to enter Canada, his presence would be noted.

"No, no stalkers," I said, pointing to the screen. "Look at this."

Peter leaned over me and read the message out loud:

Dear Nazanin,

   A teenager, with the same name as you, is desperately in need of your help. The Islamic Republic of Iran has condemned her to death after she stabbed a man who was attempting to rape her. Can you help?

   Sincerely, Vincent

Peter sighed. "She's a girl who is on death row in a prison in Iran," he said. "And you are a girl here in Vancouver, Canada. There's nothing you can do. She's probably already dead."

I glared at him. "I can't ignore this!"

"You don't know anything about this girl," Naz butted in. "What if this is a hoax? What if this man Vincent is just trying to get close to you . . . like the stalkers?"

"I'll research it to see if this is true—if this girl, Nazanin, really exists," I said.

"When are you going to have the time for that?" Peter asked. "You have your voice lessons in the morning, we're writing songs in the afternoon and you're in the recording studio until nine or ten at night."

"I have to do something, Peter," I said sternly.

All three of us gazed again at the computer screen. "I didn't even know Iran executed teenagers," I eventually whispered. "I know nothing about Iran's prisons except . . ."

"Baba's story," Naz finished my sentence. She was referring to our father, Afshin.

"If this girl Nazanin exists, she needs a lawyer, not you," Peter said.

"Yes," I said softly. "But maybe I can help her get one. Let me at least look into it."

"Nini." Naz spun me around in my swivel chair so that I was looking into her black eyes.

"Naz," I started to protest, thinking that she was about to tell me all the reasons not to take on this challenge.

Instead, she put her hand in the air and told me to shush. "I know you always follow your heart, so see what you can find out about this girl, but try not to let your career fall behind. And be careful. Be very careful."

"Why?" I asked.

"Because it is one thing for you to raise money to help orphans and earthquake survivors back in Iran. It is a completely new and dangerous world you will be entering if you start condemning the fundamentalist government in Tehran. You will be slandered, at the least, and risk your own life, at the most," she said sharply.

THAT EVENING, all I could think about was Vincent's email. Doubts crept in. I had heard many stories about Iranian political dissidents. Rumours abounded that the regime had secret agents in many cities where there were large concentrations of Iranian immigrants and refugees. Certain outspoken activists said these spies followed them. Some opponents of the Iranian regime had even been killed in the West, their deaths made to look like accidents or suicides. There was, for instance, the case of Shapour Bakhtiar, the last prime minister of Iran under the shah, who was murdered in Paris by assassins sent by the regime. Assassins also killed three

Iranian Kurdish leaders in Berlin at the Mykonos Restaurant in September 1992.

I shuddered at the thought. Naz was a mom, and she and Peter had a comfortable life, as did my parents, Afshin and Jaleh, after years of hard work. The last thing any of my family needed was me involved in politics, potentially threatening the safety and security my father had worked very hard to achieve since leaving Iran after nearly being killed himself by regime officials.

"So it is settled," I said to Peter and Naz before I left that night. "I will email Vincent in the morning and say I can't help."

BEFORE I WENT TO BED, after I had put on a pair of warm fuzzy slippers and a housecoat, I peeked out from the crack in the curtains at the twinkling lights of the city below. *I wonder what Nazanin in Iran is looking at.*

I closed my eyes and summoned my only memory of Iran. I was just a year old, so my memory was more one of snapshots of images and feelings than anything else. I can see a house with bright yellow flowers out front. I can feel the heat of the sun on my face. I can hear the sound of water lapping up against something hard—my father told me when I was a child after I had recounted this memory to him that it must have been the water in the swimming pool in the backyard. It was a big house, three storeys, and belonged to my maternal grandparents. When I think of this house, I think of laughter, comfort and happiness. When I think of this house, I think of Iran.

My mind drifted next to my fourth year of university. I was a volunteer global youth educator for the Red Cross. I led workshops in an attempt to get young people engaged in issues related to poverty and disease, children affected by war, the humanitarian crisis of land mines, and natural disasters. I always ended my talks with two questions: "If not now, then when? If not you, then who?"

"Exactly!" I now whispered to myself. "If I don't do something for Nazanin, who will?" So many people seem to think that some-one else will do something—whether it be end poverty, end war or even simply end the suffering of the homeless right below me on the streets of Vancouver. But few people actually step up to the plate and act. Women have been raped in broad daylight—from the slums of Calcutta to the bushes along Lake Kivu in the Democratic Republic of Congo to the streets of New York City—and no one intervenes, either out of fear or passivity—they assume someone else will do something. I had come to appreciate that the voices and positive actions of common people united in a goal to end strife hold the most power for change in the world. But simultaneously, the greatest problems in the world are fuelled by the inactivity of these people when they become bystanders.

There are two types of people in this world: those who dare to dream, create and make history, and those who wait around, con-sume and let life happen to them. I do not want to be the latter, the bystander. I do not want to be the one who throws my hands up in the air in surrender. I want to try to create positive outcomes and make change for the better.

I felt something stir deep inside me, some deep connection to this young woman with the same name as me. It was as if I had been here before, faced with this same decision. *What if it was me? Who would come to my help?*

The alarm clock flashed 11:11. I heard my mother's voice in my head offering me the advice she had given since I was a young child. It was a quote from Albert Einstein: "The world is a dangerous place, not because of those who do evil, but because of those who look on and do nothing."

Whenever I saw the digits 11:11, I felt that God was giving me the message that I was on the right path.

I stepped back from the window, my view of downtown Van-couver and my memories. "I'm going to do it," I said. "I will help Nazanin."

CHAPTER 1

NAZANIN AFSHIN-JAM

November 2003, Hong Kong and China

———

I took a deep breath as the flight attendant announced that the airplane would be soon starting its descent to Hong Kong International Airport. I had been in the air now for thirteen hours. I had tried to eat, tried to sleep, but my nerves hadn't let me do either. I was excited and absolutely petrified.

I stood up, stretched my legs and then headed to the washroom to change out of my track suit and into a tailored suit for arrival. A beautiful young woman wearing a similar track suit, also with a change of clothes in her hands, was waiting in line for the washroom. We looked at each other and smiled.

"Are you going to a competition in Hong Kong?" I asked her.

"Yes," she replied. "I was going to ask you the same thing. I'm Joyceline Montero, Miss Puerto Rico, birthplace of Ricky Martin, and I'm on my way to Miss World."

"Nazanin Afshin-Jam," I replied. "I'm from Canada, birthplace of hockey, toques, sirop d'érable and more hockey."

We both laughed. Good, I thought, someone travelling for the same reason as I was, and she was nice. Joyceline told me she had been flying for more than twenty-four hours. She had started out in San Juan, first stopping over in New York and then Vancouver, where she boarded the flight to Hong Kong. "Even before I left," she explained, "my life was non-stop—dress fittings, workouts and media interviews. I've been at this for months. I'm going to pass out from exhaustion on arrival."

"It's been busy for me too, except I just won my national competition two weeks ago, so I've been in a frenzy getting ready for this."

"Wow, two weeks!" she exclaimed. "Most of the women have an entire year to prepare for Miss World."

On October 22, 2003, I had become Miss Canada. A Canadian designer originally from Trinidad named Bobby Ackbarali had taken me under his wing to help me prepare for the world competition. He designed and custom-tailored several beautiful and unique evening gowns for me, all the while mentoring me. Over breakfast Bobby would recount his life in Trinidad, where he made costumes for his nation's largest carnivals and gowns for the beauty pageants. Over lunch, he would tell me about the other competitors I'd be meeting at Miss World. "Those from the Philippines, India, Venezuela, South Africa and a few other countries receive big sponsorships from jewellers and clothing designers. Even car manufacturers gift them expensive sports cars," he said in his Trinidadian accent. "They rehearse for months how to walk, how to stand and how to answer questions. In this industry, we call these ladies 'pageant Patties.' But don't let the support they get versus the lack of support you get hold you back. I've been around this business for thirty-five years. You've got something. I think you might be able to bring home the crown."

Joyceline exited the washroom, giving me a hug before returning to her seat. "Good luck," she said. "I hope we get some sleep soon. Your family must be so proud!"

"They are," I said, smiling.

As THE FLIGHT ATTENDANTS prepared for landing, I leaned my forehead against the windowpane. Before flying to Hong Kong, I had spent a week with my family in Vancouver. My sister, Naz, accompanied me as I travelled from workouts with my personal trainer to media interviews in advance of the pageant. Naz reminded me that two billion viewers would be watching me on television at Miss World. "And I will be one of them," she said, rubbing her stomach. Naz had just found out she was pregnant and was suffering from morning sickness. "I'll be recording it for the baby. You'll be her role model, not because of your beauty but because of your intelligence and because you have always been a hard worker and leader."

As our plane continued its descent, I smiled thinking of Naz and my soon-to-be niece. I thought of my boyfriend, James, and our long walk with our dogs, Chutney, Hershey and Paprika, before I left Vancouver; I pictured my mother, Jaleh, who when I left for the airport was painting my portrait in acrylics on canvas, with my Persian cat, Shahtoosh, watching her every brush stroke, and my father, Afshin, who pulled me into his big arms and kissed me goodbye. I could still smell his scent of Drakkar Noir on my scarf.

I felt a comforting warmth move through me as I realized that what had given me the confidence to do all that I had so far, at age twenty-four, was the support and love I have from my family and friends.

I'm ready for Miss World, I said to myself.

My eyes scanned the lobby of Hong Kong's Mandarin Oriental hotel. The chandeliers swayed ever so slightly from the energy moving around me. The scents of Chanel and Dior and the music of Harry Connick Jr. filled the reception area, where various competitors, most of whom towered over my own five feet nine inches, were busy talking to one another. Despite never having met each other, the South American winners hugged each other like long-lost friends. They were definitely the loudest in the room. Watching them, I thought, *I'm at a speed-talking competition, not Miss World*.

I looked over to the lobby's revolving doors just in time to see a beautiful tanned brunette enter the hotel. She was wearing a glittery white sash on which her country's name, Venezuela, was embroidered in gold thread. A valet pushing a trolley piled high with her suitcases and garment bags followed her.

"Bobby is right," I murmured, looking down at my two battered suitcases with stickers of the Canadian flag slapped on the sides. "These other women seem way more prepared than I am."

"What did you say?" came a voice from behind me.

I turned quickly and found myself looking into the sparkling brown eyes of a dark-haired woman. She, like me, was not wearing her country's sash. "I'm Irna Smaka, from Bosnia-Herzegovina," she said, shaking my hand.

"I'm Nazanin Afshin-Jam."

"Are you Persian?" she asked.

"Yes," I replied. "Born in Tehran, raised in Vancouver, Canada. How did you know?"

"By your name," she replied. "*Man Farsi harf meezanam*," she said in a Slavic-Persian accent. "I took Persian language classes in high school. What do you do?" she then asked me.

"Three months ago I let my acting agent know that I had to take a break from acting because I was going to be starting an intensive two-year program in broadcast journalism, hoping one day to make a difference by reporting from conflict zones or other areas in need of help," I replied. "What about you?"

"Well, I am studying law and want to help the people in my country still struggling from the conflict. Do you know anything about our war?"

"Of course—I studied it at school," I said. "I will never forget a documentary I saw called *Romeo and Juliet in Sarajevo*. I did a bachelor's degree in international relations and political science. I also volunteered for a few years with the Red Cross," I told her. "My job was to get high school and university students involved in humanitarian projects. I'm here . . ." I paused, thinking of how comfortable I felt talking to Miss Bosnia-Herzegovina despite having never met her before. "I'm here because while I love speaking to students, I reach only about thirty of them at a time, yet the problems of the world are so monumental."

"I hear it's very difficult to get North American students engaged in world issues. But in my country, students are literally dying to be involved. It seems to me that the public in your part of the world only ever listens to famous people," she said.

"I know." I sighed. "They listen to sports stars and celebrities. That's why I entered the Miss Canada competition. My goal is to gain some kind of public profile, so that I have a stronger platform for my messages, to reach more people. When I learned about Miss World and its motto, 'Beauty with a Purpose,' and that it had raised $250 million for children's charities, I thought this would be a great way to increase my humanitarian efforts."

"I agree," she said. "Miss Universe is trying to find the most beautiful woman in the world. Miss World is trying to find the well-rounded woman who will be a great ambassador for the charities the organization supports."

AFTER GETTING THE KEY CARD, I headed to my room. My room-mate hadn't checked in yet. I unpacked, changed into a pair of silk pyjamas my mother had snuck into my suitcase in the hope that they would replace my worn flannel checkered pyjamas and then plugged in my laptop to check my emails.

There were about fifty just from Naz, who was forwarding me messages from my website, almost all from fans wishing me good luck at Miss World. Then my pulse quickened as I read three emails from women criticizing me for taking part in the competition. "You are objectifying women and using your body and beauty to exploit others and get what you want," one wrote.

"You are an embarrassment to all women," another said.

"You beauty queens are creating a shallow, superficial and unat-tainable image of what beauty is and, as a result, are responsible for causing girls to grow up with body-image issues and eating disor-ders," another penned.

Feeling hurt and attacked, I flipped shut my laptop just as a beau-tiful brown-eyed blond entered the room. She introduced herself as Rosanna Davison from Ireland and then sat down, crossing her tanned legs, on the bed opposite me. I introduced myself.

"Nazanin from Canada, nice to meet you," she smiled. "You look a little flustered," she continued with some apprehension. "Everything okay?"

"I got a few emails from women in North America who are criticizing me for taking part in this. It bothers me; they just don't understand," I told her.

"I know all about that!" Rosanna said. "People back home think I won the title of Miss Ireland because my father is the musician Chris de Burgh."

I sang a line from "Lady in Red" and then stopped quickly. "I am so sorry, Rosanna. You must be so annoyed at people who sing that."

"No," she giggled. "I'm tired of the people who say that I do well only because of my father."

THE NEXT WEEK was a whirlwind. While in Hong Kong, all 106 of us competitors were whisked around the city in red double-decker buses to sightsee and attend festivals with dancers and acrobats doing the Dragon Dance. We also met many of China's top business people, government officials and an adoring public. We then toured Mainland China, including Shanghai and Beijing, visiting schools and orphanages by day and at night dining at five-star hotels and banquet halls with various diplomats, actors, writers and filmmakers. I learned that millions of dollars had been pumped into paving new roads to make a good impression on us and on the press. Hundreds of thousands of dollars had been spent renovating the local hotels and on our meals, which were always five to eight courses. We received gifts and memorabilia wherever we went. Mayors gave us the keys to their cities and celebrated our presence with elaborate firework performances. China wanted to show the world its best face, knowing that the media were following us, documenting everything.

Our days would start at four or five o'clock in the morning, when we would have to catch our flight to the next city. During the long bus rides, I got to know the other competitors, though there were so many of us that we couldn't always remember each other's names. So we slipped into calling each other by the country we represented. Slowly my unease at having the fewest suitcases, dresses, shoes and purses lifted as many of the women began referring to me as their sister. I found myself translating for several of the Spanish-, French- and even Portuguese-speaking competitors.

Midway through the competition, we were in Beijing, touring the great historical sites, such as the Summer Palace and the Great Wall of China. It was a very cold day when we reached the Great Wall, and it had started to snow. The women were so eager to get off the bus, they were almost trampling each other. The South American and African young women were jumping up and down and squealing like children on Christmas morning. Some made snowballs and threw them at each other.

"What is going on?" I asked Miss Colombia, who had a smile that stretched from ear to ear. "Why are you all so excited? Did a cameraman ask you to perform like that?"

"No. But this is so wonderful—it's the first time many of us have seen snow."

"Really?" I exclaimed, not realizing until that moment how I took having four seasons for granted.

"So, you are from Canada," said Miss Colombia, running her manicured red nails over my sash. "Do you live in an igloo? Do you travel around in a dogsled?" she asked innocently.

It was my turn to laugh. I told her that Canada doesn't get snow year-round, nor do Canadians live in houses made of ice, except the Inuit if they are sleeping overnight away from their homes when they are hunting or fishing for food. "In fact, our summers, in parts of the country, reach over forty degrees Celsius sometimes."

"Oh," she said. "But you must ski?"

I told Miss Colombia that I lived about two hours from Whistler, which was located in the Coast Mountains and where many World

Cup skiing events took place. "In fact, Vancouver just won the bid to host the 2010 Winter Olympics," I told her. "And yes," I continued, "I started skiing at age six. My teacher called me 'the yellow ski demon' because I wore a bright yellow ski suit and would whiz down the mountain. I didn't like to do turns. I liked to take the fast route. I liked to take risks.

"But with every risk comes the chance of failure. I broke my knee at age eleven, and when it healed I turned to snowboarding. This lesson taught me that to achieve great things, one needs to take risks. Sometimes you navigate the moguls with finesse, other times you fall. But you get back up, dust the snow off and continue to try it in a different way."

"I thought Canadians were blond-haired and blue-eyed," she said. "Are you sure you're Canadian?" Some of the other competitors leaned in close to listen.

I laughed. "Yes, I'm sure I am Canadian. Canada is made up of people from all over the world. This diversity is one of the riches of our country. I was born in Tehran, Iran. My family left when I was one and lived a year in Spain before immigrating to Canada. I am Iranian-Canadian."

"Ah, I thought so," she said. "Many of us Latinas talked about how you look more Spanish, or something else—not Canadian."

"I don't remember much about Iran," I told her. "I have never been back."

Just then, we were all asked to huddle together for a group photograph wearing our puffy red ski jackets and jeans bejewelled with the Miss World motto on the back, donated by a sponsor.

"Miss Canada, where is your hood?" one of the chaperones asked.

"I took it off," I replied. "It has a fur lining and I refuse to promote anything of the sort."

I could see the dismay on the chaperone's face and thought, *Oh no, that's one strike against me—but I don't care. My principles come first.*

A week later, I had breakfast with Marie-José Hnein, Miss Lebanon. She was all alone at a corner table, sipping tea, and waved me over when she saw me enter the room.

"I just got off the telephone with my mother," I started the conversation. "I told her that, in China, wise women can read a person's future from their tea leaves. I think mine would say I am a fish out of water."

"That would be right," Marie-José replied. "You and I both are fish out of water!"

"What do you mean?"

"See Miss Israel over there, sitting alone at that table?" She pointed to Miri Levy.

"Yes," I said. "Let's join her."

"No, we can't. Before I came to Miss World, I was told to never, ever stand beside Miss Israel or have any photographs taken of us together."

"But I would think it would be a sign of peace, tolerance and solidarity to be seen together, to show that political differences don't mean anything here at this competition."

"You are smart but naive," Marie-José laughed. She shook her long dark hair and smiled. "Everything is political about the Middle East, even beauty pageants. At night, Miss Israel and I sneak into each other's rooms and talk, mostly about clothes, our friends, our dreams. Sometimes we talk about what we can do to bring peace to our countries. But we can never have these conversations in public." She then said in a low voice, "At least not with each other. Surely you must understand. You, me and Miss Israel are the Middle Eastern women. Your life also must be political and full of paradoxes."

I slowly shook my head in disagreement. What I was loath to admit to Miss Lebanon was that I knew little about Iran's current political situation other than what I overheard my family talk about with friends at dinner parties.

"I can tell you," Marie-José said, "that if you had remained in Iran, your life would be very different."

CHAPTER 2

NAZANIN FATEHI

September 1996 to February 1997, Sanandaj, Iran

===

It was a sunny day, though the east wind that blew the smog over Sanandaj toward the Zagros Mountains was cool. Eight-year-old Nazanin woke early and, after washing her face, donned the dark brown *manteau* and matching headscarf and pants that made up her school uniform. When she was dressed, she sat on a Kurdish kilim cushion on the floor of the room where she slept and ate a breakfast of *lavash*, a soft, thin flatbread; *panir*, feta cheese; and *chaee shirin*, sweetened tea. After breakfast, she took the hairbrush she often used on her younger sister Shahla, and smoothed down the scuffs and scratches on her brown loafers.

Nazanin's mother had been given the clothing and shoes when she registered her daughter for school. The administrator hadn't asked whether there was enough money in the family to pay for the uniform. Instead, she had studied Nazanin's mother's dirty fingernails, wrinkled eyes, round body and well-worn black chador. She could hear the children wildly running up and down the hallway: Nazanin and her younger siblings, Hojat, six; Shahla, four; Parastoo, three; and Ghomri, two. The school administrator had ordered Nazanin to step inside the office. After Nazanin's feet, waist and height were measured, her mother had been handed the used items without a word.

Nazanin didn't care that her uniform had once belonged to

another student. She was happy that she wouldn't be at home all day, sweeping the house, washing dishes and doing the laundry in big aluminum buckets out back, a task that in the winter numbed her fingers with the cold.

"*Achm bo madrasa*. I am going to school," she sang in Kurdish. Nazanin's father had already left for his job, and Nazanin could hear her older sister, Leila, who was fourteen, and mother bathing her siblings. "Tell them goodbye for me," she said after kissing Parastoo on the forehead, "*achm bo madrasa*." She slipped out the blue wooden door that had fallen off its upper hinges.

Though it was not quite seven-thirty in the morning, the neighbourhood was alive with activity. Boys, sitting on idling motorbikes, hung out at the end of the alleyway beside Nazanin's home. Nazanin scurried past them, keeping her head and eyes lowered, and followed the smell of fresh bread coming from the bakery. Once on the main street, she passed the fruit and vegetable stands, her mouth watering for one of the bananas, which she had tried only once, since they were too expensive for her mother to buy. Nazanin slowed as she passed a used-clothing store. T-shirts, pants and dresses hung on pegs out front. She covered her nose with her hand to block the smell of the disinfectant the clothes had been sprayed with as she ran her fingers over a pink dress with a white lace collar and trim.

"One day," she said out loud, "I will have a pretty dress like this." She then resumed her walk, skirting the newspaper and magazine stands that jutted out into the sidewalks.

Nazanin had to leap over big potholes and tiptoe around puddles when crossing at the intersections. Garbage, from chicken bones to outdated magazines, was strewn everywhere. After fifteen minutes of walking, Nazanin entered the middle-class neighbourhood where her school was located. The roads were paved and there were bins for the trash. She breathed in the smells of the blossoms, including the roses, whose long stems stretched out over the fences she passed.

She breathed more easily when she reached this middle-class neighbourhood of single-family homes made of granite and marble blocks, for she felt safe here. Nazanin, who had attended part of her kindergarten and grade one years, had once overheard her classmates from this neighbourhood comparing what their fathers did for their jobs. Two were engineers for the city, another owned a furniture and trading company and yet another was a lawyer. The children of these fathers brought biscuits and fresh fruits for their school snacks. Nazanin usually didn't bring anything.

Nazanin's dream was to learn to read. A few years earlier, she had found a children's picture book of fairy tales with beautiful paintings in a grocery market garbage bin, which the children of her rundown neighbourhood often scoured for snacks. That night, by the light of a candle, which she used instead of turning on the electricity that would have awakened her mother, she stared at the pictures—a forest, a wolf and some goats—and ran her fingers over the Persian words.

"I want to learn to read Persian," she had whispered to Shahla, who was sound asleep beside her.

While her brother, Hojat, never missed any school, Nazanin had attended only about half of her required schooling before grade two, as her mother was pregnant with first Shahla, then Parastoo and then Ghomri. Nazanin was needed at home to do the chores and look after her younger siblings. But a few weeks before the start of grade two, her mother surprised Nazanin by gently taking her hands into her own. "I don't want you to miss any school this year," she said, tears glistening in her dark eyes. "I don't care that your father says girls shouldn't go to school. I want you to go. I see you looking at that book at night when you think I am asleep. I once had dreams too."

NAZANIN ENTERED the school's courtyard and moved to the back of one of the lines of children waiting to be informed of their classroom number. She crossed her arms and kept her head lowered, afraid to make eye contact with any of her classmates. When it was finally her turn, she said her name and a small woman with a mole above her lip told her to go to the third classroom on the right-hand side on the second floor.

Children of all ages ran past her as she climbed the metal staircase and walked down the hall, stopping at her classroom door. The teacher, writing something on the chalkboard, didn't notice Nazanin, so she scanned the room, looking for a vacant seat. All of the benches at the wooden desks were taken except for one at the very back. As she slipped into the empty seat, Nazanin smiled sheepishly at the green-eyed girl beside her, who glanced at Nazanin and then quickly looked away.

The teacher, a pretty woman with rosy cheeks and soft brown eyes, finally introduced herself in Kurdish, which she explained she would not be speaking for long, as Persian was the official language of the school and, indeed, of all Iran. She explained that she could be disciplined if she spoke Kurdish too often, even though it was the native language of most of the students in that area. The teacher then asked the girls in Persian to introduce themselves one by one, starting at the front, where the students from the wealthy neighbourhood sat, ready to learn, with their brand-new bags by their sides.

"And what do you want to be when you grow up?" she eventually asked Nazanin in Kurdish, as if she knew that the girl's Persian was limited.

Nazanin's classmates covered their mouths and whispered to one another as she answered. "A sccchhhool . . . tttteacher," Nazanin gave her answer in Kurdish, stuttering, her face flushed and her hands perspiring from the nervousness she felt speaking in front of the others.

"I will help you," said the teacher over the snickers of the other girls.

THE NEXT COUPLE OF MONTHS blurred one into the other. Nazanin would arrive in the courtyard by 8 a.m., where she would line up with her class. Like the others, she would hold her arms out in front of and then beside her to ensure she was arm's-length from any other child, and then sing the Islamic national anthem, which was followed by a student reciting verses from the Qur'an. On a crisp and clear autumn day, the leaves of the platanus tree having turned from a deep green to a burnt brown, the green-eyed girl who used to sit beside Nazanin recited part of the Yaseen Sura in Arabic. Once back in class, Nazanin's teacher translated the recited verse from the Qur'an into Persian. Nazanin had by now learned enough Persian to understand that the sura was about the sun and moon. She wanted to learn more and her teacher seemed kind—unlike her classmates and many of the other teachers—so afterward, when the others had left, she asked her teacher to translate the text into Kurdish for her. Nazanin recited the verse in her head all the way home.

> *And the sun—it runs to a fixed resting place; that is the ordaining of the All-mighty, the All-knowing—And the moon—We have determined it by stations, till it returns like an aged palm bough. It behooves not the sun to overtake the moon, neither does the night outstrip the day, each swimming in a sky.*

ALL NAZANIN HAD KNOWN about Islam before she reached grade two was that as much as five times a day, when her father was at home, he pulled out his black-and-white prayer mat, gestured for the family to be quiet, and then mumbled some words that she did not understand, all the while doing prostrations on the mat.

"What is that you do?" Nazanin had asked when she was younger.

"Praying," he replied.

"What do the words mean?" she probed.

"They mean many things. They are in Arabic."

"Why don't you say it in Kurdish?" she asked. "What is this 'Arabic'?"

"Arabic is a language, and the Qur'an, which is the word of God, was written in Arabic," he explained in a calm voice. "In order to keep this word of God sacred and pure, we have to recite it in the original language."

"Can I learn?"

"Ask your mother," he said, patting her on the head and leaving the house without another word.

But Nazanin's mother was always too busy to teach her about prayer. And at school, she was hearing passages from the Qur'an translated into Persian only. As a result, she understood just a few words of what was ever said, and she dared not ask her teacher a second time what the morning prayers meant for fear she would be kicked out of school and her teacher punished for speaking Kurdish. Nazanin instead focused on and soon became mesmerized by the parts of the Yaseen Sura she had heard. In her mind's eye she saw the sun on a midsummer's day, and then the cool icy full moon of midwinter: "It behooves not the sun to overtake the moon," she would whisper before closing her eyes at night, "neither does the night outstrip the day, each swimming in a sky."

The teacher never explained what the sura meant, but Nazanin felt safe as the words slipped off her tongue, knowing that Khwa—God—made everything work in some kind of order, even when it made no sense to her, and that, somewhere out there, for her moon there was a sun directly opposite.

Nazanin also began to indirectly learn a little about her Kurdish roots during religion class. "The *dini*," the teacher explained one day, speaking about the religious book for children in the schools, "is for students in all of Iran. The majority of people in Iran practise Shia Islam. Most of us in this room are Kurdish, including me, and most Kurds practise Sunni Islam. Almost all of the population of Sanandaj is Kurdish. Sanandaj is located in what is called Iranian Kurdistan." She then walked around the room, passing to each student a *dini* with a section, she explained, that discussed the four general schools of thought of Sunni Islam.

Uncharacteristically, Nazanin flung her hand into the air. "Does it teach us how to pray?" she asked.

The teacher, whom by now everyone simply called Khanoom Moalem, or Miss Teacher, shook her head.

Nazanin typically never spoke in class unless the teacher called on her. She swallowed hard and cleared her throat. "Khanoom Moalem, can you teach me how to pray like my father?" she asked in Persian with a confidence that surprised even Nazanin, for now every eye in the room was on her.

"Of course," the teacher said, smiling. She gestured for the girls to stand up and follow her to the *namaz khooneh*, the prayer room, on the third floor.

Nazanin entered slowly, smelling the stale air. Two posters nailed onto the white walls, their paint peeling, caught her eye. The first was of a boy showing how to wash properly before prayer, with the word *"vozoo"* written across the top. The second showed the boy in the same poses of prayer that she had seen her father in with the word *"namaz"* written across the top. Without realizing it, Nazanin had walked into the centre of the room, the floor of which was covered by a burgundy carpet.

"Shoes off!" yelled the teacher, pulling Nazanin by the arm out into the hallway. Nazanin slipped off her loafers and put them outside the door of the *namaz khooneh* as the others had done. The teacher instructed the girls to find a place on the floor and then described the various prostrations to be done during prayer.

"Khanoom Moalem, what do we think of when we pray?" asked one of Nazanin's classmates.

The teacher tapped her fingers on her chin. "Think of being a good person," she finally said. "Think of the story of Dehghane Fadakar, the selfless farmer who noticed the railway tracks had a problem just when a train was approaching. The farmer ripped off his shirt, attached it to the end of a stick and set it on fire. He waved and waved until the conductor noticed him and stopped the train. It was a bitterly cold day and the farmer got very sick afterward. But he saved people from death. Think of leading your life to help others. Think of being a martyr."

Nazanin tried to focus on what the teacher was saying, but every crack of a knee, a seam ripping in someone's pants and even a fart got her peers giggling, and even made Nazanin smile, revealing her crooked front teeth. "*Ssss . . . saket,*" the teacher hissed for the girls to be quiet several times before the room grew silent. When Nazanin could finally concentrate, she focused her thoughts not on Dehghane Fadakar but on the Yaseen Sura.

"JAASH! JAASH!" THE CHILDREN SHOUTED as Nazanin walked quickly past them. It was January and snow was falling. Nazanin pulled the collar of her manteau up around her neck.

"Do you know what that means?" a boy about ten years old yelled at her. He ran up beside Nazanin, pulled off her headscarf and spit into her hair. She choked back the tears and quickened her pace. She was very near to the school. She was so close, in fact, that when she rounded the corner, she could see the big black metal gate. She knew that safety lay in the courtyard, which the boys were not allowed to enter. The girls there would not dare tease her for fear of getting in trouble with one of the teachers.

"It's people like your father who are *jaash*, a traitor," the boy spat, running beside Nazanin. "They trade in their own people. They're spies."

Nazanin slowed her pace, turned her head and saw that the small group of children were following her. Most of the children were her own age, though the girls were not in her class and the boys attended the all-boys school down the street. One of the boys picked up some stones and threw them at her back while the girls continued to call out "*Jaash! Kanishki jaash!*"

Daughter of a traitor? No one had ever called Nazanin this name before or accused her father of being a traitor. She was uncertain what to do or even what to think. Another boy ran up and pulled on the back of Nazanin's manteau, causing her to lose her balance. She slipped on the ice and fell. She lowered her eyes and sank to the ground, and the children stopped to pull her hair. She remained in this position long after they had left, listening to the national anthem being played in the schoolyard, followed by the morning prayer. She didn't move from the cold, icy ground even when she heard the students shuffling into class. Only when the sound of the clasp on the heavy gate closing reached her did she stand up on shaky legs. But, instead of going toward the school, Nazanin headed home.

"Why are you here?" her mother asked when she saw her daughter.

"I don't feel well," Nazanin lied, heading past her and Leila to get a cushion. "I'm going to lie down."

Nazanin's mother stopped folding Ghomri's clean diaper rags and stared at Nazanin. "Your coat is ripped. And you have dirt on your face. And look," she said, wagging a finger at Nazanin's right knee. "Your pants are torn too. I will have to mend those. What happened to you?"

Nazanin stood silently, shifting her eyes back and forth, not knowing what to say. She finally opened her mouth to speak but found her throat too dry. She collapsed to the floor and cried. As her sister Leila pulled her into her arms and rocked her, Nazanin recounted what the children had said to her. "What do they mean I am the daughter of a traitor? I am not jaash, am I?" Nazanin asked her mother.

"Ah, Nazanin," her mother sighed. "There are some things you need to know. I think it is best if I show you. Come, we'll all go," she said, waving to the smaller children. "Leila can stay behind and finish the laundry."

After donning their coats and shoes, Nazanin, Shahla, Parastoo and Ghomri headed outside with their mother. It was still snowing. Parastoo and Nazanin walked in silence while Ghomri whimpered to be carried rather than walk. The group retraced almost the same path that Nazanin took to school each day. Her mother detoured, however, just before the spot where Nazanin had fallen and led the family downtown to the main square.

"Over there." She pointed to a wide opening in the square.

"What is that?" Nazanin asked.

"Go on, Ghomri, go play!" her mother said, pushing the young child to join Shahla and Parastoo, who were already running about in the square. When the children were out of earshot, Nazanin's mother drew Nazanin close. "This is where the government once hanged people," she said in a quiet voice. "It's where the government killed Kurdish people for being enemies of the state. And your father, he works for Sepah-e Pasdaran-e Enghelab-e Eslami, the Army of the Guardians of the Islamic Revolution, which wants to stifle, even by death, any Kurdish threat of uprising. The government doesn't hang people in public here anymore for fear of prompting protests like those that erupted over the hangings of the past. But many Kurdish people have been murdered."

"I don't understand." Nazanin looked quizzically up at her mother.

"He works as a Revolutionary Guard," her mother continued, her eyes staring straight ahead. "I don't know what he does exactly in his job. He has never told me. Husbands don't have to tell their wives things. But I do know that Kurdish people have been killed for speaking out against the government. Some people in this city think your father is a traitor, because he is a Sepahi. The rumours are that he turned over to authorities some of those who were killed. Why do you think none of the other women talk to me in the market?" she asked. "And your cousins, kids your own age? Where are they? No one comes to visit. We are the only family around here who eats alone."

Abruptly, Nazanin's mother ran off calling out for Ghomri, who was teetering toward the street. Nazanin looked over at Parastoo, who was spinning around in circles, her unbuttoned manteau flowing around her. As she watched her sister, Nazanin's mind drifted to the previous Yalda, the celebration to mark the longest night of the year. During the day, the women and girls in her neighbourhood had separated the seeds from the pomegranate and used *robb*—tomato paste—to make the evening stew of chicken or lamb. At night, with a half moon rising over the city, the guests had begun to arrive, wearing traditional Kurdish outfits with coins sewn into the fabric. Nazanin had cradled her head in her arms folded on the window ledge and stared out at the relatives and friends arriving at her neighbours' houses. They carried watermelons under their arms and hugged and kissed each other. Throughout the night, Nazanin had heard singing and laughter, followed quickly by shushing, for the Iranian government didn't like people to celebrate Yalda openly. Yalda, an ancient winter solstice celebration that predates not only Islam but also Zoroastrianism, was seen by the Muslim clerics as un-Islamic.

When they returned home from their walk, the mood was dark. Leila helped her mother prepare *shalamin*, a thick soup made with wheat, vegetables and bone. Nazanin's father did his prayers while Ghomri jumped on his back. Her mother spanked Parastoo across the bottom for knocking over the tea. Nazanin didn't eat much at dinner and afterward went straight to bed, laying her blankets on the floor and listening to the sounds of happiness from the houses around her, wishing she were somewhere else.

RELUCTANTLY, NAZANIN RETURNED TO SCHOOL. Weeks passed and she didn't see the children who had taunted her. She stayed as much as she could completely to herself. That included during recess, when she sat under a tree and tried to make out the words in her fairy-tale picture book.

One day when spring was just around the corner, her sister Leila appeared.

"What are you doing here?" Nazanin asked, jumping up.

The children playing nearby had stopped their games and were staring at Leila in her burgundy headscarf and cream-coloured floral dress, which billowed out below her faded and too-small brown manteau.

One of the teachers walked up to Leila. "Do you have permission to be here?" she asked, eying Leila's dishevelled appearance.

"I am her sister," Leila said nervously, pointing to Nazanin. "There is a family emergency. Nazanin must come with me now."

"And what could that emergency be?" growled the teacher, narrowing her eyes.

Nazanin's mind began to race as other students crowded around her and, with their arms folded, clicked their tongues and tapped their feet. "*Jaash, jaash,*" she imagined the teacher and the children saying. Nazanin took a step toward the teacher and clenched one of her fists, motioning that she was prepared to fight.

"Don't," Leila cautioned, cutting in front of Nazanin. "It is not worth it. You need to come with me right away. Don't fight. You will end up paying for it in the end."

Nazanin shook her head and took a breath. She nodded. She grabbed Leila's hand and they ran out of the schoolyard. They didn't stop until they had passed through the wealthy neighbourhood of rose gardens and had entered their own. "What's happened?" Nazanin asked, bending over to catch her breath.

"It's terrible," Leila cried. "It's terrible . . . our lives are ruined. Father has been shot. He is going to die."

CHAPTER 3

NAZANIN AFSHIN-JAM

November to December 2003, China

After we had all finished breakfast, we flew from Beijing to Xi'an, in Shaanxi Province, to see the Terracotta Army. After we had settled in our hotel, we made our way by bus to where the famous statues were housed. For most of the bus ride, I was quiet. I stared out the window at the dusty roads and tall, boxy grey apartment buildings. I mulled over Marie-José's comment that if I had remained in Iran my life would be very different, and wondered why I kept being defined by my Iranian heritage rather than my Canadian one. I breathed steadily, all the while my inner voice asking, *Why now?*

I had thought I was prepared to compete at Miss World. I had thought I was worldly. After all, I had studied classical political theorists, from John Locke and Thomas Hobbes to Jean-Jacques Rousseau and Immanuel Kant. I knew Third World economics and dependency theory. I had studied the French Revolution, the world wars, the politics of the post–Cold War period and liberation movements in South America. But Iran . . . How could I have been so foolish as to not know much about the current political system of the country where I was born?

At the excavation pit, we were greeted by a slender male Chinese tour guide. "Welcome to the Terracotta Warriors," he said. "The statues you see today represent most of the 8,000 found buried close to Emperor Qin Shi Huang's tomb in about 200 BC. We believe he wanted the warriors with him to defend him in the afterlife. The emperor was famous for unifying China under one dynasty," he said.

My attention soon moved to the warriors themselves, many of which looked to be twice as tall as me. I admired their facial features: strong, powerful lines that showed distinction and bravery. I wanted to jump down into the large pit and run my hand over one of the cavalrymen's faces.

"Were there any female warriors?" I asked the tour guide, surprising myself, for I had interrupted his talk.

"Not that I know of," he replied politely as he turned to me before addressing the group. "Forced labourers, numbering in the hundreds of thousands, constructed the emperor's tomb . . ."

I squatted low and looked into the face of a cavalryman. I imagined that maybe he was actually a woman, like Fu Hao, a female warrior and queen consort of King Wu Ding of the Shang Dynasty, or Joan of Arc, who rode into battle for France during the Hundred Years War, wearing the armour of her male colleagues. I slowly made my way along the periphery of the exhibit, all the while making stories up in my head about the warriors. The archers, for example, I imagined were also women, perhaps Chinese versions of the Amazons who helped the Trojans against the Greeks. Perhaps the general was Pantea Arteshbod, the great Persian military commander who was part of an elite force called the Immortals during the conquest of the Neo-Babylonian Empire in 547 BC—during the reign of Cyrus the Great.

As I walked back to the bus, I passed the guide, who was speaking to one of the girls. "We Chinese have sayings," he said. "Be not afraid of growing slowly. Be afraid of standing still."

Be not afraid of growing slowly. Be afraid of standing still. I repeated the lines to myself all the way back to the hotel.

A FEW DAYS LATER, the other contestants and I flew to Hainan Province. We were greeted, as usual, by a red carpet on the tarmac, children presenting us with flower leis, a full band with trumpets and a line of photographers blinding us with their lights and cameras. It was only when we were on the buses that we would get a bit of rest from smiling and truly be able to relax.

As we travelled through the countryside from Haikou to Sanya I looked out through the window at the rolling hills, mangrove trees and water buffalo, and at the locals walking along the highway while motorbikes, cars and buses whizzed by at full speed. A few times I grimaced, afraid someone was going to get run over. But it slowly became apparent that within the chaos there was a system. People had adapted to the dangers.

At one point, we pulled over for fuel at a village of about forty small cement houses. After applying lip gloss and primping our hair in anticipation of the arrival of the media vans that had been constantly following us, we all climbed off the buses. One of the chaperones told us we could walk around, so I made my way down a side street. I was immediately taken aback by the rundown houses, with their chipped walls and doors hanging off their hinges. Some of the windows were broken, patched up with duct tape and cardboard. As I was looking up at a roof that appeared as if it was about to collapse, I stumbled in a pothole and fell.

A woman came rushing over and helped me up. A small group surrounded us. "Thank you, thank you," I said, bowing. I finished dusting myself off and looked around to make sure no photographers had caught my fall on camera. I heard Bobby's voice in my head saying, "It takes only one bad photo during the entire month of the competition and you are ruined for the entire pageant."

I turned my attention to the woman, who told me in broken English that I was welcome. When she smiled, I could see her rotting teeth. She timidly reached over and took my hand. Her skin was callused and I noticed that her nails were split and brown from malnutrition.

"My name is Ah Cy, which means 'lovely,'" she said.

"I am Nazanin, which means 'lovely' in Persian," I told her and the two small children standing by her side.

"These my," the woman said in broken English, pointing to the children. The lines and wrinkles on the woman's face and her hunched back made me think she was close to sixty, certainly not young enough to have small children. "Mama, Papa, Auntie," she said, motioning to the others standing around us.

At the end of our brief exchange, we bowed our heads and said thank you. "Thank you for helping me up," I repeated, but I was startled. I wasn't expecting to see so much poverty while so much money was being lavished on us, the Miss World competitors.

When I neared the buses, I saw that we were not quite ready to go. I walked up the dirt road about a hundred metres and stared off into the barren fields.

"Life is full of contrasts," I whispered into the wind. Until today all I had seen of China were the fancy hotels, golf courses, banquet halls, shopping centres and the highly modern tour buses they shuttled us around in. "We see what we want to see . . . or rather, they show us what they want to show us." I said quietly, tilting my head up to watch a sparrow flying overhead. "But this country isn't just the pomp and splendour our hosts want us to see. It is also full of poverty. This competition is rife with politics. The world is full of night and day . . ."

"May I join you?" asked a quiet voice from behind me.

I turned and faced Miss Angola. "My English is not that good," Selma Katia Carlos said in Portuguese.

"I don't speak Portuguese. But French and Spanish, which I do speak, are Romance languages, like Portuguese, so I can make out what you are saying." I smiled and took her arm, and we turned to look out over the hills together. Glancing over at her, I saw that her eyes were full of worry. "What is it?" I asked, giving her a hug.

"I don't feel comfortable here," she said in Portuguese.

"Why do you say that?"

Her shoulders slumped as she sighed. "I can't communicate with anyone except you, Miss Portugal and Miss Brazil," she said, wiping her eyes with a tissue.

"Don't worry, I'll help you."

We turned as we heard the other contestants getting back on the bus. "Thank you," Selma said as we started to make our way back. "I haven't met many friends yet, but that is okay because I know why I am here."

I was about to ask Selma what she meant, but before I could, Miss Belize, a dental surgeon who had told me earlier in the competition that she had started a charity to help care for people with HIV or AIDS, came running over to tell us it was time to go.

FINALLY, WE ARRIVED IN SANYA, dubbed the Hawaii of China, where we were to stay at the Sheraton Sanya, a beautiful, spacious beach resort. We spent the week taking part in fashion shows to raise money for various charities, recording videos promoting the competition, doing press interviews and rehearsing our routines for the main evening competition, which was to be telecast around the world.

On the day before the main event, my stomach churned as I stood in the middle of the auditorium of the Beauty Crown Cultural Center, staring up at the ceiling lined with chandeliers. The entire room, shaped like a crown, shimmered with tiny lights embedded in the walls and lining the floors. The government built the facility just for Miss World. When we first arrived, all 105 contestants and I posed for photographs outside the complex.

I was told by my chaperone that a third of the planet would be watching the final event—*which is more viewers than for the World Cup*, I thought with apprehension.

It was late afternoon when we returned to the hotel. I felt light and airy as I joined my parents and James, who had arrived the day before, for tea. James recounted how earlier, wanting to explore the countryside, he had rented a hotel scooter and, map in hand, headed east. At dusk he noticed that the scooter's fuel was getting low. From his map, it looked as if he could take a shortcut over a low mountain pass. To conserve gas, he pushed the scooter up a hill, thinking that on the way down the mountain, he could coast and have enough fuel to get him safely back to the hotel. Just as he reached the top of the hill, a military van pulled him over, and he was arrested by what looked like military police. They threw him and the scooter into the van. They could not understand each other because of the language barrier, and James tried to call the hotel for help but could not get reception on his cellphone.

Finally, the van hit a pocket where James got cellphone reception and he passed the phone to one of the military men. The concierge explained to him that James was a guest at the hotel, there to see the Miss World pageant. James was driven back to the hotel, where he was interrogated further, this time with the help of a translator. The military men made him delete all the photos on his digital camera. Afterward, the receptionist explained to James that no one usually ventured that far from the hotel and that he was lucky he was returned. Years later, thanks to Google Earth, James and I learned that he was headed toward a secret underground nuclear submarine complex, which apparently was not so secret anymore.

The chaperones had told us to go to bed early so that we would be fresh for the next day, so after a while I hugged James and my parents goodnight and headed back to my room through the courtyard and then down a path of softly lit palm trees. I pondered my chances of winning. Earlier in the day I had heard rumblings among a few other contestants and some of the hotel staff that I might win. I knew I had made it to the top-twenty round, for it had been announced that I had won the sport competition, which involved, among other things, a swimming and running race and timed push-ups and sit-ups. Leading up to Miss Canada and Miss World I had trained hard with one of the top personal trainers in the world, Yvan Cournoyer. During the sports competition I had pushed myself to my limit and felt nauseated and sick afterward. I was also a finalist in the talent competition, in which I performed a Middle Eastern dance in a turquoise silk belly-dancing costume Bobby had designed for me, which was adorned with gold coins. One of those coins was a lucky gold coin from Iran that my maternal grandmother had given me on one of her visits to Canada.

All the contestants crowded around computers at night in the hotel business centre to review the betting websites, which listed where we were anticipated to place based on that day's events. I was listed in the top three each day. Some of the young women who never placed on the betting lists were very distraught. Some admitted it was hurting their confidence.

Just as I reached the door leading into the wing where my room was located, I stopped and looked up at the moon and said a prayer.

> *Dear God,*
>
> *If it is your will for me to win this competition, then let the lights shine bright on me tomorrow. I vow that if I win I will do what is required of me as Miss World. After that I will change out of these glamorous clothes and wear only a simple white linen dress and follow in Jesus's footsteps, living a minimalist life and distancing myself from what I see more and more as a superficial world, where everyone seems to be looking out for only their own self-interest. If you have a different plan for me and what I was meant to do on this earth, then I will remain your patient servant to see what path you would like me to take.*
>
> *Amen.*

I slowly made my way to my room, only to find Miss Angola standing at the door. She wanted to talk some more, so I invited her in. She told me how nervous she was. I told her I had been petrified until I said my prayer, and that now I felt at peace. "You said you knew why you were here—then why are you scared?"

"My country is very poor," she replied in Portuguese. "We've been in a civil war until just last year. Many people in my country live in small villages, and children, especially during the conflict, often didn't go to school. Many had to get water from wells that were an hour walk from their village. The well water was more often than not polluted. Some children were attacked by crocodiles while collecting water from the river, some were maimed by land mines and others were forced to become child soldiers. Many girls and young women were raped during the war or forced into marriages with older soldiers.

"So much sadness, Nazanin," she said, shaking her head, her eyes swelling with tears. "But everyone kept telling me I had a gift. I was beautiful and smart and could help raise awareness of my country's suffering. I could speak to people. I could make friends. You know I am the first Miss Angola to compete since our war ended?"

I had read about Angola's twenty-seven-year-long civil war, which ended in 2002. It started right after the former colony gained its independence from Portugal in 1975 and involved various internal factions, including the new nation's two leading liberation parties. Both Russia and the United States were drawn into the conflict, making it even bloodier. Angola had played host to one of the continent's worst humanitarian disasters.

"I won't win tomorrow," Selma said in a soft voice. "I have not been confident throughout the competition. But I have come further than any girl in my country, and my goal is to work for a charity in Angola that helps protect women and girls from abuse."

"You know, I've been getting emails from women in North America saying that my taking part in Miss World is derogatory to women," I said, glancing over at my laptop. "I contemplated many things before entering the competition. I thought about whether I would be contributing to a Western stereotype of beauty. But I realized it doesn't have to be that way. We all come in different shapes and sizes. God gives each and every one of us different blessings, and we need to celebrate them all. I vowed that if I did well in the Canadian competition, I would champion, as best I could, the idea that beauty is what comes from within. Plus, I have the duty to also showcase that women can do, say and wear whatever they please. Runway models," I continued, "tend not to smile and are paid to be waif clothing hangers for designers, whereas the young women who enter Miss World generally have healthier, athletic bodies, are smiling and are trying to be role models for their communities."

"I don't understand the problem," she said, her eyes searching mine for an answer. "In my country, most girls would trade places with me tomorrow, just to have the chance to be here with all these amazing women from all over the world. To go to charity events. To learn about the world. To be the most beautiful they can be."

"I haven't quite figured out how to respond to those emails," I said, shaking my head.

"You will. Everything happens for a reason, that much I do believe. An aunt of mine used to say, 'The bone is to the meat what a person is to life.' I can now go back to Angola with a much bigger platform than when I left and raise awareness of the impact of war on women. I have always had lots of meat on me, but now, being here, my bones are a bit stronger."

BEFORE I FELL ASLEEP that night, I checked the emails that Naz had forwarded to me from my website. There were about twenty messages, which I read quickly at first and then more slowly. All of them were from Iran, from young women in Tehran, Shiraz and Isfahan. I found myself reading one email about four times.

Dear Nazanin,

I heard about you on the Internet and wanted to write. I am eighteen. I was imprisoned and received lashings to my back for being caught wearing a short skirt at a friend's party. All of my friends and I love to dress up, wear makeup and be beautiful. But we risk so much if we even dare to look this way in public.

I look at photos of you in your beautiful clothes and I wish I had your freedoms. You represent Iran so well. Please make us proud and win. All of my friends and I are cheering for you.

Taraneh from Isfahan

Officially, I represented Canada, but I was also now, unofficially, representing Iran. I was overwhelmed by the women in Iran who were reaching out to me. I began to feel pressure—so much was riding on my shoulders, in particular, their dreams that a Persian woman can just be herself. Most Islamic countries don't field candidates or have beauty pageants because women who take part in such competitions are seen to dress immodestly. Miss Lebanon was right. We were fish swimming alone in a big pool.

I sent Taraneh a quick message, thanking her and asking her to keep in touch. I then wrote Naz.

> Dear Naz,
>
> Tomorrow is the big day.
>
> Before, I told you that if I win I would devote my reign to raising awareness that a woman's beauty isn't just things she puts on but internal qualities of grace and goodness. That I would use my platform to speak on global issues so that people would see our interconnectedness, not our separateness, and that simplicity, honesty and integrity matter more than the people we know and the things we acquire. Well, I still want to raise awareness that a woman's beauty is not what she puts on but her confidence and inner strengths. But I now also want to do something else. I want to learn more about Iran . . . how Iranian women live today. I feel, in a strange way, that everything I have done in my life has led me to this moment, where in front of me is a path I need to take.
>
> I love you,
> Nini

THERE WAS AN ELECTRIFYING ENERGY in the air at the convention centre. The spotlights were bouncing around the stage. The audience was abuzz. There were just five of us left in the competition: Miss China, Miss India, Miss Ireland, Miss Philippines and me. One by one we were brought out to centre stage and asked a random question.

"Excluding tonight, what is one event in your life this year that has most changed you?" the master of ceremonies, a petite woman wearing a blue traditional Chinese dress, asked me.

That year, my mother's sister Shahin had died of cancer. A couple of days before her death she told me a story that a Kurdish woman had once told her. It involved an eagle and a raven and a choice. The eagle was given an opportunity to extend his life, but that extension would entail him having a much poorer quality of life than that to which the soaring bird of prey was accustomed. In the end, the eagle discovered the meaning of his existence and chose accordingly. He chose quality over quantity. My aunt always chose quality too.

That story flashed through my mind as I decided on my answer.

"When my aunt took her last breath, with our family gathered around her," I replied, directing my response to the audience, "I realized what was truly important in life. Health, love and family." I felt my aunt's spirit with me as I continued on for the remaining minute I had.

SHORTLY AFTER THAT, the five of us stood in a small semicircle as Julia Morley, president of Miss World, read the winners in reverse order. Guan Qi, Miss China, was named second runner-up.

"Miss Canada," Julia Morley then said, announcing that I was first runner-up for Miss World. At first, I didn't catch on. As I was being crowned, all I heard was my father screaming in the audience, along with Connie McNaughton, the Miss Canada franchise director, who in the 1984 competition also had been runner-up—the highest any Canadian had placed at Miss World—and the other organizer and former beauty queen Caroline Frolic, who had come all the way from Toronto to China to support me. Then the winner was announced: Miss Ireland—my roommate, Rosanna Davison. Azra Akin, the former Miss Turkey and the 2002 Miss World, crowned Rosanna, who moved down the stage, waving to the audience.

It then hit me. I had come second. My heart sank.

I didn't realize until that moment how much I really did want to win. But I quickly focused my mind on the positive. I had placed— and placed well. It went through my mind that there were many notable beauty queens who didn't end up competing or placing first in international competitions but still went on to have very success- ful careers, including Oprah Winfrey, Diane Sawyer, Sophia Loren, Michelle Pfeiffer, Raquel Welch and Halle Berry—the first African- American competitor at Miss World. She placed sixth at the pageant, in 1986.

As confetti floated down from the stage's ceiling, I found myself feeling at ease with the knowledge that God had a different plan for me. I tilted my head up and closed my eyes, letting the sparkling gold pieces of paper bathe my face.

CHAPTER 4

NAZANIN FATEHI

February to June 1997, Sanandaj, Iran

———

Nazanin and Leila skirted stray dogs and laundry hanging on clotheslines as they ran through the alleyways of their neighbourhood. They slowed only when they neared the single-storey brick building that served as the medical clinic for their community.

Nazanin had never been inside the clinic, which was staffed by two nurses and a doctor who left his main practice at Tohid Hospital two days a week to work with the poor. When Nazanin was six, she had a high fever and her mother attempted to take her to the clinic, but the lineup stretched an entire block. An elderly woman walked up and down the line, ordering the sickest people to enter first. The nurse felt Nazanin's head and told her to wait. Some people behind Nazanin began to leave their posts, declaring they were going to see their *doanoos*, a person believed to have healing powers, for a *nooshte*, a prayer to heal their ailment instead. Nazanin's mother decided to go home, where she made her daughter chaee.

Leila and Nazanin didn't have to wait this time. Leila told Nazanin to follow her into the clinic's reception area. There they were met by five Revolutionary Guards, who quickly turned, their hands on their semi-automatic weapons. Leila and Nazanin lowered their eyes as one of the Sepahis started to walk toward them. But a nurse in a black headscarf, white lab coat and white pants emerged from behind the group of men and waved for them to lower their weapons.

"You are his daughters?" she asked Leila and Nazanin, who nodded. "You need to come with me."

The girls followed the nurse down a dim, narrow corridor lit by dull fluorescent light bulbs hanging from the ceiling by wires. The cement walls of the clinic echoed with the coughing, wheezing and wailing of the patients and their pain. Her eyes still lowered, Nazanin peered into one of the rooms. It was full of men, some lying on beds, others sitting on the floor cradling bloody arms and legs, rocking themselves back and forth.

At the end of the corridor, Nazanin and Leila saw two more Sepahis standing on either side of a door. The nurse mumbled something to them under her breath before guiding Leila and Nazanin into the room, where their mother waited with their younger siblings. "What happened, Dayah?" Nazanin asked her mother once the door shut.

In between sobs, Nazanin's mother managed to tell them that there had been an accident at their father's work and that he had been shot in the chest. "I just don't understand," her mother murmured. "I was told that one of his colleagues' guns went off while it was being cleaned. If that is true, why all the Sepahis? Something is terribly wrong, I can feel it."

"Will he live?" Nazanin asked.

"We don't know," her mother said, stressing the "we" as she motioned to the room with her hand.

Nazanin looked into the long, thin faces of three other women sitting on plastic chairs, their arms tucked underneath their black chadors. "Who are these people?" she asked, bewildered.

Leila's eyes moved first to her mother and then to Nazanin.

"You might as well tell her," urged her mother.

Leila took Nazanin's hand and pulled her to the side of the room. Leila stared at the ceiling as she tried to find the words to explain what she wanted to say, a character trait Nazanin knew all too well. Since she was a small child, Nazanin had always looked up to Leila, whose high cheekbones, doe-like eyes and lithe figure had brought her four marriage proposals before the age of fifteen. To Nazanin, Leila was like one of the kittens in the alleyway, at times playful, at other times fragile and vulnerable.

"Baba has another wife," Leila eventually whispered into Nazanin's ear, waving her arm around the room, indicating she was speaking about one of the three women.

Nazanin stepped back and looked quizzically at her sister.

"He is married to two women," Leila said, leaning in close. "I only found out today. Mother knew. But she never told me."

"Do we have half-brothers and sisters?" Nazanin asked with a weak smile, thinking of the special occasions—Yalda and Nowruz—when they might now get together.

"Yes. But they are much older than I am. They are grown and have families of their own, including girls who are your age. Nazanin, you cannot tell anyone," Leila said in a serious voice. "Father is in trouble at his work, I know it. Those Sepahis, they came with Baba. And he should have gone to the main hospital in the city, not here. It is like they want to hide him. People don't like us in our neighbourhood because of his work. They will like us even less when they find out that he has two wives—this may have been done in the past, but it isn't common anymore and people will shun us, think the family is dirty, if they find out. No one in your school can know."

NAZANIN RESTED HER HEAD on a cushion, waiting for news from the nurse as to whether her father would live or die. Nazanin thought back to times she had spent with her father, including one of her first memories, when she was no older than three. Her father had picked her up in his arms, hoisted her onto his shoulders and walked down the alleyway to the market, stopping along the way to say hello to the older men leaning against the walls of their homes, smoking cigarettes and sipping chaee. When they reached the sweet shop, her father dug out his change to buy her a piece of *gaz*, a traditional Middle Eastern nougat.

At night, Nazanin would sneak up to where her parents were sleeping on the floor, crawl over her mother and nuzzle her face into her father's neck, feeling his warm breath on her hair as he slept.

But this all changed when her brother, Hojat, was born. By the time Nazanin was five and Hojat was three, he was clearly his father's favourite. When Nazanin woke in the night to cuddle up beside her father, she would find Hojat already in her spot. On Fridays, when he was not working, Nazanin's father would choose Hojat for the shoulder rides around the neighbourhood. "This is my son," Nazanin could hear her father say proudly to the old men. Nazanin would sit on the ground of the alleyway and stare after them, choking back tears, for she thought she had done something wrong that caused her to lose her father's affection.

Then, the year she was six, she entered the main room of their house, where her father was eating. Beside him was Hojat, nibbling on some meat, the juices spilling down his chin.

"May I have some?" she asked.

"No, no, no, Nazanin!" her father, scolded, standing up, pushing her out of the room and slamming the door. "Go help your mother. Your place is with her," he called after her. Nazanin stood beside the closed door, her forehead pressed against the wall.

Eventually, Nazanin moved slowly to the box where she kept her clothes and slipped on her brown cotton dress and shoes. She then wrapped a scarf around her head to cover her hair, like her mother did, and went outside. When she was several blocks from her home, she hid behind an abandoned building, where she curled herself up into a fetal position and cried. She stayed like this, her head tucked into her knees, her scarf and manteau concealing every part of her body, long after her tears had dried. It wasn't until the late afternoon that she finally lifted her head and held her face up to the sun. She pulled her scarf away and let the rays blanket her face. For a brief moment she felt loved, the warmth of the sun satisfying her yearning to be wanted and held.

She got up, her legs stiff and cramped, and made her way home.

En route, she passed the supermarket, where the children in her alleyway often dug through the store's garbage bin out back. Sifting through soggy newspapers, rotten lettuce, used tea leaves and eggshells, she found the picture book, her fairy tale, which she wiped clean with the sleeve of her dress.

NAZANIN SAT UP when the nurse entered the waiting room. Nazanin's mother and the woman Leila had pointed out as her father's other wife both stood up. "He will live," the nurse told them. "The doctor removed the bullet, but we do not know what long-term damage it has caused."

Nazanin smiled at her father's other wife and the two women with her, hoping they would talk to her and arrange a time for her to meet their children. But when the nurse left, they left too, not looking at Nazanin or even saying goodbye.

In the days that followed, Nazanin waited and waited for her mother to talk about the cousins that she dreamed about at night: girl cousins, with whom she could run home from school and enjoy a snack of biscuits and walnuts. But a heaviness descended on the house, especially after her father arrived home after his operation.

Nazanin returned to school and Leila looked after the children while their mother spent the day preparing the meat the nurse had told her to include in the soups and stews. Only Nazanin's father and Hojat were allowed to eat these meals; Nazanin and her sisters lived on *dokhawa*, a soup made of yogurt, chickpeas and herbs, and *doghrme*, a cold meal of yogurt and cucumber, eaten with bread.

When Nazanin's father eventually did get out of bed, he was as thin as a child, for he never really ate the food—Hojat did. Her father's hair stretched down his neck and his beard was long and bushy.

On a sunny June day, Nazanin's mother sat her father outside in the sun and trimmed his hair. Just as she was done, two Sepahis in neatly ironed green uniforms walked down the alleyway. One of the men, wearing a black cap with a gold symbol on the front, which Nazanin knew from her father meant he held a high position in the Revolutionary Guard, jerked his head to indicate to her father to step inside the house.

Nazanin remained outside, imagining her mother serving the guards chaee and whatever biscuits she had, and the men commending her father for his bravery on the job, for taking a bullet, perhaps to save someone's life.

After an hour or so, the guards left, marching down the alleyway as women and children pushed their bodies up against their houses to give them plenty of room to pass. Just as they rounded the corner, Nazanin heard a crash, followed by her mother's screams. She flung open the front door and ran into the house to see her mother lying on the floor, a plate broken by her side and her father about to heave an aluminum pot at her head.

"Baba?" said Hojat, who had run in after Nazanin. "What are you doing?"

Nazanin's father stared first at Hojat and then at Nazanin's mother, who was curled up in a ball, shaking, her hands covering her face. "Nothing," he sighed, lowering the pot and letting it fall to the floor. "Nothing at all."

Nazanin's father left, grabbing Hojat on his way out and slamming the door behind him. Nazanin rushed to get a wet cloth to put on her mother's forehead and swollen, bleeding lip.

"He has never hit me before," her mother whispered when she was settled. "I don't know what got into him. All I asked was if he still had a job."

"Why were the guards here?" Nazanin asked.

"I don't know," her mother replied, wincing in pain as she tried to move the leg her husband had kicked. Nazanin gently lifted it and tucked a pillow underneath her mother's knees.

"You know, Nazanin, when I was a little girl, I had dreams too," her mother said after a long silence. "I had a fairy tale, which I never told anyone. But I want to tell you now.

"Once upon a time there was a little girl who was born on the dirt floor of her parents' house in a tiny village. The little girl never went to school, but she would watch the other boys and girls head to the small schoolhouse in a distant village for lessons. This little girl had to stay home and help her mother raise her younger sisters and brothers, as well as look after the chickens and goats on the family farm.

"I didn't mind," Nazanin's mother continued with a weak smile, despite her throbbing lip. "Because right beside this little girl, who was me, lived a boy named Sherko—*sher* for lion and *ko* for mountain. He was six years older than I was, and as I grew from a child into a girl, then a young woman, I would watch him watching me hang the bedding and feed the goats.

"When I was very little, I would close my eyes at night and see stars in my mind's eye. I just knew that all these stars were the people who would love me one day. One of those stars was you, Nazanin," her mother said softly. "And one was Sherko. He wasn't very tall, but he was well-built, with strong legs and arms. He had dark brown eyes that sparkled and danced whenever he saw me. He had a deep laugh too, one I could still hear when those stars blackened into sleep.

"When I was a child, Sherko and I would run across the countryside, picking poppies and rolling down the hills. When I became a young woman, I became more and more beautiful, like Leila. My hair had silky curls. My movements were delicate and light. Sherko and I couldn't play like children anymore. He had to be careful when he was around me. I started to get many admirers from villages far and wide. These young men would walk by my house as I was spreading the chicken feed or washing the dishes outside, drape their arms over the stone fence and ask questions, such as, 'What did you dream about last night?'

"I never told them about the stars," Nazanin's mother said. "The only person I ever told was Sherko.

"I soon gained the reputation of being the most beautiful girl in the village, or that's what my father would tell me as we sat by the fire at night sipping chaee and eating dates. And the marriage proposals started to come. The parents of the boys would arrive at our door just before the evening meal, the men and women dressed in Kurdish outfits. My mother would listen to the proposals and then politely my father would thank them, saying that I was still too young—maybe in a year or so.

"Not long after that, my mother announced that because I was so beautiful, I was going to get some *nekhsh* tattoos. It was a long-standing tradition among rural women who were very pretty. We believed the tattoos kept the evil eye away. 'When people pass you, they will look at the tattoos, not at your features,' my mother said, 'preserving your beauty for the man you marry.'

"On a rainy afternoon, we skirted the puddles along the dirt road and arrived covered in mud at Frmesk's house. Frmesk, who told me her name meant 'tears,' was the village beautician for weddings. She also did the tattoos. Once I was lying on the floor and she had admired my full lips and high, wide cheekbones, she decided on what tattoos I would have. 'A cross here,' she said, drawing a cross with her right index finger on my chin. 'And a sun here,' she continued, touching my right cheek. 'And on your hand should be another sun and moon. A sign of beauty.'

"Now, I had not been forewarned that tattooing would be painful. Frmesk dipped a long needle into a jar of blue ink and then pierced my skin with the tip. My mother and Frmesk's daughter held me down as I wailed in pain. Another daughter came when I started to kick and spit, and she held my head as Frmesk carefully kept the needle steady and drew her designs. When it was all done, I closed my eyes, breathed heavily and drifted into a light sleep.

"I could hear someone telling me to wake up, and I felt a kick on my leg. It was Frmesk's great-grandmother, whom I had never met but had certainly heard about. Mahtab was famous for her predictions of the future, and for casting prayers that helped young women conceive their babies and old men stop hitting their wives. She was the best *doanoos* in the region.

"'Tell this girl to get up,' Mahtab said to my mother, who pulled me into a sitting position. As she did so, a few drops of blood from the *nekhsh* landed on my blue dress. Mahtab, whose brown eyes had turned cloudy from her cataracts and whose skin was pale, almost white, and sagging, pointed a bony finger at me. 'I see your future. It is not good. The happiness you seek will be taken from you and also from your children. Your curse is that of the *bawbakht*, the wretch. You will not die young, but you will live a wretched life, as if dead.'

"'Is there anything she can do?' my mother asked, taking out a small velvet sack containing all of the family's money. 'Please let me know how much for a prayer.'

"'No money,' said the grandmother. 'But you can paint the eye on the forehead. That might protect her.'

"As she said this, Frmesk started to prepare her tattoo needle and ink again. My mother had me lie back down, while Frmesk's daughters took hold of my arms and legs. But it wasn't necessary. Not this time. I braved the pain, wanting to escape the future that had been predicted for me. When the eye was done, Mahtab held a cracked mirror up to my face and I stared into that *nekhsh* positioned just above my eyes.

"'I also predict that for a brief moment in time,' Mahtab continued, taking the mirror from me, 'the entire world will see this tattoo.'

"She then quickly turned and left, disappearing into the darkened rooms at the back of the house.

"As long as I lived in that village, I never saw Mahtab again."

"Did the eye work, Dayah?" Nazanin asked, pulling the damp cloth off her mother's forehead and looking closely at the tattoo, now blurred from time.

"A few weeks after I got my tattoos, Sherko's mother and father arrived at my house with pastry, flowers and a marriage proposal," her mother said. "This time, my father surprised me, for he said yes. As was our marriage custom, Sherko first handed my father a satchel full of money and a promise of goats, my *shirbaii*, bride money. Sherko then bent down to kiss my father's hand, which he, by custom, immediately pulled away. Instead, my father kissed Sherko's forehead and declared, 'You are my son now.'

"Within one moon cycle, we were married in a ceremony at Sherko's house. My family cried when I left to live with his family. But his family, including his mother and sisters, embraced me. They showered me with rosewater. They adorned my face with heavy blushes and lipstick. For our wedding ceremony, I wore a light pink Kurdish dress and large gold necklaces and earrings. At the ceremony I did the usual slow Kurdish dance, one of the *helperke*, with Sherko, surrounded by our family and friends. My parents left early, as is also customary, and I sat quietly and watched the other guests dance for the rest of the night. I was demure and said 'thank you' only when others approached me to wish me well.

"But, Nazanin, not long after that, Sherko was called away to join the army," her mother said, her voice becoming more solemn. "He had just turned eighteen, and he was ordered by the government to go and fight. I told him how sad I would be, and he said he would write me every day. I reminded him that I could not read and did not even know how to write.

"A few days later, just before Sherko was to show up at the *pasgah gendarmerie*, the local army base, he took me out into the field where we used to run and play as children. In a sandy part of the ground, he taught me how to read and write simple words like 'love,' 'heaven,' 'moon,' and 'stars,' which he wrote in the loose earth with a stick.

"I got one letter from him when he was about to leave for the front lines. He was killed a few days after the postmark on the stamp, blown up by a land mine. 'At least he had the keys to enter heaven,' I overheard his father tell some of his friends, echoing the mullah who had said that young men who died in combat for the regime were martyrs and would be justly rewarded for their sacrifice in the afterlife.

"'I wish I had entered heaven with you,' I had whispered back as I prepared food for the funeral.

"After my forty days of mourning, during which I wore no kohl around my eyes, a long black scarf that I draped around my body and a black, simple dress with no design, embroidery or coins, Sherko's mother told me that the Iranian government saw me as a martyr's wife. 'But instead of feeling pride, I want you to feel shame,' she told me, grabbing my arm. 'Sherko had a good life until you and the bloody war came into it. I believe you are to blame for his death. You are cursed. You are *bawbakht*.'

"She then beat me with a cane on my back and legs until I was so black and blue I limped for a week. From that day on, my dreams at night were pierced by her voice saying, '*Bawbakht, bawbakht . . .*' And by what else she had told me: 'You will marry Sherko's older brother. He has homes in Bandar-e-Bushehr and Sanandaj, and he has agreed to take you. I don't ever want to see you again.'

"I never again wore makeup. I no longer watched my figure. I still wear the black that I wore to Sherko's funeral. My life was over when he died. I am *bawbakht*, just like Mahtab predicted. A dark veil now covers my eyes where I used to see stars. I am alive, but I walk in shadows."

CHAPTER 5

NAZANIN AFSHIN-JAM

December 2003, Sanya, China

After celebrating my first-runner-up finish with my parents and James back at the hotel, I returned to my room. I felt light-headed from the excitement of the evening. I slipped off my high-heeled shoes and then called Naz.

"I got your email," she said after congratulating me. "Emails are coming in from Canadians and also Persians from around the world, including those in Iran. So many people stayed up to watch the competition because of you. They are so proud."

I lay down on my pillow, still wearing the light pink satin gown with chiffon wings that Bobby had designed for the final night of the competition. I took off my crown and stared at it. My mind then drifted to the time when my father gave me a sparkling tiara for a present. I was a small girl in Canada.

LIKE OUR HOUSE IN TEHRAN, the house in which I spent my early childhood in Vancouver was also full of laughter, comfort and happiness. But it was a house that contained a secret too.

For as long as I can remember, I have always internalized what others feel. I first noticed this when I was about four and a friend I was with fell off a swing. My stomach knotted as blood trickled down her leg from a scraped knee. When she cried and held her knee, it was as if I too had injured myself—I could feel her pain in my body. From that day on, whenever I witness or hear of human or animal suffering, I feel the pain in my stomach as if it were my own. And so it was the same in my house. Even as a small child, I knew that my father and mother were in some kind of pain, particularly when I asked them why we lived in Canada while my grandmothers, aunts and other relatives remained in Iran. And why I had never met my aunt, uncle and cousins on my father's side.

For many years, the response was always the same. My father would smile and reply in a calm, soothing voice, "We want you to get a good education."

When I would ask why we couldn't live all together as a family, he would pull me into his arms, stroke my back and change the subject by telling me a story in Persian. "You like *Shangool o Mangool Habbeyeh Angoor*," he would declare, even though he knew my mother had recited it to me a thousand times before. "Let me tell it to you again."

"*Yeki bood yeki nabood ghair as Khoda hichki nabood*," my father would say, reciting, the way Persians do, the conventional beginning of all fairy tales, the equivalent of "Once upon a time": *There was one, there was no one, other than God there was no one.*

"There were three little goats," he would continue, sitting me down on his lap. "The mommy goat had to go out shopping. So she told the three little goats to not open the door unless it was her.

"A wicked wolf knocked at the door while she was away. 'I am your mommy,'" my dad would say in a high-pitched voice, pretending to be the mommy goat. "'Let me in!'

"'Show us your hands through the mail slot,' the three little goats said.

"The wicked wolf put his hairy brown paws through the mail slot.

"'But your hands are not soft, white and pretty like my mommy's,'" continued my father in a childlike voice, as if he were one of the goats. "The wolf left, only to return with flour on his paws to make them appear more goat-like. The three little goats fell for the ruse. They opened the door, and the wolf burst in and gobbled them up. But when the mommy goat returned and saw the wolf licking his lips, her three little babies nowhere to be found, she knocked him over and with her horns slit open his tummy. And all the little goats came tumbling out.

"Be careful," my father warned me at the end of the story. "Always be careful, when you answer your door, whom you let in."

My mother, Jaleh, is so very different from my father. She can never conceal her sorrow the way he can. Jaleh is an artist. She lived and studied art in Rome for seven years before returning to Tehran and marrying my father. She has the true heart, soul and torment of an artist. The walls of all our homes when I was growing up were adorned with her silk paintings and acrylics on canvas. Many elements of her pieces reflect our ancient Persian heritage—harem-style pants, which billow out like butterfly wings on the women when they are seated, Persian calligraphy, images of horses resembling those that guarded the palace of the Achaemenid kings in Persepolis, and ruby-red pomegranates, symbolizing fertility. But her paintings reveal Jaleh's torn soul as well. One of her silk pieces is of a lone wounded white dove with blood on its wing, symbolizing that the world has no peace.

None of the townhouses in which we lived in West Vancouver was big, so Jaleh painted her canvases on the kitchen table. She cleaned up before meals by piling her paints, cleaners, rags, brushes and papers along the walls. The houses were also full of Jaleh's music—Charles Aznavour, Adamo, Plácido Domingo, Billie Holiday, Frank Sinatra, Nina Simone and Julio Iglesias. The great symphonies were also part of my mother's soul. Every day when she was a child, she and her two sisters would return from school and spend an hour in front of the radio listening to classical music while their father quizzed them on what they had just heard. "Music," she would say to me when I sat beside her painting my own pictures, which were sometimes typically childish—rainbows, flowers and smiley suns—and other times quite grown-up, of girls riding horses into battle and Persian female warriors—Apranik and Artimisia—"music is the soul of life. When there is no music, there is emptiness."

Every now and then when we visited another Persian family for dinner or to celebrate holidays like Nowruz, Persian music would be played. Usually it was music set to the great Iranian poets such as Hafez or Omar Khayyám. Jaleh's honey-brown eyes, heavily lined in dark brown kohl complemented with smoky-green eyeshadow, would tear and she would gaze off into nowhere.

I would rub my cheek against her silk blouse and ask, *"Chi shodeh?"*—"What happened?"

"It is nothing," she would eventually say. She'd then wipe her eyes, her eyeliner now smudged. She'd run her fingers through my hair and kiss my forehead. "Don't worry, Nini, my love; I'm just feeling nostalgic," she would say with a smile, but I knew the smile was faked, to make me feel better.

In Vancouver, I attended Hollyburn Elementary School. I took my classes in French but spoke Persian at home with my mother, English with my sister and a mix of the two with my father. Naz turned seven the year we moved to Canada. I was two. We both learned English by watching *Mr. Dressup* and *Sesame Street*.

The first townhouse we lived in was on a quiet street. My group of friends and I could walk back and forth across the street, from one house to another, as there was so little traffic. In the summer months, we played games outside like double dutch skipping and hide-and-go-seek. We would go from one girl's bedroom to another, where we squirmed our way into each other's clothes or rummaged through each other's dress-up boxes and then put on plays that we made up ourselves. We always ended up in a kitchen, where we snacked on crackers and cheese, apples, or carrots. My house was often ignored for snack time, since my mother served Iranian staples like pistachios, figs, feta and *lavashak*, a sour fruit roll-up made of prunes. Certainly not the Western foods that my friends were used to.

None of the adults on the street worried about young girls roaming about on their own. For one, we had my tomboy sister, Naz, who was always watching over me, "like Napoleon would his armies," she would say, standing with her back straight and arms folded in front of her, a portrait of the great leader himself. When she was eleven and got a paper route, she used most of the money she earned to buy me toys and chocolate. I shared a bedroom with my sister. Her side was full of Transformers and toy cars and, as a teenager, posters of Ferraris and Porches. My side had bookshelves filled with stuffed animals, Barbies and arts-and-crafts sets. While Naz skateboarded outside or rode her boy's BMX bike, I would sneak inside and dress up in my mother's velvet shawls, clunky necklaces and high heels. We couldn't be more different, but I loved her deeply. With Naz I felt safe.

Naz was my keeper, while my mother reflected my own soul. It was the running joke in the family that my sister acted more like my mother, and my mother, more like a sister.

SHORTLY BEFORE my eighth birthday, I learned my family's secret.

I was lying on my parents' bed after dinner one night in my pyjamas. The rain was softly hitting the windowpane outside. Georges Bizet's *Carmen* was on the stereo in the living room, and I could hear Naz in the washroom down the hallway brushing her teeth. I was reading *Curious George*.

"What is that little monkey doing this evening?" my father asked as he walked into the bedroom.

I was lying on my stomach, my elbows propping up my torso, my bare feet splayed in the air, and mumbled a response.

"How was school today?" my mother asked as she too entered the room, slipping off her gold clip-on earrings.

I didn't look up. My eyes didn't even leave the line of the page I was reading. Curious George was lost in Central Park in New York City and the man with the yellow hat was looking for him.

But then I stopped and looked over at my father. His back was turned toward me. He had taken off his white button-down work shirt and was about to put on a cotton pyjama top. I caught a glimpse of his back. White scars ran horizontally in the middle of his back. I'd seen them before, but I had never been told what they were from.

I swung my legs off the side of the bed and sat up. My mind drifted to a conversation I had put away somewhere in my mind—a conversation I had had about a month earlier with my friend Arlene, whose mother was my godmother. With our Sunday-school class we had been visiting a soup kitchen in Vancouver's Downtown Eastside, one of the poorest neighbourhoods in all of Canada and known as one of the worst communities in all of North America for drug use and addictions.

Our class was helping hand out food. I was nervous at first, for I had never seen people so dirty and wearing such tattered clothes. Their fingernails were yellow and their hair greasy. They smelled and some had obvious mental illnesses, which I could tell by their twitching bodies and mannerisms.

We had been told—which had shocked me—to give the patrons, mostly homeless men and women, whatever was set in front of us. As a result, some people I gave a box of doughnuts to; others, a loaf of bread. I had been expecting that the food would be meals of turkey and mashed potatoes, like I had seen actors on television shows hand out when they visited soup kitchens. I thought the clientele would be rough and mean. But I was surprised: they were extremely kind, and grateful for the food.

The poverty of the people, the rundown establishment and the nutritional value of the food had startled me. I was still thinking about it when we drove home over the Lions Gate Bridge and into one of the most affluent areas in Canada, West Vancouver.

"Can you believe that people live like that so close to this?" I said to Arlene as we drove past a mansion with four expensive cars sitting in the driveway.

"No," she gasped. "I heard some of the men talking at the soup kitchen about just being released from prison . . . like your dad."

"*What?*"

"I heard from my mom that your dad had been in jail in Iran."

"No. Why would you say something like that!" I hissed, shuffling away from her and staring out the window in silence the rest of the way home.

I asked my father about it now. "Arlene told me that her mother told her that you were beaten up and thrown in prison in Iran. What is she talking about, Baba? Do the scars on your back have something to do with that? Only bad people go to jail. Are you a bad person?"

My mother, who was unravelling her long purple cashmere scarf from around her neck, stopped still, her eyes staring straight ahead without blinking. Silence filled the room. I looked at my father, who was also standing absolutely still and wide-eyed. Naz appeared at the doorway with her toothbrush still in her mouth. My father shifted slightly and waved for her to stay where she was. He then took a deep breath and looked at me with pleading eyes.

"What are the marks on your back that you never tell me about?" I persisted.

My father sat down beside me on the bed. Naz took the toothbrush out of her mouth, placed it on my father's dresser and then crawled along the bed to sit on the other side of me. My mother took a package of cigarettes from her sweater pocket. With shaking hands, she struck a match and lit one. She stroked her chest with the long elegant fingers of her free hand as she inhaled. All the while she stared out at the raindrops dripping down the window.

My eyes darted from Naz, who was biting her fingernails, to my father, who was looking at the ceiling fan. The room started to spin, so I focused my gaze on my favourite painting of my mother's, of ten white birds flying toward a diamond. Another white bird, however, flies confidently toward a white heart. I remembered my mother telling me the significance of the painting. Those birds flying toward the diamond represent all those who choose the path of greed and riches. The lone bird has chosen the path of love and goodness. I identified with the bird flying toward the heart even though the flock was going the other way. "Are you the good bird or a bad bird?" I asked my father almost in a whisper.

"I'm the good bird." He sighed, then said, "It is complicated. It is getting late." He cupped my chin in his hand and held my head at such an angle that our eyes locked.

"But, Baba," I pleaded, "you never answer my questions about Iran. It's not fair. Arlene even knows things I don't know. You are hiding a secret from me."

"You are right," my father replied, jolting me so much so with his response that my sobs immediately stopped. I was expecting him to change the subject to a fairy tale. Instead he said, "You are growing big, and you are right to ask about these things. Tomorrow, I will tell you what it is all about. Tomorrow, I will tell you about Iran."

CHAPTER 6

NAZANIN FATEHI

Early 1988 to 1997, Sanandaj, Iran

————————

Nazanin Fatehi came into the world the second eldest daughter of her mother, Maryam, and father, Habibollah, whom everyone called Habib for short. Premature by about a month and weighing only two and a half kilograms, she was born in the family's small stone house at about midnight to the sound of a stray dog howling at the moon, and into the arms of an aging midwife. She didn't cry. She didn't even pucker as if to suckle at her mother's breast.

"Can I see the baby?" Leila asked, emerging from the shadows of the kerosene lamp–lit room, from where she had watched the delivery, squirming at her mother's screams and squeezing her hands together with every push, all the while praying to Khwa that the baby would come.

Leila had known for several weeks her mother was carrying a girl. "I heard her say her name in my dreams," Leila told her mother one day as the two were mending clothes.

"And what is that name?" her mother asked, not looking up from the button she was sewing onto one of her husband's shirts.

"Nazanin," Leila whispered. "'I am coming now, sweet sister,' she said to me in my dream. And she said, 'I want to be called Nazanin.'"

Her mother stopped what she was doing and stared at her six-year-old daughter, who had never set foot in a school and who

Maryam at times thought was not bright thanks to her happy-go-lucky, flighty nature. "I think that's a Fars name," her mother said with a scowl. "And dreams are for Fars, not for us. If you don't dream, you won't be disappointed."

Leila tilted her head to the side and looked intently at her mother's fleshy face. "You're wrong," she was about to say, when her gaze landed on her mother's forehead. Leila did not know then the story of her mother's life. But in a flash, looking at that tattoo of the eye, Leila felt all of her mother's pain. "I understand," she said, lowering her head. "I will love my sister whatever you call her."

That same day, when Leila was out in the alleyway banging the crumbs and dust off the family's old Kurdish rugs, she saw a sparrow leaping along the roof of a building. She imagined that the little bird, with its brown and green feathers, was her sister Nazanin. "I can't wait to see you. We will fly together," Leila said, cupping her hands and blowing her words up to the creature. The bird looked at Leila. Then it quickly flew away, escaping a rock fired from a slingshot by a boy on the street.

THE YEAR NAZANIN WAS BORN, 1988—the Persian year 1366—was also the year the Iran-Iraq War, which started in 1980, ended. Both countries were bankrupt and tired of fighting. The reasons for the conflict were complex. It is widely believed that Iraq thought that, since Iran had just gone through its revolutionary period (which Iraqi elite supported because they had their own issues with the shah), it would be an easy victory, especially if the most important oil-producing province, Khuzestan, was conquered. Ayatollah Khomeini, the leader of Iran, on the other hand, did not hide his anger toward Iraq for the bad treatment he had endured while living in exile there. During the height of the Iran-Iraq War, Khomeini used the slogan *"Rahe Quds az Karbala mi gozarad"*—"The road to Jerusalem is through Karbala"—Karbala, Iraq, being among the holiest cities for Shia Muslims, along with Mecca, Medina and Najaf. This was also an indication of Khomeini's hostility toward Saddam Hussein. Khomeini viewed the defeat of Iraq as the first step to freeing Jerusalem from Israel and handing it over to the Palestinians.

The Kurds in both countries were often the ones who bore the brunt of the fighting. Stories abounded in the Iranian Kurdish cities of Mahabad and Sanandaj of their men, soldiers in the war, taking Iraqi prisoners and torturing them in darkened cells with acid baths and drilling of body parts, only to later discover that the victims were Kurdish Iraqis, and in some cases relatives of people they knew.

There was no reprieve for the Kurds when Iran and Iraq began to withdraw their troops. Starting in 1986, the Iraqi regime, led by Saddam Hussein, used its exhausted and battered soldiers to wipe out the Kurdish people in northern Iraq. The Kurds were holding peaceful protests and engaging in acts of civil disobedience in an attempt to gain more cultural autonomy and a federal government system that would allow them voting rights and representation. It was a crime to ask for such rights, according to Saddam Hussein. The regime ordered Iraqi troops to use any means to eliminate and disperse the Kurdish population. They called this campaign or war against the Kurds "Al-Anfal." Saddam's cousin, Ali Hassan al-Majid, head of the Ba'ath Party's northern region, rounded up Kurdish men and boys physically strong enough to carry guns. Most were murdered and buried in mass graves, some of which are just being discovered today. Others were sent to concentration camps, the most famous of which was the Nugra Salman, which confined as many as 9,000 people at a time, the majority of whom were starved, dehydrated, savagely beaten and raped before being shot by firing squads and buried in mass graves or fed to wild dogs. All of this was done in an attempt to Arabize the Kurdish region of Iraq. Kurds were expelled from the oil-rich cities of Kirkuk, Mosul and Makhmour and replaced by Iraqi Arabs.

Al-Anfal was touted as a religious war. Al-Anfal, after all, is the name of the eighth sura of the Qur'an, which speaks of the victory of the followers of the new faith of Islam over pagans in the Battle of

Badr in AD 624. Al-Anfal is what a leader recites to those under him to encourage them to do well. But Al-Anfal in the Kurdish genocide came to mean the fruits of war and was used by Iraqi soldiers to justify their taking whatever they could from the Kurds—the looting and razing of Kurdish villages; the kidnapping, rape and sale of girls and young women to other countries as prostitutes and housemaids; and the theft of the region's cattle, sheep, goats, money and weapons, which were given to Iraqi Arab villages in the south. Western human rights organizations dubbed Ali Hassan al-Majid "Chemical Ali" for his use of mustard gas, sarin and tabun on the Kurdish people, including the infamous attack on the Kurdish town of Halabja in 1988, which killed 5,000 civilians instantly. Between February and September 1988, the slaughter of Kurds reached genocidal proportions. More than 180,000 were killed. Many more went into exile, most walking through rough mountainous terrain in sub-zero weather to reach Turkey, Syria, Iran and even as far as Lebanon.

Nazanin's father, the brother of her mother's first and only love, fought on the front lines of the Iran-Iraq War as a Sepahi. On a break from his duties, he and Nazanin's mother quietly said their vows in the groom's mother's home. There was no asking the bride's father for permission, for Nazanin's mother was now considered the property of her former husband's family. The wedding was a sombre affair. There was no music or dance, just a simple exchange of rings. Days later, the couple travelled to the port city of Bandar-e-Bushehr, where they lived in a one-room stone house that smelled of smoke and saffron.

For many years, Nazanin's father did his job dutifully. But by 1988, the year Nazanin was born, he had begun to question the war and his place in it. The news had reached him of the Kurdish people's plight in Iraq. At the end of his shifts, when he smoked his hand-rolled cigarettes, his mind would wander to all that he had seen and heard during his time in the war.

What he knew of the Kurds in Iran was that, after the revolution of 1979, Kurdish political parties began to ask for their equal rights and representation in the newly formed government and for autonomy, resulting in Ayatollah Khomeini declaring a jihad—a holy war—against Kurdish activism. In a speech in December 1979, Ayatollah Khomeini claimed that the concept of ethnic minorities was contrary to Islamic doctrine. He ordered the Revolutionary Guard to clear Kurdistan of the infidels. In the spring of 1980, government forces bombarded most of the Kurdish cities with an all-out military offensive, closing off roads to prevent food and other necessities from entering. The regime then enforced a military state in the region with a large presence of Revolutionary Guards.

One night just before Nazanin's birth, her father stood alone outside his house. As he watched the smoke from his cigarette drift up to the sky, he began to plan what he would do once his military service ended. He would look for a new job, perhaps doing construction work or as a porter, or even settling on a farm near his family home and raising goats and chickens. "I want to be a better man," he vowed.

When Nazanin was much older, her father told her of his pledge and his longing for a different life that never came—that is, until he was dismissed from Sepah for reasons Nazanin never fully understood.

Despite her tender age, the one thing she took with her from Bandar-e-Bushehr when her family moved to Sanandaj, just a year after her birth, were the distant sounds of gunshots, which punctured her dreams for many years to come. Leila seemed to be the only one who was pleased with her birth.

"May I hold the baby?" she asked, peering into her sister's red, puffy face.

The midwife guided Leila into a seated position on the cushion beside her mother and passed the baby to her. Leila held her cheek to her little sister's and rocked her back and forth, singing the lullaby her mother used to sing to her: "Sleep, sleep, my pretty-eyed daughter. *Lai lai lai lai kizholei chaw kazhalm . . . Lai.*"

"I wanted a boy," Nazanin's mother cried out as Leila finished her song. "Habib wanted a boy. When he finds out, he is going to be very disappointed."

Leila's smile left her face and she looked over at her mother, whose hair was wet from the exertion of the delivery, her eyes ringed with dark circles.

"*Khwa koro pe bat* . . . Next time may Khwa give you a son," the midwife said.

Leila's mother burst into tears. Leila, thinking she wanted the baby back, passed her the child, swaddled in a grey blanket her mother had saved up to purchase at the market. Her mother pushed the baby away. "No," she screamed, swatting her hands in the air. "How can I have two daughters? I am so cursed. I am *bawbakht*."

"Next time," the midwife repeated, waving Leila back to the corner of the room. "Next time you will have a boy. We will make sure of it." The midwife put the child into Maryam's arms. But Maryam didn't even look at the baby.

"She needs a name," the midwife said as she gathered the bloody sheets to throw out. "Do you have a name?"

Leila hopped from foot to foot. "Her name is Nazanin," she wanted to shout, but she knew to hold her tongue.

A tear trickled down Maryam's face and onto the child's cheek. With her free hand, Maryam slapped her chest to choke back the cry she had started to let out and then looked to the corner of the room, where Leila stood, holding her breath.

Nazanin's mother sighed and shook her head. "It doesn't matter," she said, handing the baby to the midwife. "You choose the name."

"Mahabad. I am from the city of Mahabad," the midwife said. "It's not such a bad city."

"It's not such a bad name," Maryam replied after a brief pause. "Mahabad."

"MY NAME IS NAZANIN," a four-year-old Nazanin said, stomping her foot on the ground and sending dust up into the air. "Why does she always call me Mahabad?"

"I know," Leila said, slipping her arm around her sister's shoulders.

Moments earlier, the two had been helping their mother make *robb* over the fire in the backyard, when their mother, stirring the pot, had tipped it over, burning her hand and spilling the contents on the ground. She had screamed at Nazanin, calling her Mahabad and throwing a tomato at her face as if she were responsible for the accident. Nazanin wiped the tomato pulp from her cheek. She wanted to lash out against her mother—Nazanin had *told* her she wanted to be called by a different name! But she saw her mother's piercing dark eyes and puffed up chest and knew better.

Nazanin, though young, had become all too familiar with her mother's mood swings. There were moments when her mother's demeanour was warm and welcoming; sometimes, on balmy summer nights, she would pull Nazanin into her arms, humming the lullabies Leila sang to her. It was on these nights, as Leila tended a fire in which she was roasting sunflower seeds and potatoes and Nazanin watched the embers float up into the sky, that her mother would call her Nazanin. "My sweetest daughter, *bawanm* Nazanin."

But on other days, her mother was possessed by a fury that Nazanin could sense with a shiver that came from deep inside her, even if she was a block away from home. Nazanin's first memory of this wrath was the day she was playing house with two other girls in the alleyway. They had used discarded boxes taken from the back of the supermarket and a rough grey blanket to construct their playhouse. One of the girls had run off to get her doll and some of her mother's cushions. Nazanin stepped out of the playhouse and spied her mother watching her from the window. Nazanin smiled and waved, but her mother only scowled back.

Nazanin's body shook and she stepped backwards. Tripping over a box, she fell onto the playhouse, crushing it. The other girl pulled herself out, her hair standing on end, her clothes rumpled. She glared at Nazanin. Nazanin, who didn't have many friends, turned and ran home in a panic, thinking the girls no longer liked her. She flung open the door. "I ruined our game," she cried out as she ran into her mother's arms. But instead of comforting Nazanin, her mother pushed her away and Nazanin stumbled into the corner of the room, hitting her head on the wall.

Five years later, when her mother recounted her life story of broken dreams after Nazanin's father had hit her, Nazanin did what good daughters do: she stayed by her mother's side, held her hand and listened. But when her mother pulled her into her arms to sleep side by side, Nazanin's body stiffened and her lips trembled, for she was uncertain whether it was her loving mother holding her tight or the one who hurt her. She closed her eyes tight and imagined herself as the little sparrow Leila had told her she had seen before she was born, flying toward the sun. When her mother's heavy snores filled the room, Nazanin unwrapped herself from her mother's embrace and moved in beside Leila, whose soft, sweet breath lulled her to sleep.

Nazanin woke and followed the sound to the washroom, where Leila was filling the aluminum tub one bucket at a time with hot water. Leila pulled off Nazanin's dress. Nazanin curled her legs up as she crouched into the warm water and Leila ran a sponge over her skin. After, Leila combed her long, silky hair. "Mother loves you. I know she does," Leila said, adding some cream to Nazanin's knots. "She is just sad."

"She told me why she is sad," Nazanin replied. She then related their mother's love story.

"I have a crush on a boy," Leila said in a very low voice when Nazanin was done.

"Who?" Nazanin asked, wide-eyed. "Will you marry him?"

"I hope so," Leila smiled. "You've seen him. He waits for me on his motorbike every morning. He has curly black hair and blue-green eyes. You walk past him on the way to school. He follows me to the market. His name is Shaho."

"I thought father had met with another family that asked for your hand in marriage?"

"Baba didn't accept," Leila said, her eyes sparkling. "He said the *mareii*, the money owed to our family by the groom in case we divorced, was too little. So I have hope. When there is a full moon, I always wish for Shaho, and I always hear a little voice in my head saying, 'You will be together,' so I know everything will be all right."

"Mahabad, get in here," her mother bellowed.

Nazanin quickly dried herself off and slipped on the same dress she had been wearing the day before and a pair of slacks that Leila handed her. With her hair loose and wet, she ran into the room her mother used as a kitchen, although the family was too poor to have a fridge and the stove was small and portable. Her mother was inspecting a pot with burned rice at the bottom and plates with dried beans caked on them. "Clean this up," Nazanin's mother ordered.

Nazanin began to pour water from the jug on the floor into the rubber basin used for cleaning dishes. "You can't go to school anymore," her mother said coldly as she sat down on a stool and spread her legs out in front of her.

Nazanin's back straightened and her body trembled. She closed her eyes tight and thought positive thoughts, something Leila had taught her to do. *I am going to school*, she repeated silently to herself.

"Did you hear me?" her mother bellowed again, leaning forward and slapping Nazanin's back with the wet towel she had been pressing to her lip, which was swollen from Habib's beating the night before. "You can't go to school anymore."

Nazanin slowly turned and faced her mother. "Why?" she asked. "The school year is almost finished. I will then have time at home to help you. You promised this would be the year I could go all the way through," she sobbed.

"Your father can no longer work," Nazanin's mother said, leaning back against the wall and covering her face with the end of her chador. "Sepah refuses to give him a pension. I have heard that for this to happen the guard must have done something terrible on the job, but what, I do not know. And my money for being a martyr's wife is gone. I don't know where. All I know is that we have nothing.

"Leila is getting married," her mother continued. "She is moving to her husband's house. You have to care for your sisters and younger brother."

A few days later, Leila was told that her father had agreed for her to marry a man nearly three times her fifteen years. He had been a prisoner of war during the Iran-Iraq conflict; Iraq had released him in the early 1990s. He now worked as a driver for the City, Nazanin's father explained. "He has a good job that the government has promised he can keep for life for his sacrifices made during the war," he told Leila. When the man arrived, Nazanin winced, for he was missing some teeth, was as thin as her brother, Hojat, and smelled of onions, sweat and urine. Nazanin shrank to the back of the room as introductions were made. "This is Karim," Nazanin heard the man's father say.

Karim's mother said her son's name meant "kind," but she herself was not kind, or so Nazanin thought. She wouldn't even look at Leila. "We will take her," she said sternly as Karim's father offered bride money, *shirbaii*, of fifty gold coins.

"I don't want to marry Karim," Leila told her father when everyone had left.

"It is done," he sighed. "You have no choice. You need to marry him, for us." Her father ordered Leila to never see the boy on the motorbike again. "I know you like each other. Your mother sees everything. But you will bring shame to this family if you are caught together . . ." A tear escaped from the corner of his eye. "Leila, you now belong to another family," he continued after gaining his composure. "Don't bring us shame and make me have to do something I don't want to do."

LEILA HAD TAKEN TO SHUFFLING slowly around the house like one of the women Nazanin often saw in the Sanandaj cemetery: her eyes never fully open and the black of her pupils seeming dulled to grey. Leila still brushed Nazanin's hair, as she brushed Shahla's, but none of the girls in the house said much, even when their mother had left to clean the houses with the rose gardens, which was becoming a steady stream of part-time work for her.

"I saw a puppy at the market when we went to look for dresses for Leila's wedding," Hojat said one morning before school—being a boy, he was still allowed to attend classes. "Remember when Shahla and I ran off to look at the skinned goats hanging in the window of the butcher? In front of the store was a basket of puppies. I want one," he told Nazanin. "I will ask Father for one."

"I don't think that is a good idea, Hojat," Nazanin said. "Dogs are, well," she bit her lip, afraid of Hojat's wrath. "Dirty," she finally managed to get out.

"No," Hojat said, placing his hands on his hips and glaring at Nazanin. "I want a dog."

"How are you going to feed him?" Nazanin asked, cautiously standing up to her younger sibling. She knew that Hojat was her father's favourite. If he allowed Hojat to get a puppy, Nazanin would be beaten for protesting. "We don't have enough food for us, let alone a mongrel," she said, her voice cracking.

"But you're all mongrels," Hojat spat, "all you girls, so one more won't make a difference." He punched Nazanin in the stomach as he moved past her to get to the door. "I'll get my dog on Friday, when Father is home," he called out as he left.

Nazanin's father now spent most of his days in the home of his other wife, which gave Nazanin and her sisters free range of their house. He picked up Hojat right after morning prayers that Friday. Hojat, too big by then for shoulder rides, skipped alongside his father, who walked with the help of a cane following his surgery. When they returned to the house, Hojat had his puppy, a brown-and-white short-haired dog with tiny ears and a piercing bark. Hojat also had a lollipop in the shape of a rooster and a fistful of other candies, which he refused to share with his sisters.

LEILA'S WEDDING PREPARATIONS were not joyful. Her mother chose a dress from a rental store, a cream-coloured Western-style dress with gold embroidery. The day of the wedding, Leila sat in the kitchen and stared into nowhere as the beautician applied a cake-mix-like white powder several shades lighter than Leila's olive skin, lip liner that was a far darker shade than her lipstick and thick black eyeliner to create a cat's eye effect. The groom and his family arrived. After one Kurdish line dance, the bride and groom said goodbye to Leila's mother and father and headed to the groom's house for the rest of the ceremony and celebration. As Leila walked away, Nazanin's mother started to wail, as is customary, to show her sorrow that a daughter had left the home. But Nazanin felt that her mother's tears were not real. She doesn't care that Leila is gone, Nazanin thought. It's all show for the neighbours. Only I care.

The wedding, as was also customary, ended with the bride and groom heading to the wedding chamber. A female relative of the groom's wrapped up the bloody sheet indicating that Leila had been a virgin, and she and several other female members of the family took it to the bride's home. Leila wasn't allowed to return to see her mother, at least not right away.

As the days after Leila's wedding drifted into weeks, Nazanin's mother woke each morning before the sun rose and headed to her cleaning jobs, lugging around her supplies in a shopping basket. She always returned well after nightfall, after Nazanin had fed her sisters *dokhawa*, while Hojat chewed on lamb or goat and sometimes chicken pieces that Nazanin's father brought only for him.

While Hojat was at school, Nazanin would tie the dog, named Rocky after the American movie Hojat wanted to see, to a post outside the house. She then pretended she was the mother of her sisters, preparing their food, taking them to the market, bathing them and scrubbing their clothes. She sat them outside in the alleyway and then read her book to them.

One day, a woman who regularly passed by stopped. She had

noticed Nazanin reading the same book over and over. "What are you doing?" she asked.

"Reading," Nazanin said.

"Do you like to read?" the woman probed, sitting down on a rock beside her. Nazanin had often been curious about this woman, who wore new Kurdish dresses with real coins sewn into the fabric. The woman carried a brown leather shoulder bag, wore high-heeled shoes and smelled of jasmine. "My name is Hana," she said. "May I?" she asked, taking the book from Nazanin.

With animated speech, as if she were the characters, Hana read the popular fable *Shangool o Mangool Habbeyeh Angoor*, about the three little goats. Parastoo and Shahla moved in close, gasping at the high points and covering their mouths and screaming "No!" when the wolf ate the goats.

"How come you aren't in school?" Hana asked when she had finished reading the story. She pulled a small knife from her purse, then felt into her paper shopping bag and pulled out a pomegranate, which she cut into pieces for Nazanin and her sisters. "How come you can't read the whole book?"

"How did you know?"

"I watch you when I pass by. You can read some of the lines from the book but not all. At your age, you should be able to read chapter books, not struggle with picture books."

"I have to look after my sisters," Nazanin replied, wiping pomegranate juice from Shahla's face with a tissue Hana had handed her. "Mother has to work, because Father can't work anymore."

"I live alone and I have a big library, and I would like to teach you to read," Hana said, smiling, as she started to gather up her belongings. "I don't work on Fridays. Why don't you and your sisters come and I will fix us a nice meal and we can read?"

Nazanin felt a great joy bubbling up inside her. But she didn't want to show Hana anything but her reserve. "Thank you," Nazanin said politely, lowering her eyes and tenderly kissing the knuckles of Hana's hands. "I would like that very much."

But the following Friday, Nazanin could not attend. Rocky had bitten a three-year-old boy, and Hojat's father was furious when he heard the news. He slapped Hojat for the very first time. "The dog is sick, Hojat," he said. "He has rabies."

"But I will keep him on the leash at all times. I promise I will watch him. He won't bite again."

"It has nothing to do with you," his father replied as the dog, locked up in the washroom, howled. Nazanin could hear the irate dog pushing around the watering can they used to clean themselves. "That boy may die. His blood is now on my hands, for you are my son and that dog is yours. I got these," he then said, holding up two orange pills. Hojat started crying when his father tucked the pills inside some raw red meat.

For most of that night, Nazanin, Hojat and Shahla lay side by side, listening to Rocky's breathing. It wasn't until the early hours of the morning, when the rooster first crowed, that the children fell asleep. When they awoke a few hours later, Rocky was dead, his mouth half open, his legs stiff. "Dogs are *najess*"—"dirty," her mother said to Hojat as he wrapped the carcass in a torn sheet to take to the outskirts of town for burial. "I never could understand why your father allowed it. Your father couldn't even pray in the house when he came to visit with that dirty dog around. Now, at least, Khwa will bless our home again."

CHAPTER 7

NAZANIN AFSHIN-JAM

April 1987, Vancouver

———

The morning after my father promised to tell me about Iran, I woke early. I looked over at Naz on the other single bed in our bedroom. Her Snoopy bedspread had fallen on the floor during the night and her blankets had been pushed to the side.

Naz stirred slightly and began talking in her sleep. *"Baba koo?"* she said in Persian. I remember shuddering, for she was asking, "Where is Dad?"

"I don't want to leave," she cried out.

I sat up and had started to pull back my pink comforter to go to Naz and comfort her when she mumbled, "Don't hurt Baba. Please don't let them take my baba away." She then rolled over and was quiet again.

I lay back down on my pillow and stared at the stucco ceiling, mulling over the meaning of Naz's words, when the clock struck six. I heard my father clear his throat and shuffle past the closed bedroom door. I quickly got up. My father only woke early when he had to go to work.

Baba wasn't supposed to go in today. He promised he would talk to me about Iran!

I ran so fast that when I entered the kitchen and saw my father standing there with a frying pan in his hand, I had to skid on the linoleum floor in order to come to a full stop.

"Good morning, Nini," my father chuckled. "How are you this morning? Ah . . . I can see you have had a rough night."

I turned and looked at my reflection in the mirror that hung on the wall. My long hair was tangled and frizzy and I had tied my belt so quickly that the front of my housecoat was a good foot shorter than the back, but I didn't care. I looked at my father.

"Baba," I said slowly, tilting my head to the side. "You said you would tell me some stories today about, well, you know."

"I know. I promised," my father replied, startling me, for I was convinced he was going to put me off again. "I thought you and I could talk before the others wake up. Shall we have breakfast? How about an omelette?"

I nodded. When my father turned to prepare our food, I whispered "Thank you," and placed my hands in front of me as if in prayer. I then sat down on one of the kitchen chairs and watched as he put olive oil in a frying pan and heated it on the gas stove.

I tapped my fingers on the kitchen table until my father set my omelette and a big glass of freshly squeezed orange juice in front of me. He then grabbed his own plate. "So, Nazanin," he began after taking a few bites. "You want to know about . . . Spain? No—Sweden!"

"Baba!" I glared at him.

"I'm just playing with you," he laughed, and took out a parcel wrapped in tissue paper. He pushed it toward me, saying, "I was saving this for your birthday, but I want to give it to you now because you are growing up so fast."

I opened the gift and smiled, for it was a "diamond" tiara.

"You want to learn about Iran. So, my little Persian princess, let's start," he said, as I slipped on the tiara.

After he told me his story, I cried. Looking back, he didn't tell me much then other than what I as a small child could understand at that time.

Not very often, but a few times over the years on special moments when we found ourselves alone together, he would tell me more of his story and in more depth—especially one time in my last year of high school, just before I was about to enter university. "When I myself entered university, Nini, it was an interesting time," he began in a nostalgic, soft tone. "I felt our great nation's demise."

"THE UNIVERSITY OF TEHRAN was a hotbed of political activity in the late 1960s, when I started my undergraduate degree there," he said. "I had attended an all-boys school until then and was immediately struck by the women's movement on campus. About half of my classes consisted of females, wearing miniskirts and fashionable outfits mimicking the models in the Western magazines that they read in the cafeteria during lunch. There were women taking physics courses and working in the laboratories too.

"I was so impressed with the liberation I saw," my father said, smiling at the memory. "But at the same time, there was this one table in the cafeteria that was always taken by a group of young women. Over the years, the group got bigger and bigger, eventually spilling over and taking up as many as five tables. These women wore modest, floor-length dark skirts and bulky tops and sweaters. They would not socialize with the more stylishly dressed women or the men, no matter how much my peers and I tried to persuade them to join us at our table."

"The young women's parents won't let them socialize with boys," a friend later told my father. "They go to school and then return to their homes. They are instructed by their families to speak to no one other than their professors and each other. They will be married soon and will have to wear the chador from then on. We are seeing more and more women leading lives like this."

"Why?" my father asked.

"This country is a paradox," his friend replied. "We are modern and we are backward. It is now just a matter of time before we see which force will be stronger."

When my father entered university in 1968, Iran was booming economically, thanks mostly to oil revenues. Workers from overseas, particularly from the Philippines, were coming to the country in droves to work in construction or on the oil rigs. Tehran's streets were full of expensive cars, from the German-made BMW and Mercedes-Benz to the British-made Jaguar and Bentley. Many of the women who passed by the front desk of the hotel where my father had taken a part-time job to pay his living expenses and university tuition wore furs, pearls and diamonds, and the men tipped with crisp large bills. To my father, even people employed in what he thought would be low-paying positions appeared to be doing well. "The valet at the hotel had seven children," he explained. "All were fed, attending good schools and vacationing in the summers at the seaside."

By his third year at the University of Tehran, however, some of the students were condemning the excesses. The discussions at the cafeteria often turned to Communism, the events occurring in Eastern Europe and the Cold War between Iran's neighbour to the north, the Soviet Union, and the United States. The shah of Iran, Mohammad Reza Pahlavi, was fearful that these events would sway Iranians toward socialism, and so books such as Karl Marx's *Das Kapital* were banned. Nonetheless, many prohibited books and essays could be found in underground bookstores, and some of my father's professors were even diverting from their course lessons to debate world politics and political theories.

Simultaneously, another group on campus was becoming more and more vocal about the importance of religion in daily life and calling for a return to more traditional Islamic values.

"I was invited to attend evening get-togethers with my peers, where politics were discussed over wine, but I always declined," my father said. "I was busy, Nini. By second year, I'd given up my dreams of playing professional football, but I still played on the university team. I had football practice before and after classes, then my part-time work at the hotel, then studying after that, followed by whatever sleep I could find and then classes at the university again. I also didn't know what I could add to these conversations. I was happy with my life and optimistic about the future."

Then my father met my mother, Jaleh. They fell in love. After a year of dating, the couple wed. And a year after that my sister, Naz, graced their lives. For them, it was a golden time. They moved into an apartment in the Yousef Abad area of Tehran. The businesses were booming. Champagne flowed, and my father, now working full time as the general manager at the hotel, arranged concerts by pianists and famous musicians from Europe and the United States. Jaleh, who had quit her job to raise Naz, returned to painting in her spare time. Over long dinners and fine wine, as Naz slept quietly in a bassinette beside them, the two talked about the future, including putting their daughter into a good school and vacations. "And we did go away, much sooner than I thought," my father sighed. "But it foreboded dark times to come."

In 1978, his employers asked him to move temporarily with the family to Munich, then to Frankfurt and finally to Paris. Partly this was so that he could study European hotel-operating styles and eventually gain a higher position within the Sheraton hotel chain. But it was also because Sheraton was debating cancelling its management contract for the hotel in Tehran. The corporate brass, my father was informed, felt the political situation in Iran was becoming increasingly unstable and they were preparing to leave the country if something happened to the shah's government. It was in Paris that my mother found out she was pregnant with me.

My family was supposed to stay in Europe for a year and a half. But in January 1979, my father's boss in Tehran called to say he wanted him back. Tehran had virtually shut down. Protests and marches were taking place almost every day. Several industries had gone on strike, and many foreign hotel employees had left the country, fearing for their safety. "It's better that we have Iranians running the hotel," one of the hotel's vice-presidents told my father. "We're not sure how this is going to turn out."

The political tensions he first noticed as a student at the University of Tehran had escalated. The pockets of discontent from the Communists, socialists and freedom-fighting groups in Iran had spilled over to the masses. A very odd marriage had taken place between the Islamists and a variety of Communist factions. They buried their hatchets and cooperated, saying they wanted to unify the nation for a common cause, the achievement of democracy and freedom of speech.

When my parents and Naz arrived back at Mehrabad International Airport in Tehran, it was full of people thrusting their passports into the hands of officials, some with thousands of toman, the local currency, slipped between the pages. Women were crying as their husbands pleaded with airline personnel to find them a seat on a plane, any plane, leaving for anywhere. "As long as it is outside Iran," a man screamed at the person behind the ticket counter.

When they landed in Shiraz, where my father's boss wanted him to manage two hotels for a while, he exclaimed, "I've never seen anything like this!" As the taxi inched forward, children, some no older than six years, walked up to the windows and with dirty, outstretched hands asked for money. Many of the women on the streets wore black chadors. "I couldn't believe Iran could change so quickly, Nini," he told me. "You weren't even born yet."

My pregnant mother, my father and Naz settled into a two-bedroom suite on the fifth floor of Shiraz's Kourosh Hotel, one of the two hotels my father was managing. Everyone except night staff went to bed early, leaving Shiraz's once vibrant nightlife struggling to attract visitors. No one talked politics in the hotel, but when BBC reports ran on the television in the lobby, everyone, including the staff, stopped to listen before quietly and quickly returning to their duties, their heads lowered.

Taxi drivers would talk at great length about Iranian politics and the movement underway. "I heard today that even the clerics in the mosque are telling people to support the shah's downfall," my father told my mother one night. "The mosque, Jaleh! Never before have I heard about mullahs getting involved in politics in this fashion and so openly."

"On January 16, 1979, I woke to the sounds of shouting coming from the street," my father told me. "I dressed and opened the thick curtains and then the window. The streets for as far as I could see were swimming with people. They were all chanting '*Na Sharghi, na Gharbi, Jomhoori-e Eslami*'—'Neither East nor West—Islamic Republic!'"

"Something has happened, Baba?" Naz asked, the noise from the street having awakened her.

My father nodded as Naz and my mother walked up to stand beside him. "Yes. I think the shah has left the country."

"Down with the shah! Down with the shah!" The chanting was so loud that at first my father didn't hear the telephone ring.

"What do you mean? Explain this to me!" he yelled into the receiver.

My mother rushed over, while a now sobbing Naz crouched below the window hugging a pale yellow blanket she called Tati. With shaking hands, Jaleh rubbed my father's back as he continued to shout into the phone. Then he slammed down the receiver.

"A group of protestors wants to set the hotel on fire," he said to my mother. "Don't panic. Get Naz dressed," he ordered before getting back on the telephone and arranging for his secretary to take Jaleh and Naz on the last military airplane leaving for Tehran, all commercial airlines having been grounded. Then he pulled Jaleh into his arms. "Be strong, for Naz," he whispered in her ear. "I love you."

He rushed down the stairs—the elevators weren't working. When he stepped into the lobby, he came face to face with hundreds of protesters, including some of the hotel employees still in their uniforms. The upholstered chairs had been pushed to the sides of the room.

And then my father saw them: protestors carrying gasoline tanks and poles that had been wrapped with layers of fabric, which he suspected would be lit to be used as torches.

"There is the manager!" someone screamed, pointing at my father. "Get him!"

My father quickly jumped onto a stool. "Stop!" He held his hands out in front of him. "Stop!"

"Take us to the basement, Mr. Manager," a protestor spat out. As my father looked around the lobby his gaze fell on the hotel's entrance, which had been boarded up with sheets of plywood. In August, while living in Germany, he had read in the Iranian newspapers how Islamic militants in the city of Abadan had set the Cinema Rex on fire and that 400 theatregoers had perished because the doors had been barricaded shut. "Down with America! Down with the shah! Burn it down, burn it down, burn the symbol of the shah down!" the protestors shouted.

"Please listen to me!" my father yelled over and over. Eventually, some in the crowd in front of him quieted enough for him to continue.

"I am not a political man. But I know you cannot do this to the hotel."

The mob surged and grumbled, and my father motioned with his hands for them to give him a chance. "I know you want to set the hotel on fire," he said as people began to hush one another, indicating that they were willing to hear what he had to say. "But what will happen when it is gone? Many of you work here. How will you support your families? You won't have a job if there is no hotel. We all need to think logically about this. Even if this regime goes and another regime comes in its place, they will need to build another hotel. This is your hotel. Why burn down your own property?"

"For the next hour, I reasoned with the crowd, who slowly began to see my point," my father told me. "The hotel employees returned to their jobs as cooks, waiters, bellhops and maids, some even volunteering to take shifts guarding the hotel, while others headed back to the streets to join the march."

About a week after my birth on April 11, 1979—Easter Day—my father was transferred to the Sheraton hotel in Tehran. It was a tense time. Gangs of men brandishing semi-automatic weapons roamed the streets. One group called itself the Mobile Units of God's Vengeance, and pulled women over for not wearing the hijab, shouting, *"Ya roosari, ya toosari!"*—"Scarf on your head or we'll bang on your head!" Many of these unorganized militant groups merged to form Sepah and Basij.

A Mobile Unit first showed up at the Sheraton in the summer of 1979. The men ordered my father to take down all the portraits of the shah and replace them with photographs of Ayatollah Ruhollah Musavi Khomeini. The Mobile Unit then asked my father to take them to where the liquor was stored in the basement.

"That wasn't the end of it, Nini," my father pressed on. "It was an evening in the late fall of 1979 when Revolutionary Guards, part of Khomeini's new military, showed up. When I received the phone call that soldiers were in the lobby, I told Jaleh that I would not be long. This was routine. I had done nothing wrong."

But my father was greeted on the first floor by four men pointing Kalashnikov rifles at him. He slowly raised his arms as one of the men pushed him into the corner. Another man stepped toward him and started accusing him of still serving alcohol. "You are allowing men and women to talk with each other in the bars and restaurants," the man shouted. "And you are playing music. It's like opium," he said. "You are drugging Iranians. You are a drug pusher."

My father shook his head and denied the accusation of having alcohol on the premises. "It is gone, all gone. Your men poured it down the drain."

"But what about the music, and men and women mingling and dining together?" another shot back, jabbing his rifle into my father's ribs. "Only husbands and wives can be together in public. You are the devil we are trying to rid this country of. Was it your mother who raised you to be a traitor to the regime? I suspect she is nothing but a whore."

"I snapped, Nini, when he insulted my mother. The irony is that, unlike me, she was a devout Muslim. I slapped the man standing closest to me across his left cheek," my father explained. "After that, all the men aimed their rifles at my heart. I lowered my head. 'Take me,' I told them. 'I will not fight you.'"

One of the Revolutionary Guards started hitting him in the head with a baton. He fell to the ground, and another man started beating him with a club. Lying on his stomach, my father saw blood, his blood, coming from any number of head wounds, forming a pool on the white-and-black marble floor. He then felt a rough hand grab him by the collar of his shirt and drag him through the lobby to the street. Some of the employees started to move forward to help, but the soldiers ordered them to back off or they would be shot. Once outside, four men tossed my father headfirst into the back of a waiting van, where they beat him some more. Before he passed out from the pain, he heard one of the men say to him, "You're going to love where we're taking you."

CHAPTER 8

NAZANIN FATEHI

1997 to late October 1998, Sanandaj, Iran

———

"What do you smell?" Hana asked.

"Saffron," Nazanin replied.

"What else?"

After a long pause, Nazanin exclaimed, "Roses! I smell roses."

"Yes," chirped Hana as she slipped off the scarf she had used to cover Nazanin's eyes. As Nazanin stared at the blue glass vase of red roses sitting on the desk in her friend's library, Hana said, "I got these for you. To inspire you so that one day you can have a real rose garden of your own."

"Hana," Nazanin exclaimed, "I can't accept these. My mother would—"

"No need to say anything," said Hana, raising a hand. "The flowers are for you to enjoy when you are here."

Nazanin ran her fingers over the delicate petals and breathed in the scent. "Thank you," she said. Then added silently, *You are the best friend I have ever had.*

Nazanin and her sisters had been going to Hana's every Friday morning. That first day they had met, when Nazanin had been reading to her younger sisters from her picture book, Hana had drawn a map to show Nazanin how to get to her place. Nazanin assumed the home would be small, like her own, and attached to many others. She was wrong. Although not far away, Hana's house had four large rooms, one of which had been converted into a library. The house was also one of only a few that stood alone, surrounded by a vegetable garden and wire fencing.

Hana explained that her grandfather had built the house when he moved to Sanandaj from a small village in the north of Kurdistan Province. He had left his family's home with his young bride in search of spirituality. He wanted to follow a mystic path and so became a disciple of the famous Naghshbandi Sufi order in Sanandaj. Hana's grandfather had four sons, and as they grew and wed, the family kept adding on rooms to the house for their families. "At one point, this house had eight rooms," Hana beamed. "And outside we had cherry trees and rose bushes, and jasmine ran up the stone walls and on trellises. I had four of the rooms removed when I moved back from Tehran. It was just me," she sighed, "and I didn't want to have such a big place and draw attention to myself."

Each week, Nazanin was allowed to choose one book from a shelf that Hana had stocked with children's picture books. She and Hana would sit on one of the cushions in the room and read through the book together as the other children played games with each other. After, Hana would leave Nazanin to read the book on her own while she taught Shahla and Parastoo their letters in both Persian and Kurdish.

"A for *aab*"—"water," Nazanin would hear Hana tell the children in the kitchen, where she was teaching them the alphabet. "B for *baba*. Now, write *Baba aab daad*"—"Dad gave water."

"Excellent," she would say, clapping. "You are doing very well."

One time, Parastoo asked Hana why she always wore white gloves.

"Because I use chalk on the blackboards all day long at my work as a high school teacher. My skin is allergic to the calcite. Some of my skin is now peeling off," she replied, taking off the gloves and holding up her red chafed hands for the girls to see. "I wear the gloves to protect myself."

"I want to wear gloves too," Parastoo said.

"Well then, let's find some for you," Hana said, leading the girls from the kitchen to her bedroom, which had been decorated with burgundy velvet curtains and a matching bedspread on a real wooden bed, which the girls had never seen before—at their home they slept on mats on the floor. Hana opened a chest at the foot of the bed and started pulling out its contents: Kurdish dresses, Western skirts and tops, scarves and fur collars. "You can try these on," she told the children as Ghomri toddled into the room, rubbing her eyes from a nap. "And here you go," she said, holding up a small tin box. "Gloves. Lots of gloves."

From that day on, after their lessons, Shahla, Parastoo and Ghomri would play dress-up. In the early afternoon, Hana would feed the girls herbed stew with meat and rice, followed by sweets, including cake she'd made from scratch. While they ate, Nazanin read the book she had chosen for that day out loud to everyone. Their Fridays together ended with all the children putting on a skit, in their dress-up clothes, based on the story.

One day, Nazanin had chosen a book about Persian heroines, including Gordafarid, one of the heroines in Shahnameh's *The Book of Kings*, and Pantea, a Persian commander whose name means "strong and immortal." "Do you have any books about Kurdish women and their stories?" Nazanin said after she had read what she could of the book and Hana had finished it for her.

"Nazanin, we don't have much. A bookstore in Mahabad publishes our stories written in our language, but usually only in magazines and journals that we distribute among ourselves. The regime has banned Kurdish fairy tales," Hana said, closing her eyes and shaking her head.

"How do you know so much?" Shahla piped up.

"I went to university and I have travelled, and I come from a political family. While at university, I studied the great poets and fell in love with Rumi. I too then began to ask, where are the Kurdish writers?

"A Persian student named Farzad introduced me to Mawlawi

Tawagozi, also known as Mawlawi Kurd, the great Kurdish poet and mystic. Mawlawi Kurd spoke about love, humanity and caring for each other, and said that this world is not our destination, we are all merely passengers. When we die, we go back to source, to God, to Khwa." Hana closed her eyes and drifted off, as if in a dream. The girls sat quietly and watched.

"Kurdish stories were told orally," Hana said so suddenly that Ghomri jumped. "One of the reasons was that, historically, we were a peasant or village culture, and most people were not literate. School didn't reach the Kurdish people until relatively recently. And even then, Kurds in almost all regions in Turkey, Iraq and Iran have not been allowed to write in their own language. Long ago, we Kurds passed on our traditions, our values, our culture through stories that professional storytellers would travel far and wide to share, and fathers would tell their sons, and mothers their daughters, at night in the winter, when the winds howled through the mountains and the premorning chills drew ice designs on the glass windows."

"Tell us a Kurdish story," Parastoo asked, taking off Hana's red scarf, which she had tied around her head.

The room became quiet, except for the hum of the refrigerator and the gurgling of the kettle simmering on the gas stove. Nazanin sipped a glass of *doogh*, a drink made of yogurt and herbs, and Shahla silently counted the pearls on the necklace Hana had let her wear.

"*Yake boo, yake naw,*" Hana eventually began, reciting the traditional Kurdish opening to fairy tales—"Once upon a time"—"there was an eagle, which was about to die. He sat on a bare tree branch in midwinter, icy wind ruffling his feathers, and looked up at the cold blue sky. 'It is time,' he said out loud.

"'Time for what?' a voice called from below.

"The eagle looked down, and there on the road in front of him was a black raven.

"'It is time for me to die,' the eagle told the raven.

"'Why?' asked the raven. 'It may be winter. You may not have anything to eat. You may be old, but if you come down here to the ground, you can live with me and feed on all the dead animals. You will grow younger from all the food, and you will never want for anything.'

"The eagle looked at the raven. He then looked up to the sun. 'No,' the eagle told the raven. *'Lay haloy barza fri, barza mji, chon bji sharta nawak chanda bji'"*—"For an eagle that flies high and lives high, quality of life matters more than the number of years he lives."

LIFE IN HER MOTHER'S HOME was becoming more and more unbearable for Nazanin. Her mother was now working night shifts cleaning offices in Sanandaj in addition to her day jobs cleaning the homes of the city's wealthy. Many of the women wanted her to clean and cook for them on Friday, the holy day. "The rumour going around is that your mother is a gifted *doanoos*," Hana told Nazanin.

"Why?" Nazanin frowned. "She's not a witch."

"I know," laughed Hana. "But her tattoos . . . well, some of the women in Sanandaj who aren't from the villages think that because your mother has such tattoos on her face she has the gift of sight and touch. One of the women whose house your mother cleans boasts that she had been trying for years to conceive a child and all of a sudden, when your mother went to work for her, she became pregnant. Maryam has become the most sought-after cleaning woman in Sanandaj."

On her days off, Nazanin's mother mostly slept, complaining that her chest hurt from the fumes of the cleaning products she used. Nazanin dared not ask, but she wanted to know how her mother was getting any sleep, for she often was working both day and night. Most of all, she wanted to know where all the extra money her mother was earning was going, for Nazanin and her sisters still ate only *dokhawa*.

"It has been a while since you have been coming here. I'll tell you what," Hana announced one day after the children had devoured two heaping pots of meat stew and a warm, freshly baked flatbread. "Nazanin, Shahla and Parastoo—if I pay for someone to watch

Ghomri during the mornings, why don't the three of you go to school? I will also pay for your books and supplies and new uniforms," she added as the girls began to protest.

"But mother will never approve of someone other than us watching Ghomri," Parastoo piped up.

"We won't tell her," Nazanin butted in, desperate to return to the classroom. Reading one day a week was not enough.

"Then let's go tomorrow and I will register you," said Hana.

"But you have to teach," Nazanin said.

"For the three of you, I will take the day off. And you can meet the young woman I want to hire to look after Ghomri. I think you will like her. Her name is Leila."

"You mean *our* Leila?" she asked timidly.

"Yes," smiled Hana. "I mean *your* Leila." Nazanin was startled. She had only seen Leila a few times since her wedding.

And so Nazanin was back in school in the mornings and Leila, whom Hana had tracked down, became Ghomri's babysitter. Nazanin had moved from picture books to early readers and then on to simple chapter books. She learned mathematics and she prayed. Fearing that all the students believed her to be the daughter of jaash, she kept her head lowered at school and talked to her classmates only when she needed to for assignments or class projects. And every Friday, she and her sisters would head to Hana's house.

"I am so happy," Nazanin confided to Hana on the Friday before Nowruz. She was ten that year. For Nowruz, Hana had given her and Shahla Kurdish dresses with real coins sewn into the fabric. Parastoo and Ghomri received books, and Leila a scarf, corn oil and rice, since she needed extra food, being pregnant with her first child. Nazanin's outfit was pale pink. "I knew one day I would have my very own pink dress," she said, beaming.

"I've never owned anything so beautiful," Shahla hummed as she spun around the room in her dress to the music of Kurdish singer Naser Razazi. "Listen," she said when the coins clanked together. "I can make music."

"Rumi said that we rarely hear the inward music," said Hana, "but we're dancing to it nevertheless, directed by the one who teaches us, the pure joy of the sun, our music master."

LEILA MISCARRIED later that spring. Nazanin's mother also was pregnant and she was due right around Yalda. It was a difficult pregnancy. For one, Maryam was no longer young. She also continued to work and the cleaning products were not only hurting her lungs but also burning her hands, in much the same way that the chalk scalded Hana's palms. Parastoo suggested that she wear gloves, but Maryam couldn't afford them. "But what about all the money you are making working all day and night?" Nazanin got up the courage to ask.

Nazanin's mother's face turned red and clammy. Nazanin knew that what she called "the bad" was about to erupt from inside her mother. But, miraculously, it faded. With a sigh, her mother sat down on the floor and began to cry. "I don't know. I give it all to your father and it just disappears. I wonder if he is supporting his other family on it. I just don't know," she sobbed, holding her face in her hands. "He can't work because of all his medical problems," she then wailed. "And I can't quit. He is in charge of all the money, but if I don't work, he will beat me."

IN OCTOBER, Nazanin's father told her mother to try to earn as much money as she could before having to take time off to deliver the baby. He would take Nazanin and the other children to the home of his other wife, Aylar. Nazanin would have to leave school for a month or so. She was distraught. Nonetheless, she did what she was told.

The next morning, Habib took the girls and Hojat on the bus to Aylar's. She lived on the other side of Sanandaj, in another poor area made up of factory-like buildings, with rows of single- and two-room houses and dirt roads full of beggars. Habib introduced the children to Aylar, and her eyes lit up when she saw Hojat. She pulled him into her arms, smothering him with kisses. Then she patted his bottom and sent him out back to have some stew, which she said her daughter, Nahid, had prepared especially for him.

As for the girls, Aylar lined them up against the wall. With a scowl, she inspected them one by one, examining their nails, their hair, even lifting up their dresses to feel the muscles on their legs through their pants. "You're the eldest, Mahabad," she said, "and the strongest."

"No, I have an older sister."

"I know about Leila. I mean, you are the eldest of all of you," she said, pointing to Nazanin's sisters.

Nazanin nodded and held up the tin with a cake inside, which she had brought as a gift.

"You cook?" Aylar scoffed, prying off the lid. She grabbed a big piece of cake and stuck in her mouth, then spat it out on the floor at Nazanin's feet. "How wretched. I knew a Kurd couldn't cook." She stuck out her tongue as Nazanin's father merely looked on. "No one will ever want you, or this horrible food. Take it and give it to the stray dogs out back."

Aylar informed Nazanin and Shahla that since they were strong and healthy, they would be put to work helping around the house. "You can watch the two little ones while you do your chores," she told them. She then showed the girls how she liked her floors cleaned with carpet shampoo, the dishes washed and the laundry done. "I am Turkish," she explained, watching Nazanin sweep out the ashes from the fire. "I am from Urmia, a city in West Azerbaijan, near the city you are named after, Mahabad," she said, making it clear that Nazanin would never be called by any other name in Aylar's house.

"Your father was visiting a cousin of his in Urmia, and that is how we met. I swore I would never marry a Kurd, but we fell in love. I am your father's only love."

EACH DAY, NAZANIN AND SHAHLA woke before the sun rose to start their duties. Nazanin's father was never there. He told Aylar he was going to wait in line with other unemployed men, on the chance that he'd be picked to do construction work. When he didn't come home some nights, Nazanin was hopeful that he had found a job. But when her father did come back, his eyes were always bloodshot. He slurred his words and took Aylar out back, where Nazanin could hear them arguing and then him beating her with his belt. He then left the house immediately, and Aylar would sheepishly come into the room where the children were huddled together. "What are you looking at?" she would ask, grabbing Nazanin or Shahla, ordering her to clean the dishes or put her little sisters to bed on the floor, only a thin mat underneath them.

"MY NAME IS SOMAYEH," the little girl said in a soft voice, sneaking up behind Nazanin, who was washing clothes in the backyard. "I am Nemattollah's daughter. Ne'mat is your father's eldest son. I am your niece," she said, beaming at Nazanin. "Do you want to come and play with me?"

Nazanin looked at the two large baskets of laundry. "No," she said, shaking her head and turning her attention back to scrubbing the collar of her father's shirt. "Shahla and I have to finish laundering the clothes."

"I'll help you," said Somayeh, pulling up her manteau and kneeling between Nazanin and Shahla on the cold ground. Somayeh was a few years younger than Nazanin and was small-boned and tiny in stature. She reminded Nazanin of a newly hatched chick, fragile with her wobbly, thin legs and fine, delicate features.

"I heard about you," Shahla whispered, looking around to make sure it was just Somayeh and Nazanin within earshot. "We also heard about your mother. She left you and your dad."

"Ignore her," Nazanin hissed at Somayeh, scowling at her sister. "She says things she shouldn't."

"I don't mind." Somayeh smiled, revealing a chipped tooth.

"Tell me about your mother," Shahla prodded, ignoring Nazanin.

"Shush," Nazanin said, scolding her younger sister. She turned to Somayeh. "Shahla is just curious. You don't have to answer."

"It's okay," Somayeh said. "I don't mind answering, and besides, you can trust me. I won't tell anyone you are asking such questions. I am not going to stay here long. I am going to go find my mother."

"Ohhh," Shahla exclaimed. "But I heard she was a horrible person!"

"That's what my father and Aylar say, but my mother is beautiful. She was soft and smelled like fresh air after a rainstorm when she held me."

"Why did she leave?" Shahla asked.

"She didn't leave. My father yelled at my mother all the time, calling her lazy, fat and stupid. He hit her with her own pots and pans. I would close my eyes and wish I was somewhere else." Somayeh choked on the words. "I saw my mother threaten to burn herself with a container of gas if my father didn't stop hitting her. My father told her to do it, but she couldn't. Instead, she took me and ran away. But my father found us, beat my mother and brought me home."

"Do you know where your mother is now?" Nazanin asked.

"No, but I will find her. I can't stay with my father anymore. Look." She lifted up the right sleeve of her manteau and showed Nazanin and Shahla her arm, which was covered in burn marks and bruises.

AT NIGHT AS SHE DRIFTED off to sleep, Nazanin pictured Hana's rose-coloured lips telling her stories of Kurdistan and the poetry of Mawlawi Kurd and Rumi. She had a deep yearning to be back in Hana's house, warmed by the two large fireplaces. One chilly late-October day, Nazanin told Aylar that she had to return home to get more clothes for her sisters and Hojat. "It's too cold. We need our sweaters and blankets."

As she started on the four-hour walk that lay ahead of her, she briefly felt sorry for Shahla, who would now have to do all the laundry on her own. She also wished she had told Somayeh to come with her, but she dared not. Two days earlier, when Aylar was at the market with the other children, Somayeh had popped around to show her the lipstick and blush she had bought from money she had stolen from her father. Somayeh and Nazanin were putting the makeup on each other when Hojat and Ne'mat walked in from outside, slamming the door behind them and bringing with them the stench of cigarette smoke.

"What are you doing?" Ne'mat spat, slapping the lipstick out of his daughter's hand before hitting her hard across the back of her head.

Hojat grabbed the mirror from Nazanin's hands and tossed it to the ground, where it shattered into pieces. He picked up Somayeh's lipstick and yelled at Nazanin to lie down on the ground. She slapped her brother's face, at which Ne'mat punched Nazanin in the stomach and ordered her to do what her brother said. Both girls, lying side by side on their backs on the ground, stared at the ceiling. "What are you going to do?" Nazanin cried out, her body trembling. "What are you going to do?"

"Don't say a word," Somayeh said calmly. "If you do, it will be worse."

Ne'mat wrote *"jonna"*—prostitute—across Somayeh's forehead, while Hojat did the same on Nazanin. They then spat in the girls' hair. "Don't ever use makeup again," Ne'mat said, standing up and kicking Somayeh in the groin. "Only a *jonna* like your mother wears makeup."

"And don't see each other anymore," Hojat yelled at Nazanin as he and Ne'mat turned to leave. "If you do, I will tell Father about all of this."

The house fell silent. Nazanin closed her eyes and recited, first silently in her head and then in a soft voice, the only part of the Yaseen Sura she knew.

HER MOTHER'S HOME was cold and pitch-dark, and the air smelled of feces. Nazanin fumbled around for the matches and lit a kerosene lamp. She went to the washroom and discovered that it hadn't been cleaned since before they left. She then inspected the kitchen. There were no bags of rice or beans, nor any *robb* sitting in the covered tin pot, ready to be heated. "Mother hasn't been home," she said out loud.

But she didn't want to think about this. Nazanin couldn't wait another minute to see Hana, whom she knew would by then have returned from work.

As she ran up the cobblestone path to Hana's front door, Nazanin could hear Arabic chanting coming from the record player. She peeked in the front window and saw the salon lit by tiny white candles, and the back of her friend, who was praying. Nazanin leaned in close, her breath steaming up the window, and heard Hana reciting what she had told Nazanin was Sufi *dhikr*, or prayer, along with the record. Hana was wearing a long, white dress with gold stitching. "You look like a *freshta*, an angel so beautiful you don't belong on earth," Nazanin gasped, thinking of the pictures she had seen of Mary, the mother of Jesus, in her religious book at school. Suddenly, as if she had heard, Hana turned quickly, her eyes full of tears, and stared at Nazanin.

"Nazanin," she called out, running to the front door to let her in. "You startled me. Where have you been?"

"I'm sorry," Nazanin said.

"It's fine," replied Hana, rubbing Nazanin's cold hands. "You must be hungry."

As Hana heated up some food, Nazanin told her about staying with Aylar, and how cruel she was to her. She also told Hana about Somayeh. But she did not tell her about Hojat or the violence, and there was no telltale trace of the lipstick he had used to write on her forehead, Nazanin having washed it off thoroughly.

"I am very intuitive," Hana said as she sliced up a pear to serve to Nazanin with some walnuts. "Something happened while you were gone."

"I don't want to talk about it," Nazanin said, lowering her eyes.

"You know, our culture, we have been so oppressed by so many nations over our history. It is said that no one is our friend other than the mountains. The poverty of the region, mixed with other cultures not liking us, mixed with, well, one class of Kurds not liking another, has created a tension in all of us that is so deep-seated. People don't act normally. For one, when men get angry, they blame the women for making them angry, as opposed to looking inside themselves and taking responsibility for their own actions. Some even start using *taryak* as a way of escaping their responsibilities," she said, referring to the cheap opium found on the streets. "Men take out their frustrations on women. And women take it out on their children. This is most common with the poor, like you. I know you are being abused." Hana put her hand over Nazanin's heart. "Even in your darkest hours, something bright will happen if you allow Khwa in. It is only when we shut God out that we prevent magic from happening."

"Why were you crying when you were praying?" Nazanin asked, changing the subject.

"I was deep in prayer. I was feeling the divine."

"Khwa?"

"Yes . . . and no, sweet dear. I was once in love," Hana began with a sigh. "In love with a Fars man I met at university, the same man who introduced me to Mawlawi Kurd. We wanted to marry, but his family wouldn't allow it. He came from a wealthy family, and his parents sent him away to America for graduate school. He never returned, and I have never stopped loving him. He is my divine."

"I am so sorry," Nazanin said. "I hope one day I feel love."

"Me too, for you," said Hana, smiling. "'Lovers don't finally meet somewhere. They're in each other all along.'" Hana stared at the candle flame. "Rumi said this, and it couldn't be more fitting. My lover, Farzad, has never left me. I feel his presence, along with God's, when I pray. And their presence is so beautiful, I cry."

AFTER SPENDING THE NIGHT sleeping on cushions on Hana's floor by the stone fireplace, covered in blankets made of mohair, Nazanin knew she had to return to Aylar's. Her father would think she had run away. She said goodbye to Hana and told her she would be back soon, for she didn't want to be away from school for much longer. "I'll tell my father right away that I want to return home, and we'll come every Friday just like before," she promised Hana as she handed Nazanin a box full of fruit, nuts, homemade jam and cookies.

Nazanin decided to see if her mother had returned home before heading back to Aylar's. It was about midday and as she turned down her alleyway, she saw Mohsen, her father's friend, knocking at the front door.

"Where is your father?" he asked when Nazanin drew near.

"He's not home, Mr. Mohsen. We're all staying on the other side of Sanandaj," Nazanin answered timidly, for she was nervous speaking to him alone, without her father present.

"Then what are you doing here?"

"I'm with my mother," Nazanin lied. "She's sleeping inside. The baby is due soon."

"She's not home," Mohsen snarled. "She's been living at her boss lady's house. She brought them a baby and now she cares for it."

No. She's supposed to be caring for us. But Nazanin kept her composure. "I'm telling you, Mr. Mohsen, my mother is inside. And Father is not home."

A shiver ran through Nazanin as she smelled Mohsen's foul breath and body odour.

"Your father is right when he says you are a stupid girl, like Leila," Mohsen said, revealing his yellow stained teeth.

Nazanin shook her head. "Don't speak badly of Leila," she wanted to yell. Instead she looked down at the box of food in her arms.

"Come on then, prove it to me. Prove to me your mother is sleeping," Mohsen hissed.

Nazanin slowly unlocked the front door and watched as it creaked open. *Please, please be home, Khwa help,* she prayed silently.

"Go inside," Mohsen said, gesturing as his eyes darted about the laneway.

As soon as they were inside, Mohsen slammed the door shut. The box of food fell from Nazanin's arms as he threw her face down onto the ground. He lifted up her manteau and tore off her pants. Nazanin scratched the ground, trying desperately to turn around to poke her fingers into Mohsen's eyes. She started to scream, but he reached around Nazanin and stuffed one of her socks that he had ripped off into her mouth.

"Shut up, dirty girl," he said into her ear. Nazanin felt as though she was about to choke. She felt his weight on her as he pried open her legs. She began crawling, her knees bruising from the effort. She managed to free herself enough to get to the wall, where she tried to turn to kick Mohsen. But he was too quick and strong for her. He pinned her to the corner, ripped off her dress and then she felt him inside her, hot, hard and ripping her apart. She tried to scream but choked on the sock. She eventually just gave in and remained lifeless as he abused her body.

On his way to the door, Mohsen grabbed the box of food, biting into one of the pears. "You are a dog," he spat out, leaving Nazanin shaking, bloodied and bruised in the corner. "Your mother raises other people's babies. Your father smokes taryak," he said. "And you are a dog."

CHAPTER 9

NAZANIN AFSHIN-JAM

December 2003, Vancouver

———

A few days after my arrival back in Vancouver following the Miss World competition, I was whisked away to a celebratory dinner with my family, including Naz and her husband. In the early hours of the morning, we returned to my parents' condominium overlooking the Pacific Ocean. It was late but I was still used to China's time zone, and instead of being tired, I found myself wide awake. My father agreed to stay up with me, so we grabbed some blankets and sat out on the balcony, silently watching the moon over the water.

"What is on your mind, Nini?" my father eventually asked. "You are always quiet when you are thinking about something."

"Baba, in my last year of high school you told me about all the changes happening in Iran, starting when you were in university. I think it was the last time you talked to me about Iran, about your life," I said quietly.

"Tell me how you got your scars," I said after a long silence between us. "I feel I need to know the ending of the story again."

He looked at me and seemed to hesitate, but then, with a sigh, acquiesced.

"NINI," HE BEGAN as I pulled the blanket around me tight, my body shivering from the cool air and my memory of my father's story.

"When I was thrown in the back of that van, I passed out from the assaults. I woke several hours later to a blinding light aimed right into my eyes."

He had been tied, sitting upright, onto a stiff metal chair. Pain shot through his legs, arms and upper back. He winced and the light suddenly switched off.

"You're in Evin Prison," a man's voice said. My father slowly lifted his head to see two men sitting directly across a steel table from him. One had a long black beard, the other was clean-shaven. Both wore civilian clothes.

"I know of Evin," my father said in a hoarse voice. He coughed, spitting up blood onto the table.

"What do you know of Evin?" the clean-shaven man asked.

"This is where the secret police, SAVAK, of the old government imprisoned political opponents," my father said quietly. "Is that what I am? A prisoner of Khomeini's?"

"Yes," the bearded man answered. Both men stood up and approached my father. The clean-shaven man grabbed an electric shaver that was lying on the table. As his colleague held my father down, he shaved his thick, full head of hair. The first shaved strip ran from his forehead to the nape of his neck. The second shaved strip ran ear to ear.

After making some humiliating comments about my father's new appearance, one of the men slapped him across the cheek so hard that he and the chair he was still tied to fell over. The two men then undid the ropes, pinned him to the floor and started lashing his back with the exposed ends of electrical cords, tearing apart his shirt.

My father tried to pull himself up by the back of the chair but was punched in the stomach and head. He passed out for a second time.

My father regained consciousness to find himself outside, soft rain hitting his face. He opened his eyes and saw in front of him a bloodstained cement wall.

"We were set to kill you," the bearded man spat. "But we need to wait for your death warrant to be signed by Judge Khalkhali. He just finished signing dozens of them at Rajai Shahr Prison. He will arrive in the morning, and then we will put you against the wall and shoot you."

My father shuddered, for Khalkhali was known for his love of killing cats and randomly issuing execution decrees.

"When the hotel staff told Jaleh that I had been taken away, she immediately contacted an official at Iran Air, the company that owned the Sheraton in Tehran," my father continued. "After taking over power, the Revolutionary Guard had assigned each state-owned company, including Iran Air, with a high-ranking clerical liaison officer. The official with whom Jaleh spoke contacted their clerical liaison, Ayatollah Mohammad Beheshti, the head of the Islamic Republican Party. Beheshti was woken up in the early hours of the morning. At first he wasn't sure he could help. He said the only thing he might be able to do was sign a document ordering the prison to release me temporarily until a proper court was summoned to try me. And even if he did this, he was worried whether the document would get there in time.

"Jaleh prayed for a miracle. Tehran's streets were more congested than ever thanks to the debris that still littered the roads from the protests. As the guard delivering the document granting me temporary freedom raced to the prison, so did Judge Khalkhali."

MY FATHER AND I became silent again as we watched the sun start to rise. I could hear seagulls and the distant sound of horns from ships making their way to Vancouver's harbour.

"You got out, Baba?" I eventually whispered, hugging my blanket tightly around my again shivering body.

My father rubbed his tired eyes. "Yes, Nini. We all got out. Judge Khalkhali was in a car accident and was rushed to the hospital with a broken arm. I was given my freedom, at least for a while. I was cautioned by that bearded interrogator, whose name I was never told, that I would be back—that I would return to Evin—that I would meet the fate he desperately wanted to carry out the day before.

"I didn't wait. About a week later, when my wounds were healed enough that I could sit upright, I was on an airplane headed to Barcelona before the Islamic Revolutionary Court could call me to my trial, which most certainly would have ended in my death. You all followed as soon as you could. You, Jaleh and Naz left Iran twenty days before Iran and Iraq declared war and the airports, which had been reopened, were again closed for commercial travel."

I felt like I had been slapped in the face. My father had never told me this latter part of the story. "You mean," I began as my eyes teared up, "that all of us really had a chance of being separated?"

"Yes, Nini," my father said with a sigh. "If any of these steps had taken a turn in any other direction, we would not be with each other right now."

"You were so close to death," I said in a whisper.

CHAPTER 10

NAZANIN FATEHI

October to November 1998, Sanandaj, Iran

———

Nazanin sat in the corner of the room, her legs pulled into her chest, her eyes staring blankly at nothing. She was numb. Like the day the children had called her jaash, she felt as though she had lost part of herself. She was conscious of her eyelids opening and closing. She felt the frigid cold of the unheated room on her bare skin where Mohsen had torn off her clothes and the moistness of the blood between her legs. But she could not move, cry or even speak. She didn't know how long she had sat there, with the sounds of wild dogs barking in the alleyway and women bickering over whose sons had hit the other boys first. It was only when she heard the pattering of tiny feet outside the window and then the laughter of little girls running home into their mothers' arms that her tears began to flow.

"No! No!" she slapped herself on the head. "I have to think. I have to think," she muttered. The numbness gave way to a panic that twisted her mind to all sorts of horrible thoughts, including Mohsen's return—or worse, her father or Hojat seeing her half-naked, her budding breasts showing from beneath her torn dress.

She pulled herself up and tied pieces of her dress together so that she was covered. She then grabbed her manteau, pants, the sock that had been stuffed in her mouth and her underwear and tiptoed to the washroom.

Once she was changed, the knots in her hair combed out and the blood wiped away, she sunk to the washroom floor. She knew that she could not make it back to Aylar's house before nightfall, but she also didn't want to stay another minute in her mother's home. So she lowered her headscarf over her forehead and set off, not daring to look anyone in the alleyway in the eye. She walked quickly despite the growing pain between her legs from the force of Mohsen's assault. When she reached the neighbourhood of rose gardens, she stopped and turned in the direction of Hana's house. But when she moved again, she headed instead the other way, toward the centre of the city. She kept her body as close to the buildings as she could, trying to remain a shadow, her thoughts now so messed up that she believed anyone she passed knew what had just happened to her.

By the time she reached Aylar's house, she felt like collapsing from the pain that ricocheted through her body and the cramps in her abdomen. She fumbled and eventually undid the lock on the door and crept inside. Everyone was sleeping, the living room echoing with their snores. Still wearing her manteau, she tucked herself in behind Shahla, whose hair smelled like laundry detergent. She pulled the blanket over her head, balled her hand into a fist and held it to her mouth so no one would hear her crying.

Nazanin woke in the morning to the feeling that she was sinking. She rolled over and looked at Ghomri, sound asleep, and felt the tears swell again. She started to reach for Ghomri when something hard hit her hand. She screamed in pain and looked up. Aylar was standing above her, broom in hand. "Take off your manteau," she said. "Only a whore would stay away from home like you did. Get your beating. Take off your clothes."

Nazanin pleaded. "I didn't come back because I was with my mother," she lied. "Please let me wash up from my walk back, and I promise you can do what you like after that."

Aylar scowled as Nazanin stood up, rocking slowly from foot to foot, feeling faint. Aylar dropped the broom and twisted a towel into a tight cord, then began swinging it, hitting Nazanin across the back, on the back of her head and even on her face. Nazanin endured the blows without tears, for she knew she could now blame any bruises and scrapes on Aylar's beating.

"And what have you been doing all this time, slut?" Aylar spat out.

"Seeing my mother," Nazanin said again.

"Your mother!" Aylar gasped. "Is she home? I thought she was . . ."

"Yes." Nazanin nodded.

"Fine . . . do your work. Shahla needs a break. Her hands are too little to do the laundry. She doesn't have the strength to wring out the clothes the way you can. Everything takes too long to dry and ends up stinking from the damp."

"SOMAYEH, WHAT HAPPENS to bad girls, you know, *jonna*?" Nazanin asked her cousin.

Somayeh sighed and rolled over on the cushions. The girls were lying in the living room, sucking on pistachios Somayeh had brought from her father's house. Aylar was out at the market. "I've heard the men talking sometimes," Somayeh said after a long pause. "In the summer, when they are sitting outside, I hear them telling stories of the neighbourhood families. One family had a daughter whom I think they wanted to marry off to a man in a village in western Kurdistan. But she told her father that she was in love with someone else. I heard my father say that one day some men followed her and saw her holding this man's hand in an alleyway. Two days after that, the girl was found dead. She jumped off a bridge. My father's brother said, 'She got what was coming to her.'"

"What did he mean?" Nazanin asked in a shaky voice.

Somayeh leaned toward Nazanin and whispered, "I think they killed her. Why do you ask?"

"I was just curious," Nazanin said. "But I've heard . . ."

"What have you heard?" Somayeh chirped. "Tell me about the girls you know who have boyfriends."

"No," Nazanin said, forcing a smile. "I don't know anyone. I just wanted to know."

"I want a boyfriend one day," Somayeh said as she lay back on the pillows, putting her hands behind her head and staring up at the ceiling. "I want a boy to love me and hold me. Do you?"

"Maybe one day," Nazanin said, blushing.

Nazanin and Somayeh heard heavy footsteps approaching the front door and then Aylar opening the lock. The girls quickly piled the cushions in the corner of the room and then ran through to the back.

"Stop!" they heard Aylar's voice order.

Nazanin and Somayeh slowly emerged from the kitchen, anticipating a beating. But when Nazanin looked up, her face broke into a big smile. There, standing beside Aylar, was her mother. Nazanin ran into her arms and inhaled the smell of her mother mixed with that of cleaning disinfectant and soap. Nazanin held on tight, tighter than she ever had before.

"I've missed you so much," Nazanin said, choking back her tears as Aylar made her way to the kitchen with bags full of rice, vegetables and fruit.

"What has got into you?" Nazanin's mother asked, pushing her daughter away so she could look into her face.

"I just . . . I thought you had left us . . ." Nazanin said after making sure Aylar was out of earshot.

"No, Nazanin," she said, rubbing her swollen belly. "I am due earlier than the midwife thought. I've finished with a big job, and I have come to get everyone. We're all going home."

But Nazanin's mother didn't have the strength to walk back to their neighbourhood. Her breathing was laboured and her feet so swollen from the pregnancy that her shoes no longer fit—she had to wear large, oversized slippers, even outside. Nazanin's mother said she'd have to take the bus back. "But I don't have any money with me," she explained to Nazanin in private. "Everything I earn I give to your father. But I don't know where he is. Sometimes he has been at our home. I meet him there every so often to give him my wages. But Aylar said he has been gone from here now for nearly a week, and he hasn't been at home at all during this time."

Three days passed while they waited at Aylar's house for Nazanin's father to return. Nazanin said barely a word the entire time, other than "sure"—"*banchaw*"—to Aylar's orders. Whenever Aylar was out, she cuddled up beside her mother, like she was a small child. Her mother didn't object the way she would have if they had been at home. She called her Nazanin and brushed her hair. Nazanin, in turn, brought her chaee, crystal sugar and an apple, to give the baby smooth skin.

"I heard you helped a woman get a baby. Is it true?" Nazanin asked her one day.

"No, Nazanin," Nazanin's mother laughed. "These women in their fancy clothes and homes, they are not as happy as they should be. They have money, but they don't like their husbands, and the things they lack, they'd do anything for. One woman wanted a baby, and she became pregnant by her husband when I showed up. So she thinks I performed some magic."

"Did you?"

"Don't be silly. But they believed I had, so they paid me well to stay with them. I let them think what they wanted."

SOMAYEH HAD HEARD that Nazanin was leaving and came to say goodbye. It was a crisp, clear day, and Nazanin was outside shelling and peeling fava beans. Somayeh slipped a pale pink lipstick into the pocket of Nazanin's manteau. "Maybe you can wear it at home when Hojat isn't around," she said quietly. "You have a nice home there. Your mother is kind."

"I never thought so until she came here," Nazanin replied. "But why are you covered in mud?" she asked, looking at her niece. Somayeh's hair had dry dirt in it, her legs were caked with mud up to her knees and her manteau was soiled and rumpled.

"I ran away," she replied, lowering her eyes. "I spent the night behind a shed a few blocks from here. I couldn't stay at home. My father was high on taryak. I came home and he started to hit me with his belt and then . . . he called me a whore and said I was worthless like my mother. Look," Somayeh opened her manteau and lifted up her dress to show Nazanin a large gash on her waist. "And he did this to me," she said, rolling up her sleeve to reveal four new burn marks. Her father had placed heated spoons on her, she told Nazanin. "He can't find work and he's gone crazy. He and your dad are smoking taryak every night."

"How do you know?" gasped Nazanin.

"Because I have snuck out and seen them. They smoke it in the alley, where no one can see."

"Where do they get it from?" Nazanin whispered, swallowing hard, not wanting to hear that maybe Mohsen was right.

"Your father gets it. From where, I don't know."

"What are you doing out here?" Parastoo asked, joining them. "Aylar is home. She wants us to unpack the groceries."

"I'll be right there," Nazanin said as Parastoo collected the bowl of fava beans and took it inside. "Somayeh, promise me you won't do anything foolish. Don't run away again. You will freeze in the cold weather. And if you don't freeze, you'll be called all sorts of bad names for not being at home. If you have to leave home, come to my house."

"How can I reach you once you leave?"

"I will tell you how you can get there," she said, and gave Somayeh the directions.

As soon as her father arrived back at Aylar's, Nazanin, her brother, sisters and mother returned to their home. Once settled, their mother announced that they could go back to school. Something had changed in Maryam. Shahla and Nazanin would eye each other with suspicion whenever their mother gave them an extra bowl of food, and one time when their father was away and Hojat was with a friend watching a dogfight, she served the girls lamb and rice.

"Where did you get the money for this good food?" Parastoo asked, licking her fingers.

"Don't tell your father . . . but I, well, I am never going to go through again what we did in Aylar's house, having to wait for him to give us money to leave that horrible woman's place. When I returned to my boss's house to get my final wages and bonus, instead of giving them to your father, I hid them away," she giggled. "Leila will help me watch Ghomri while you are at school. She needs the money, as her husband isn't giving her anything for clothes or the medicines she needs after her miscarriage. Doctors say she might never have a baby again." She then told Nazanin to go to the closet in the kitchen and bring back whatever she found there. Nazanin returned holding four coats.

"I bought the manteaus so you can have something that is just yours, not worn by anyone else before you."

Nazanin ran her hands over the soft wool of a navy blue manteau with big gold buttons. "Thank you, Dayah," she said. "Thank you for this special day."

THE NEXT DAY WAS FRIDAY, and Nazanin went alone to visit Hana while her sisters stayed with their mother, cleaning the house.

"I have a special book for you today," Hana said. Nazanin was sipping a cup of hot chocolate. "I made it myself. It is the story of the famous fox trickster."

Nazanin fingered the homemade book Hana handed her. The writing was in big, thick letters, and the pictures had been painted in watercolours. "I wanted you to have a Kurdish fairy tale," she said. "Your book, the one you always carry with you, is the Persian version of a story children were told long ago in Kurdistan. There are different versions of it around the world. I wanted to give you a story that was as Kurdish as can be."

Nazanin's eyes began to tear.

"What's wrong?" Hana asked.

"No one has ever been so nice to me," she replied, wiping her face with her sleeve. "And I just . . . just . . . I am scared."

"Of what, sweet child?"

"Of people. Of what they will do to me if they find out . . ." Nazanin sobbed.

Hana's back stiffened. A shiver ran through her. "What did someone do to you, Nazanin?" she asked in the softest voice she could find.

Nazanin's body began to shake, her shoulders collapsed and she fell into Hana's arms. "It was horrible," she managed to say in between sobs.

Nazanin didn't need to tell Hana the details of what Mohsen had done to her. Somehow she just knew.

"Shush," she murmured, choking back her own tears. "I understand. Someone touched you . . . a man," she said slowly as Nazanin's sobs grew stronger.

"You won't tell anyone?" Nazanin wailed in anguish.

"No. No. No," Hana repeated, now crying too, her tears landing on Nazanin's hair. "But, Nazanin," she said, breathing heavily to try to steady her nerves, "you cannot ever let your father find out. We need to get you to a doctor."

"No," Nazanin said, shaking her head. "Nobody can know."

"Don't worry. This woman doctor is a good friend of mine. But Nazanin, people will know, they will find out, if you don't go to her. She has helped other girls like you," Hana said. "You need to trust me. Nazanin," she said, cupping the young girl's face with her hands. "What this man did to you is wrong, very wrong. But Nazanin, your family . . ." she closed her eyes and paused. "You are poor. Your family is traditional. They hold on to practices that many in our culture no longer follow. If you tell your father, you will be blamed. And you will be scorned and the men in your family, the ones you've just visited, your half-brothers and uncles . . . they might . . ."

"Kill me," Nazanin said in a quiet voice.

"I would kill the man who did this to you with my bare hands if I could," Hana, still crying, said. "You are brave and you are beautiful. Don't ever think this is your fault."

"But what if he tells people? What if he tells my father?"

Hana sighed. "This man knows your father?"

Nazanin nodded.

"If there is anything in this world I want you to trust me about, it is this. This man will never, ever tell anyone, especially your father."

There was no one home when Nazanin returned. She stood in the empty room and looked around carefully for the first time since Mohsen had assaulted her, at the corner where the rape had taken place. Her eyes scoured the floor to make sure there were no drops of blood from when Mohsen had taken her virginity. She made sure there were no stains on the rug, even lifting it up to run her fingers over the rough cement floor beneath. She then walked to the window and looked out.

THERE WAS ONLY ONE SEAT left when she returned to school, in the front beside a young girl the teacher introduced as Favza. Favza wore black-rimmed glasses, liked to read history books at break time and brought biscuits and apples for snack time. She was Fars. Her father had been sent from Tehran to work in the government offices in Sanandaj—or so Nazanin heard some of the Kurdish girls say. Favza remained very much alone, sneaking out of the classroom much the same way Nazanin did and hiding behind the tall trees in the courtyard. Nazanin heard two of her classmates strategizing ways to become Favza's friend, for, as Nazanin discovered, the girls were seen as popular if their friends were wealthy Fars from the big cities. But then they caught Nazanin looking at them. "What are you doing, jaash?" the girl with green eyes hissed. "Listening in on private conversations?"

"Maybe you need to go home," the other girl added. "And never come back. You did leave school for a while, anyway," she said.

"Where were you—getting married? Isn't that what the poor do, marry the girls off at your age?"

"She'll never get married," said the green-eyed girl, laughing. "She's damaged already."

Nazanin felt like she had been slapped hard across the face. *How do they know?* Her body began to tingle. For a brief moment, she was back at home, staring once again into cold nothingness as the door swung shut behind Mohsen.

Nazanin shook the thoughts away. "I am pure," she said to the girls, thinking now of Hana's words. "I would say that only dirty girls like you would know to say a thing like that to another girl."

The green-eyed girl leapt as if to hit Nazanin just as the bell rang for the students to return inside. "I'll get you for this," she said as her friend dragged her by the arm toward the line heading into the school.

During math class, during the last hour of the school day, Nazanin heard scuffling behind her. When she turned her head slightly, she saw some of her classmates changing seats. *Just playing a game on the teacher.* Then she felt a sharp poke at the back of her neck. She turned around quickly to face the green-eyed girl.

"What is going on there?" asked the teacher, Ms. Heidari.

"She hurt me," Nazanin said. "She poked me . . . NO!" Nazanin jumped up and quickly took off her manteau. The girl had written "JAASH, JAASH" in big block letters with thick black marker on the back of Nazanin's new manteau.

"To the office!" Ms. Heidari ordered the green-eyed girl, pointing to the door. "I'll be there shortly, and we will discuss your punishment with the principal. Nazanin, you stay here. Everyone else leave. The bell is about to ring."

"Nazanin, I am so sorry," Ms. Heidari said when they were alone. "Can I buy you a new manteau?"

"No. Thank you," Nazanin said, looking down at her feet and

fixing her scarf. Not all the teachers in the school were cruel to her, but this time, Ms. Heidari's kindness came too late. Nazanin just wanted to go home.

"At the least, I will make that girl's family give you the money the coat cost, and I will speak to the girls."

"I want to go home now," Nazanin said matter-of-factly.

A light snow was falling as Nazanin left the building, vowing never to return. "I'll learn on my own," she said out loud as she passed through the gates. "But I never want to see this place again."

A FEW DAYS LATER, Nazanin's mother went into labour. However, the child was stillborn. After the midwife cleaned Maryam, Nazanin's father announced, "We're going to move to Karaj."

Nazanin's mother winced as she pulled herself up into a sitting position. "Why?" she asked. "This is our home! We don't know anyone in Karaj. *Shari ajamakana*"—"It's a foreign land."

"I will take a job in construction," he continued, ignoring his wife. "We will all go in the springtime, and we will have money. It will be a new life, a good life, the best life."

NAZANIN AFSHIN-JAM

December 2003, Vancouver, to June 2004, China

————————

I awoke Boxing Day to the sound of the BBC news floating through my parents' condominium, where I sometimes stayed.

"A huge earthquake has killed at least 15,000 people in south-eastern Iran, government sources said. The epicentre was near the ancient city of Bam. Arg-e-Bam citadel, a UNESCO World Heritage Site dating back 2,000 years, was destroyed. Most of its buildings have been flattened."

I snuck in beside my father, who was sitting on the edge of his bed putting on his socks. "I always wanted to go to Bam," he said, wrapping his arm around me.

"I'll take you one day, Baba," I whispered.

He took a deep breath, grabbed his newspaper and then headed to the kitchen, leaving me alone with the television.

I sighed and listened to my father, who was speaking in Persian to my mother as she made tea. Like many Iranians living in exile, my father liked to reminisce about the history of Persia, one of the oldest empires of the world, known for its scientific discoveries, education system, literature, philosophy and spirituality—Zoroastrianism being the first major faith of Persia. Whenever my mother displayed the nativity scene at Christmastime, my father would tell us that the Three Magi, the Wise Men of the East, who visited Jesus at his birth were Zoroastrian priests and astrologers travelling from Persia to celebrate and honour the birth of the new king.

"There are three tenets to Zoroastrianism," my father often told me. "Good thoughts. Good words. Good deeds. And if you live by these principles, you will have a prosperous and happy life."

I remember him saying this to me several times during high school when I was being bullied. A few girls would throw pennies at me when I was on stage during theatre class or spit water on me during gym class. They would call me names like "goody two-shoes" and "teacher's pet." One girl would confront me in the hallways and say snidely, "Nazanin, why are you so happy and smiley all the time?" The boys who called themselves the "homies"—those who wore their jeans so low that in some cases the fly was at their knees and I could see their underwear—made fun of the conservative suits and skirts I wore.

"Do you believe in those tenets?" I had asked my father. I frequently thought of what I was missing when my classmates talked about the previous weekend's parties. I felt uncomfortable attending these parties because I didn't drink alcohol, so more likely than not I would spend my weekend doing homework or taking part in my air cadets program—eventually learning how to fly a plane. I reached the top rank of warrant officer first class in air cadets, and became squadron commander, leading more than a hundred cadets. Plus I was on the student council at school and a member of many clubs, including the multicultural and environmental clubs, and the global issues club, which I had started with my two best friends. I wanted to believe that the choices I was making in my life were leading to something worthwhile.

"I don't know," my father replied. "But I do believe that there are hidden forces at work in this world, which can be either good or bad, for we have a choice in every moment as to which we follow."

In the three weeks or so since I'd returned from the Miss World competition in China, I had studied some of the great early philosophies of Iran. I was quite surprised to learn that, in addition to

Zoroastrianism being one of the world's first monotheistic faiths, there was also a doctrine of theology put forth by Persians. Known as illumination, it was the belief that God aids human thought, and I greatly identified with it. Socrates, for instance, talked in Plato's *Apology* about being influenced as a child by a voice outside himself. The early Christian philosopher Augustine spoke about divine enlightenment or illumination in human thought that came from God. And then there was Joan of Arc, an illiterate peasant teenager, who heard the voice of God telling her to guide Charles VII to coronation and lead the French army into battle to drive out the English invaders.

"I am no Joan of Arc," I whispered as the BBC announcer took a break from the station's coverage of Bam to go to a commercial, "but I am making a vow right now to do something to help the survivors of the earthquake."

So far, life after Miss World had not been quite the same as it was before I left for China. For one, thoughts of Iran consumed me. I read everything I could, including the poetry of Rumi and scientist, astrologer and poet Omar Khayyám. I even read parts of an English translation of Ferdowsi's *Shahnameh: The Persian Book of Kings*.

I also found myself inspired by and drawn to two Persian figures: Cyrus the Great and Táhirih. Cyrus the Great was the founding father of Persia. He lived over 2,500 years ago and at that time abolished slavery, advocated religious tolerance and, after conquering Babylonia, became the "Liberator" of the Babylonian people. For a conquered people to embrace their conqueror is rare.

Cyrus the Great is remembered fondly as one of the earliest visionaries and champions of the universality of human rights, as a defender of ethnic tolerance and inclusion. The Persian king's edict for equality regardless of nationality had profound social and cultural ramifications throughout his realm. Everyone under his reign, for instance, was free to choose and practise their religion and cultural traditions. He abolished slavery, and he allowed people to work and own property as long as their actions did not infringe on anyone else's rights.

Ever since the time of Cyrus the Great the region that is now Iran has encompassed people from many cultural backgrounds. Yet they lived peacefully with each other. This balance was upset when Shia Islam became the official religion of the state. Discrimination increased further after the 1979 revolution, because many ethnic minorities—including Azaris, Kurds, Turkomans, Arabs, Baluchis and Lurs—rebelled, some demanding autonomy and threatening the regime and Ayatollah Khomeini's control. As a result, official minorities in Iran are today subject to discrimination and human rights abuses by the regime. The Iranians from varied backgrounds whom I have met say that Iranians are generally tolerant and respectful of each other.

One example that stands out for me of Cyrus the Great's benevolence occurred in 539 BC. Having conquered Babylon, he freed the Jews from captivity, thereby enabling them to return to the Promised Land. Acts of this sort won him profound admiration. In fact, several passages in the Bible refer to him as "the anointed of the Lord."

His compassion for the citizens of those nations subsumed into his expanding empire was legendary. He even drafted what is believed to be the first human rights charter. It was engraved on a cylinder that became known as the Cyrus Cylinder, a copy of which is displayed today in the foyer of the United Nations building in New York City.

Táhirih, also known as Qurratu'l-Ayn, was a woman well ahead of her time. She was the first female follower of the Baha'i faith. The Baha'i faith dates back to the middle of the nineteenth century, when an Iranian nobleman, Baha'ullah, founded the new faith, abrogating the antiquated laws of Islam and instituting new laws for a new age, among them those based on equality of rights between men and women.

One August day in 1848, in front of a gathering of men during a conference in the small village of Badasht, Táhirih tore off her veil, renounced Islam and proclaimed that it was time for a new world order. One man, incensed at the sight of this immodest woman, slit his throat. Táhirih was charged and convicted of heresy and sentenced to death by hanging if she didn't recant her statements and marry the king of Persia, Nasser-al-Din Shah, becoming part of his harem. She chose martyrdom. Just before she was hanged, she said, "You may kill me as soon as you like, but you cannot stop the emancipation of women."

Sadly, the Baha'is paid—and continue to pay—dearly for their religious beliefs. Followers are denied access to higher education and to certain jobs. Their top leaders are in prison, and many have been killed under the Islamic fundamentalist regime.

When I was growing up, my father would ramble on about Iran's history and geography. And like any child or teenager, I often tuned out. But now I recalled these conversations.

Persia is one of the only Middle Eastern countries not to have been officially colonized, though the Arabs invaded the region starting in AD 632, forcibly converting many Persians from Zoroastrianism to Islam. Thus, today many Iranians call themselves Muslims, but they are not necessarily practising. Despite appearances to the contrary, particularly in the Western media, many Iranians are secular, harbouring a deep-seated resentment toward the early Arab invaders who looted and pillaged their homeland, attacking the people and imposing Islam on the nation.

Most Iranians practise Twelver Shia Islam, which maintains that the Prophet Mohammed's cousin and son-in-law, Ali, was his rightful successor. There are many differences between Twelver Shia Islam and the Sunni Islam practised by as much as 90 percent of Muslims worldwide.

There are several branches and sects of both Shia and Sunni Islam and varying degrees of strictness. Sufism is considered a branch of Islam, though it is much more liberal in thought and practice.

Under the last shah, Iran became one of the most modern, liberal, almost European-like countries in the Middle East. Many young middle- and upper-class men and women were educated abroad, in

Europe or America. Families vacationed on the shores of the Caspian Sea or travelled to Paris, London, New York or Madrid. And Iran had one of the highest literacy rates in the Middle East.

The revolution of 1979 saw a mass exodus of the country's middle and upper classes. As the value of the Iranian currency, the rial, dropped, these families could no longer afford their former lavish lifestyles of foreign travel and designer clothes. The community of writers and artists had been critical of the shah's dependence on Western governments, particularly the United Kingdom, and the granting to British Petroleum ownership of the country's vast oil reserves. This is in contrast to the 1950s, when Iranians of all social classes had supported one-time prime minister Mohammad Mosaddegh, whose policies included social reforms for the poor and middle classes, and nationalization of the oil industry. He was, however, overthrown in 1953 in a *coup d'état* backed by the United States and spent the rest of his life under house arrest.

While the intellectual elite and middle classes may have at first welcomed the changing of the guard that came with the Iranian revolution, they did not support the stricter interpretations of the Qur'an and sharia law as dictated by Islamic fundamentalists. The Islamists emerged as the stronger force and took over all organs of power, including the police and army. They systematically began eliminating any and all opposition, among other things arresting and killing Communists, with whom they had united in the revolution, and anyone else they found to be against the establishment of an Islamic government.

Millions of Iranians left, most permanently, for the West. This explained why, by Christmas 2003, I had received tens of thousands of congratulatory messages from Iranians from all corners of the globe. Universally, they echoed the sentiment that they were proud that, finally, one of them was being depicted positively in the press.

Over the past thirty years, Iran has been lambasted by the Western media, which has prompted many Iranians living in exile to shrink from publicly aligning themselves with their native country.

From November 4, 1979, to January 20, 1981, for instance, fifty-two Americans were held hostage in the US Embassy in Tehran for 444 days. Prior to this, Iranians living in the United States had been accepted. After the hostage taking, many found themselves blatantly ostracized by the same communities that once embraced them. Many Iranian-Americans went so far as to say they were Turkish, French or Greek, to avoid negative remarks and stereotyping—there was not as much public awareness of the division between regime supporters and the wider Iranian communities, both in Iran and in exile, which themselves had been victimized by their own government. Everyone was painted with the same negative brush. And so my mother, when asked about her background, often feigned Italian descent.

Then on September 11, 2001, the tragic terrorist attacks in New York City damaged Iranians' reputation for what I thought was for good. The terrorists who brought down the Twin Towers were not Iranians, but it seemed that many Westerners didn't make that distinction. Many perceived all people from the Middle East as being part of the same culture and thus terrorists too. The negative public perception of Iranians was further amplified when, in January 2002, US president George Bush declared that an "axis of evil" threatened the security and safety of all humankind. This axis: North Korea, Iraq and Iran. While these regimes' lack of human rights and democracy were justifiably so labelled, many in the general public assumed that citizens of these countries, including Iranians living in the West, were evil too. In cities on both the east and west coasts of the United States, the large populations of Iranian immigrants, who had become successful students at top universities or had risen to high positions in the workforce, broke down some of these stereotypes.

Although I was uncomfortable with my new-found celebrity within the Persian community following Miss World, I decided to embrace it. I knew we Iranians needed something to boost our reputation. Within a day of hearing about the Bam earthquake, I did a couple of news interviews, in which I implored people to donate money to the Red Cross to help the victims. Former colleagues at the Red Cross had then called to ask if I could be the master of ceremonies at a Pari Zangeneh concert put on by the Iranian Canadian Cultural Association. Pari Zangeneh, a well-known Persian singer, would be donating proceeds to victims of Bam. My mother and Pari had been friends back in Tehran.

Pari was blind, my mother reminded me. As a young woman, she had fallen asleep one night while driving her car in Tehran. She awoke just as the vehicle smashed into a building. Glass shards from the windshield flew into her open eyes. She had been married at the time, to an uncaring man, my mother said, who left Pari during her recovery.

"It will be good to be on stage with Pari and raise money for Bam," my mother said when I told her about the fundraiser. "But your audience? Does it have to be Iranian?"

Unlike my father, who talks with great affection about Persian history and literature and revels in being at Iranian events, my mother waves it all off. She has nothing good to say about Islam or the Iranian government under the ayatollahs. Her experience of Islam was that of extremism, and extremism of any kind, she feels, fuels hate and revenge; the Christianity she had experienced, on the other hand, was love and forgiveness. As a result, she always felt like she was born in the wrong country and into the wrong religion, always feeling like a foreigner in her homeland.

As I was rushing out the door to the concert my mom said, "When you see Pari, give her a big hug and kiss from me. We had such great social nights dancing at the discos together back in Tehran."

I TOOK A DEEP BREATH, then walked up to the microphone in the jam-packed auditorium at Centennial Theatre in North Vancouver. "Good evening, ladies and gentlemen. We are gathered here not only to enjoy the beautiful voice of Pari Zangeneh but also to gather as a community to help our brothers and sisters back in our homeland. I would like to introduce Pari Zangeneh and her pianist, Mr. Bastani," I said.

The theatre erupted in laughter and I was unsure why. I slowly turned and scanned the stage behind me to see what was so funny. Pari was standing behind the curtains, waiting to make her entrance, with a big grin on her face. Mr. Bastani was sitting at the piano, shaking his head.

"I would like to introduce Mr. Bastani," I said again, and again the audience broke into laughter. Mr. Bastani slowly got up and walked over to me. *"Baa,"* he whispered into my ear. "It is pronounced *baa-stani*, like the baaing of a sheep." Later, after the concert, Pari gently chided me for saying *"bastani"*—"ice cream" in Persian.

"Don't worry, Nini, you will get the hang of this," said my father, who had joined us backstage.

Other than my mispronunciation of Mr. Bastani's name, the evening went well, and I was asked immediately afterward to co-host with Jian Ghomeshi another fundraising event for Bam, this time in Toronto. I was to give a speech on the destruction that had taken place in the small southern Iranian city, which now had a death toll of 50,000, with another 100,000 injured and thousands left homeless and struggling to survive in the unusually frigid winter temperatures. Even the United States had warmed to Iran, offering Bam direct humanitarian aid.

A friend of mine, Kian Ehsan, had parents who lived just outside Bam also in Kerman Province. Kian called me before the Toronto concert to suggest that instead of raising money for a large aid agency, it might be more useful to give the money collected directly to those who lived in Bam and worked with those whose homes had been destroyed and found themselves homeless. His parents were doctors and were volunteering at a Bam clinic, he told me. At the time, I had great faith in the Red Cross, called the Red Crescent in Islamic countries. I also knew that the Persian community would trust a big non-Iranian aid group over a small Persian one.

One thing I was fast becoming aware of in my new position as a spokesperson was that Iranians could be paranoid, leaping to conclusions and mistrustful of other people's good intentions. I could understand why. Our history is full of conflict, so, whether consciously or not, we all carry the weight of being an oppressed people, constantly defending and fighting for our survival, physically and culturally. Adding to that, many Iranians today lived through the revolution, a time when neighbours turned on neighbours and when people who sympathized with the regime seemed to get rich overnight. The same phenomenon has been seen in many conflicts, including the Soviet revolution and the Khmer Rouge's reign of terror in Cambodia: people desperate to survive turned against those they once loved the most, in some cases their own parents and children.

Under the mullahs of the Islamic Republic, poor peasants now held big positions in business, the judiciary and the police, where they were sometimes responsible for the life and death of their former peers and employers. Many were not even literate and did not have any qualifications, but it didn't matter—it was preached that devotion and faith were the prerequisites for these positions.

Before I left Vancouver for the Toronto fundraiser, I called Stephan Hachemi. His mother, Zahra Kazemi, a Canadian photojournalist who was born in Iran, had been raped and murdered by regime officials after taking photographs outside Evin Prison in Tehran. Saeed Mortazavi, the prosecutor general of Tehran who was later sent to the new human rights council at the United Nations as the representative for Iran, was implicated in Zahra's death.

I asked Hachemi if he would take part in the fundraiser. He said no and echoed what Kian had told me: "I won't participate in this. All that money you are raising will go into the pockets of the corrupt officials in Iran, the same corrupt officials who murdered my mother. Why should I fatten the pockets of the people who killed her?"

I started to tell Hachemi that I sympathized with his sentiment but that the money being raised was going to the Red Crescent, not regime officials, when he interrupted me. "I've heard that some of the tents intended for the homeless are being sold on the black market.

And the medical supplies being shipped over there are ending up in pharmacies and being sold at ten times their Western value. Some of the survivors have the flu or colds that are turning into pneumonia. They're dying."

I wasn't sure what to think. I had only seen good work from the Red Cross, at least in Canada. I went through with the Toronto fundraiser, asking questions along the way as to where the money was going. I was constantly reassured that the money was reaching the victims. I wasn't as confident anymore, however. After Toronto, I was asked to take part in a fundraiser in London, England, which would take place at the yearly Nowruz celebrations.

After the fundraisers for Bam, my year became a whirlwind of activity with charity events, photo shoots, media interviews and guest appearances. I met with royalty, spiritual gurus and heads of state. I was most excited, however, to meet some of the Iranian women I had been learning about and come to admire, such as Nobel Peace laureate Shirin Ebadi and lawyer Mehrangiz Kar, who equally deserved the Nobel Peace Prize for her defence of clients, including women and girls, wrongly accused or severely punished, and her criticism of Iran's oppressive criminal laws. I also met award-winning authors Mahnaz Afkhami and Azar Nafisi, and US politician Goli Ameri.

At Oxford University's debating society, Oxford Union, I felt honoured to stand where Churchill, Einstein and Kissinger each once spoke, and presented a speech on women's empowerment and how pageantry fit in.

After all those emails I had from my Western detractors, I finally came up with a rebuttal. "Why," I asked, "is 'beauty' such a dirty word in the West? Do we not enjoy seeing the beauty of a flower in bloom? A painting by one of the great Renaissance Masters? Why is being a beautiful woman synonymous with being anti-feminist and anti-evolved? Only Western feminists equate wearing a bikini with being dumb and unemancipated. But until recently, in all parts of the world, including the West, women were not allowed to wear clothes that revealed their beauty . . . Couldn't it be argued that part of our emancipation as women is that we can wear what we want, when we want? Are not the feminists condemning pageants objectifying me as a participant and doing exactly what they are accusing men of doing?"

I also said that I felt that Western middle- and upper-class women took for granted their freedoms, which include being able to work, get an education and choose their husbands. In many parts of the world, women still don't have these basic rights. In Iran, women are being imprisoned and lashed for having a few locks of hair poking out from beneath their headscarves or wearing their skirts up to their knees at private parties. In Angola, Selma Katia Carlos is seen as a hero because she showed to the world the beauty of an African woman. She used her high profile to advocate for improved rights and freedoms for women and children.

"God gave each and every one of us different blessings, and I see beauty as one of these blessings. When I wore that bikini on the beach as part of Miss World and my ball gowns on stage, I felt strong and powerful, not weak and submissive," I said. "I felt like the Persian heroines, both mythical and factual, of old, like Scheherazade from *One Thousand and One Nights*. Scheherazade, a virgin who every night began a story but never finished it. Scheherazade, who was beautiful and clever, managed to escape death by entertaining her husband, the king, for one thousand and one nights."

IN THE EARLY SUMMER of 2004, I found myself back on an airplane to Hong Kong to meet with the All-China Women's Federation and then on to Sanya, in Hainan Province. After recovering from jet lag and learning basic martial arts from some Shaolin monks, I, along with Miss World, Rosanna Davison, and Miss China, Guan Qi, boarded a minivan and headed out to the countryside. I gazed out the window at the oxen grazing on the side of the road and the peasants on their bikes, sometimes cycling precariously close to the van. Hainan Island is a touristy part of China, with tropical weather and many plush resorts. Even in the air-conditioned vehicle, I felt hot and uncomfortable. I bemoaned the fact that Miss World organizers had asked Rosanna, Guan Qi and me to wear formal day clothing—not exactly clothes suited to the temperature. But as soon as we pulled into the first of the two orphanages, I knew this was more than just an uncomfortable mistake. I had on a floor-length, white crochet dress. The heels of my stilettos got stuck in the muddy driveway that we had to walk to the orphanage compound, made up of several small houses. But still this was just a minor inconvenience. The real problem was that I felt so out of place and disrespectful to the poverty in front of me.

We walked into one of the houses, where we were immediately greeted by barefooted girls wearing mismatched tops and skirts. We had a few boxes of plastic toys, including dinosaurs and dolls, to give to the children. The manager of the orphanage welcomed us, and a photographer took our pictures as we shook hands with the children and gave them their presents. We were then whisked away for a short tour. In broken English, the manager told us that most of the inhabitants were girls, since families in China preferred males over females: boys carry on the family name and are thought to be better providers for their families. When the Chinese government implemented its one child policy in 1978 in an attempt to control the country's skyrocketing population, which today hovers at around 1.3 billion, many women aborted female fetuses, committed infanticide or gave girl babies away for adoption to orphanages like this one.

At university, I had seen documentary footage of Ukrainian orphanages and couldn't believe the facilities were real. The floors were filthy, the walls barren and the children visibly unwell, both emotionally and physically. As I went from room to room, photographs of the Ukrainian orphanages came to life, but instead of blue-eyed children, I was now looking into soft, sweet and sad brown eyes. The girls' stainless-steel beds were small, with thin mattresses.

I was so taken aback that when I finally met all the children in a small assembly, I felt shy. I handed out more toys as the photographer snapped away. I wanted to scream that this was absurd, and how were we really helping these children?

I thought of Bam and whether Kian and Stephan Hachemi were right. What if the survivors of the earthquake were living on the streets in conditions like this or worse because their makeshift tent houses, donated to the country, were being sold by ruthless middlemen or agents of the regime?

I competed in Miss World wanting to become an international advocate for humanitarian issues. Instead, I found my world, at least the one I had known before visiting China, turning upside down. I didn't know what to believe anymore.

CHAPTER 12

NAZANIN FATEHI

Early 1999, Sanandaj, Iran

―――――――――

A little over a month after she abandoned school, on a cloudy, damp day, the neighbourhood filled with the midday call to prayer from the nearby mosque, Nazanin knelt in an open field where many of the boys played football when not at school. She had kicked together some pieces of garbage, including rumpled newspapers and discarded drink and food containers, poured kerosene, which she had taken from a neighbour's shed, onto the pile and lit it with a match. When the fire was blazing, she had placed her new coat in it and had stared as the word "jaash" slowly went up in flames.

Nazanin envisioned herself standing in the flames, her arms outstretched, her hair on fire. Without thinking, her right hand moved to the kerosene container, still half full. She picked it up.

"Allahu Akbar Ash-hadu al-la ilaha illallah . . ." sounded the call to prayer.

Nazanin felt a wave of deep sadness, deeper than any she had ever experienced, move through her. She wanted to bury herself in the earth and never show her face to the sun again. She wrapped her headscarf around her cheeks so that only her eyes were visible. Her hand moved to the matchbox.

"Heye-allal-salah"—"Rush to prayer," the words urged her. *"La ilaha illallah"*—"There is no God but Allah." Nazanin's thoughts flashed to a story she had overheard at school. An older student, one

who was not well liked to begin with, had been caught cheating on a mathematics test. The teacher told the entire class. That afternoon, her schoolmates called her names, including stupid. In the early evening, she killed herself by setting herself on fire in much the same way Nazanin was now contemplating taking her own life.

But just as Nazanin was about to douse herself with kerosene, she looked up at a tiny sparrow darting back and forth. It landed on a metal fence and chirped, as if speaking to her, and then immediately set off again, headed toward the minaret on the mosque in the distance. Nazanin thought of Leila. She remembered her sister's downcast eyes at her wedding to Karim. And Nazanin knew she had to live to be her sister's wings.

"How did you come to be called Nazanin?" Hana asked as her friend, Dr. Afsaneh Samadi, had Nazanin lie down on Hana's bed. Hana sat down beside Nazanin, who had been given a needle of opium in her arm to relax her and dull the pain. She flinched only slightly as Afsaneh gently opened her legs. Afsaneh then applied a local anaesthetic to the area of the hymen, which had been torn by the rape.

Nazanin groaned, feeling some of the pain as Afsaneh sewed up her hymen with thread.

"Talk to me," Hana prodded Nazanin. "It will take your mind away from what Afsaneh is doing."

Nazanin took a deep breath. "Leila told me that I had whispered the name Nazanin to her in a dream before I was even born. She said my spirit talked to her. Maybe she's right, because ever since I could talk, I told everyone my name was Nazanin. But I don't know if I believe in spirits. All I know for sure is that I never liked the name Mahabad."

"I don't like it either," giggled Hana, squeezing Nazanin's hand. "I prefer Nazanin too."

After Afsaneh had finished, Hana lit a candle and turned off the overhead lights. The doctor left five pills and instructions to take them as needed, though no more than two every six hours. "You will be fine," Afsaneh said, kissing Nazanin on the forehead. "When you marry, you will bleed as if you are still a virgin."

Hana saw the doctor out and then returned and stroked Nazanin's hair.

"Tell me about the photographs hanging in your kitchen," Nazanin said softly, drowsy now from the painkillers. "Who are all those men?"

"Oh," Hana began, "those are my brothers and the older man is—was—my father. They were all killed."

"Why?" Nazanin managed to get out, her mind foggy from the drug.

"My father and two older brothers were members of the Democratic Party of Iranian Kurdistan," Hana said, moving her chair in closer to Nazanin. "After the revolution, the Kurds in Iran began to rise up. We saw in the revolution a window for democracy, in which the Kurds could really be represented in government and we could preserve our heritage, including having students like you learn to read and write Kurdish in school. We Kurds wanted change.

"But the regime of the Islamic Republic cracked down on us. My father's political party was declared illegal. Sepahis took him and tortured him, and then a death squad executed him in a big open field at the airport."

"What about your brothers?" Nazanin asked.

"Sepahis killed them next. They were shot right in front of their wives and children. My mother," Hana said, now crying, "died from a broken heart within six months."

Nazanin tried to roll on her side to be closer to Hana, but the pain was too much. "Hana," she said when she was settled again, "we're moving to Karaj."

"Why?" Hana gasped.

Nazanin started to cry.

"Stay with me," Hana whispered, holding Nazanin's hand in her own as if in prayer. "You can be my daughter."

Nazanin felt warm and smiled, thinking of a life with Hana—the nice clothes, attending a new school and eating meat at mealtimes.

"Hana," she said, "tell me more about Kurdish life . . . the life that I would lead if I lived in the mountains of Kurdistan with you."

Hana smiled. "Let me see. Well, my father's youngest brother, Ako, lived on a tiny farm, where he herded sheep, near Dargala in northern Iraqi Kurdistan. When I was little, we would visit him. I remember the women. They were strong. Some were blond and green-eyed, and they wore bright red, pink and blue dresses. Many people believe that we Kurds are the first inhabitants of the Middle East, and our fairer skin and eyes could have come from anywhere, maybe even Europe. But these women could tell their husbands anything, including what to do, and no man would ever dare raise his fist. The women were not servants but heads of their families. Back then, the women worked the fields, planting and harvesting their crops of wheat and barley with their babies strapped onto their backs, singing lullabies like *Lai lai lai lai kizholei chaw kazhalm . . . Lai.*

"Once when we visited Ako, it was winter. The storyteller came from another village. When he arrived, villages far and wide held a big feast, and the village elder sacrificed a goat for the storyteller. When their bellies were full, the children were put to bed.

"But I couldn't sleep, so I slipped on my winter boots and coat and headed to the home of the head of the village. All of the adults were sitting around listening to the storyteller. He was sharing the tale of Mem and Zin.

"The storyteller remained in the village for four nights, and every night he continued with the story of Mem and Zin, two star-crossed lovers who eventually die. And every night I snuck into the head of the village's kitchen and listened. On the final night, my mother walked in. She said she knew I had been there all along. 'I want to be a teacher when I grow up,' I told her as she made me a cup of warm milk. 'I want to tell stories, like the storyteller.'

"Nazanin," Hana whispered, tucking the blankets around the now sleeping girl. "Please come and live with me. I have always missed having a daughter. I can teach you many stories. One day, maybe you will even have a story of your own to tell."

NAZANIN WOKE in the late afternoon. Despite having had surgery, Nazanin knew she had to return home. Before leaving, she told herself that she would return to Hana's and be her daughter. Once outside, Nazanin popped another painkiller into her mouth, ignoring the doctor's orders. She then walked to the sounds of canaries, sparrows and nightingales chirping, admiring the cherry and sycamore trees and the forsythias starting to bud.

But the painkiller wasn't enough to quell the surging pain. She started to feel dizzy from the medication and her feet began to feel heavy. As she pushed open the gate to her home, she slapped herself in the face. *Pull yourself together*, she admonished. *No one can know what has just been done to you.* The creaking of the rusty gate frightened a stray cat that leapt up on the cement wall separating her house from the neighbours'. Before skittering away, the cat turned and stared at her. Its fur had been worn in spots, revealing red, bloody skin. "You look how I feel!" Nazanin smiled. "But your fear made you move as if you were suffering from nothing. I am going to move like you."

The front door to her house was open. She stepped into the main room, wanting to collapse on the rug and cushions her mother had not yet packed for Karaj, but then stopped. Someone was already asleep there, a heavy wool blanket pulled over his or her head. The body stirred and then the face looked up. It was Leila.

Nazanin's happiness at seeing her sister turned to fear, for Leila's right eye was swollen and the flesh underneath had turned blue. "What happened?" Nazanin asked, running over to her sister and wrapping her arm around Leila's shaking shoulders.

Leila sat up and busied herself wrapping her scarf around her head. She would not look at Nazanin. "You are moving to Karaj in a couple of days," she said instead. "I am going to ask if I can come with you."

Nazanin clapped her hands together. "Yes! It would be wonderful to have you close. I don't like it much at home anymore. Hojat goes to dogfights every Friday. After school he goes to mosque now. He prays, he comes home, he hits me, he goes to dogfights and then he goes back to mosque with Baba to pray some more."

"Like the men," Leila said, rolling her good eye. "Some mullahs who sit around and do opium tell the men to get cross with their wives if they do something wrong, refuse to share their bed with them and then beat them. Like my husband, Karim," she said, lowering her face.

"What are you talking about?" Nazanin asked, lifting up Leila's chin.

"He beats me," she said in a shaky voice. "He says I flirt with other men when I go to the market, but I speak to no one. He says I want to be with the neighbour's husband. I don't even know him."

Leila fell into Nazanin's arms and cried. "Shush, shush," Nazanin said as she rocked her sister back and forth and sang to her. *"Lai lai lai lai kizholei chaw kazhalm . . . Lai . . ."*

When Leila's tears had nearly dried, Nazanin told her about the Yaseen Sura. "Whenever I feel sad, I think of these beautiful words," she said, reciting the few lines she knew. "I don't believe anyone who loves Khwa would ever tell a husband to hurt his wife." After a brief silence, Nazanin whispered, "I miss my prayer time at school . . . and reading. I miss school."

"Why don't you go back, Nazanin? Go back," Leila pleaded. "You have a chance at a good life. You are smarter than I am, and you are still young. Go back to school when you move to Karaj. Don't end up like me. Look," she said, pulling off her headscarf. Nazanin gasped. Like that of the cat outside, part of Leila's hair had been torn out, exposing her scalp, which was bloody from a deep gash.

Nazanin and Leila moved over to the window and stared out,

listening to the neighbourhood girls laughing as they skipped rope in the alley.

"I have to leave him," Leila eventually said. "But I have nowhere to go."

THAT NIGHT AFTER CHAEE and some fruit, Nazanin and Leila were putting their mats on the floor, getting ready to go to sleep, when Habib arrived. The whites of his eyes had turned red and his movements were slow. "He is high on taryak," Nazanin whispered into Leila's ear as their father stumbled across the room, eventually plopping himself down on the floor in a cross-legged position.

"I got a message. Your mother sent for me," he said and then, turning to Leila, "And why . . . why are you here?"

"Baba," Leila began, pulling herself up and crawling over to her father. "I . . ."

"Some chaee!" he shouted toward the kitchen. "Now, woman."

Nazanin could hear her mother clattering about in the small kitchen. "Go on, Leila," their father said as Leila lay on the ground by his dirty, bare feet. "Explain to me why you are here and why I was called away from finishing up business in town before we move to Karaj."

"Karim beats me," Leila said, lifting her head. "It has been going on since the baby died. It is getting worse every day. If I don't leave—"

"You are not leaving him," he replied, cutting her off. Nazanin's mother placed a glass of chaee, along with sugar cubes and a biscuit, in front of her husband. "Do you know what shame you will bring to the family if you do? No," he said, shaking his head. "I will not accept this! You must return."

Leila began to sob as she lay on her stomach, head down, on the rug. "But I have not conceived another child," she mumbled. "Karim is talking about taking on another wife if I don't. He doesn't want me anymore. Please, Baba, please let me come home and live with you."

"For one night, while you clean yourself up," he said. "Then you must go back, talk to Karim and get him to calm down. He will stop hitting you if you do what he asks." Nazanin's father swallowed his tea in one gulp and then left the house, leaving behind his odour of perspiration and smoke.

"He's not even my father and he has condemned me to death," Leila whispered.

"I . . . I don't understand." Nazanin turned and stared into her sister's cold eyes.

"I am Sherko's daughter. Mother told me that I had to accept Baba as my only father. While the Iranian regime may consider my father a martyr for giving up his life in the Iran-Iraq War, most Kurds don't accept this as a great sacrifice. My father's family never wanted me to speak of him again. One time when I met our grandmother, she told me that our mother was the reason for Sherko's death—that she is cursed and so must I be too."

A FEW HOURS LATER, Leila started to complain of a headache, which worsened by the hour. But Habib refused to take her to the doctor despite his wife's pleas. "You will be fine," he had said to Leila when he returned to the house to sleep there, for the first time in a fortnight.

Leila eventually fell asleep, but Nazanin could not. Hours passed as she listened to the heavy breathing of her sisters and her mother. When Nazanin finally did doze off, it was only briefly. Her dreams were full of flames and pictures of Leila's wounds. When these images flashed in her head, her eyes would pop open and she found herself gasping for air. At one point, she took another pill, but it did not make her drowsy. Instead, she found herself more awake than ever. Nazanin vowed that she would tell Leila in the morning about being raped and about Hana's offer to live with her. She would even suggest that she and Leila move in with Hana.

As the muezzin was calling people to morning prayer, light filled the room from the window and Nazanin's eyes fell on Leila. Her headscarf, which she had worn to bed, had fallen off. She was turned toward the wall, so Nazanin could see only part of her sister's cheek. But it looked blue. Nazanin looked at her sister's body. There was no movement, not even the rise and fall of breath. Slowly, Nazanin sat up on her knees and crept over to look at her sister. She gently pulled her hair back and looked into Leila's eyes, which were wide open and staring at the cement wall.

"Leila," Nazanin said, shaking her sister's shoulders. Nazanin's father came over and rolled Leila onto her back. He fell to his knees and sobbed, for Leila's dark brown eyes just stared, unblinking.

"No!" Nazanin's father cried out.

"What is going on?" Nazanin asked. "What has happened to Leila?"

"Go get a car. Ask anyone, flag someone down. Tell them your sister is sick, very sick. Hurry!" Nazanin's father shouted.

When someone eventually stopped, Leila was placed in the backseat, and Nazanin's mother slipped in beside her. "She'll be fine," Nazanin's mother said, her wild, darting eyes belying her calmness, as Nazanin's father hopped in the front. "She has the flu. That is all. We will be back soon."

Nazanin's mother and father came back that evening. Her father said nothing, except that the family wouldn't be moving for at least another week. The next day, Nazanin's mother and father woke early. They hadn't bathed at the local bathhouse in a long time, and their odours filled the room. As they were leaving the house, her father told Nazanin that they were going to the mosque.

Finally, on the evening of day three, her mother told her the truth. "Nazanin, Leila is dead. The doctor thinks she bled inside so much that her brain got covered in blood. She was dead when you saw her in the morning, with her blue skin and wide-open eyes. My baby, my first born, the child of my only true love, has left me."

CHAPTER 13

NAZANIN FATEHI

1992, Kurdistan, Iran, and 1999 to 2005, Karaj, Iran

WHEN Nazanin was just four years old, she went to a wedding with her family in a village close to the border of Iraq, past Awyar Mountain and near the city of Mariwan. Nazanin's father borrowed a friend's car, tying their bags and bundles to the roof. Nazanin's father's youngest sister was the bride. "She is my favourite sister, which is why we are going," Nazanin's father had told them. "She has a smile that makes me feel calm like the moon. And a laugh that makes me feel bright like the sun."

Nazanin's mother made arrangements to stay for a month afterward with the children, first with Nazanin's father's family and then with her own. Nazanin did not yet know the story of her mother's first husband and the great love between them, so she didn't understand why her mother seemed saddened by the visit. All the way there, she sat quietly in the front seat, looking out the window and dabbing her eyes with her headscarf. *"Dayah gian"*—"Mother dear"—"we will have fun," Nazanin said, leaning forward and hugging her mother's shoulders. But her mother did not reply.

The children ate potato-and-egg sandwiches, sang Naser Razazi songs and told each other riddles and jokes. But as the car made its way up along the winding road, the air turning cooler and less dusty, everyone became quiet as they stared at the snow-peaked mountains and gushing rivers and waterfalls. Nazanin looked over at Leila, her hair blowing out from underneath her headscarf in the breeze through the open window. *I can't wait to meet this aunt*, Nazanin thought, *for if she is anything like you, she must be beautiful.*

As the road curved its way around the mountains, Nazanin began to feel lighter and lighter, as if the weight of Sanandaj was lifting from her shoulders the higher into the sky they climbed. Leila started to sing a story about a village in Iraq.

"All of the people sing to each other," she sang in her high-pitched voice, which reminded Nazanin of a budgie's. "They greet each other at the bazaar and bargain for their okra in song."

"Where did you hear such a silly story?" Nazanin sang, giggling at the same time.

"I heard it at the bazaar from a woman begging for money, which she collected in a tin can. She wore a long black headscarf with mesh over her entire face, including her eyes, so no one would recognize her," sang Leila. "This woman said I would be a princess in the sky one day, and that my feet would not touch the earth for long."

Nazanin broke into laughter. "Maybe you need to go live in a cave up there," she said, pointing up at one of the mountains.

That night, the girls slept side by side on a colourful, newly handwoven Kurdish rug on the floor of a villager's house. The next morning, they were awakened early by one of the young women who lived in the house, who showed the girls how to bathe using a rubber hose in a small cement building out back. The woman, who had long dark-blond hair, was already dressed in a baby-blue Kurdish dress with gold necklaces and a white Kurdish hat with coins dangling from the top.

"Don't you have to wear a headscarf?" Leila asked her.

"We're safe here," the young woman said.

The wedding took place in a valley nestled in between three mountains. The bride wore white, and the blushing groom stood nervously beside her for most of the party. For hours, the party of about 400 people danced to Kurdish music, performed live by musicians, songs Nazanin's uncle, Zanyar, told her were banned in most parts of Iran. "But here . . . this is Iranian Kurdistan," he said, his cheeks red from the outdoors. "No Fars associated with the regime dares to come this close to the border. Even Sepahis are afraid of what lurks in those caves up there."

"And what is in those caves?" Nazanin asked.

"Freedom fighters," Zanyar beamed.

"Take me," Nazanin said, jumping up and down. "I want to leave the party for a bit anyway," she then said more seriously, for she felt uncomfortable in her plain dark blue dress and slacks amid the other children, who all wore bright Kurdish costumes and glittery silver and gold jewellery.

"Yes," he said, nodding. "Give me a moment." He scurried off, returning a few minutes later with a donkey. He picked up Nazanin and placed her on the handmade textile saddle. After showing her how to hold on to the rope that was tied around the donkey's neck, he led her up the grassy part of the mountain toward the caves. They walked for nearly an hour, the booming Kurdish music becoming less and less audible, until all Nazanin could hear was the sound of a trickling waterfall. Finally, Zanyar stopped, took Nazanin off the donkey and pointed to a cave about a hundred metres in front of them.

"The Kurdish guerrilla fighters once lived in there," he said.

"I don't understand," Nazanin said, shaking her head.

"The freedom fighters are our Kurdish soldiers who are waging a battle in the mountains to liberate us from our oppressors, the regimes in Iran, Turkey, Iraq and Syria."

At the time, Nazanin hadn't understood. Zanyar's words were all jumbled together. They made sense to her only when she was older and Hana began to tell her of the Kurdish plight. Back then, all she knew was that she wanted back on the donkey. "Please, Mamo, can I ride it some more?"

When Nazanin returned to the party, a young woman about Leila's age was teaching her sister how to do Kurdish dancing. The girl, dressed in a pink Kurdish outfit, held a purple scarf with fake diamonds sewn into it, which she waved in the air as the girls moved around and around in a circle.

When the music stopped, everyone stopped dancing except Leila. Instead, she took the scarf, shimmering in the sun, and tossed it around in the air herself. Leila's headscarf fell off, and she closed her eyes and lifted her face to the sky. With her hair and dress flowing around her, Leila danced like she belonged in the valley of the mountains.

WHEN NAZANIN MOVED to Karaj with her family, she found this image of Leila coming back to her more and more. Sometimes when Leila's absence was too much for her to bear, Nazanin would go to Chamran Park, where she sat on a bench and listened to the birds. "If there really is a village where all the villagers sing, I hope that is where your spirit now lives," she would say, thinking of Leila.

Nazanin had planned to run away to Hana's the day her family was to depart Sanandaj for Karaj. She had wrapped some of her clothes in a towel and hid them behind a shop garbage bin. But the day before they were set to leave, Somayeh came to visit. She had an eye that was swollen and blue, and Somayeh pleaded with Nazanin's father to let her go with the family to Karaj. "My father is angry," she told him. "If I stay, I will die."

Perhaps because Somayeh's absence wouldn't bring as much shame to the family as Leila's would have, or perhaps because they didn't want Somayeh to end up dead like Leila, Nazanin's parents agreed that the girl could join them.

That same afternoon, Nazanin snuck out the back and trudged down the alleyway in the rain. She retrieved her belongings from the garbage bin and headed to Hana's house. Soaking wet, with water dripping from her nose, she reached up to knock on the door but then stopped. "I can't be your daughter," she said, looking in the window at the warmly lit house. "I need to stay with Somayeh. But I will leave a part of myself with you," she said softly. She wrapped her fairy-tale picture book in a piece of plastic she found on the road and left it on Hana's doorstep.

KARAJ WAS WORSE than Sanandaj. Nazanin's father had developed kidney problems. The family lived in a small shack on a plot of land owned by some friends in Sanandaj. Her father eventually got jobs for himself and Nazanin at a plastic-shredding company. Hojat worked there part-time while he went to school. Nazanin spent endless days shovelling plastic into the water that flowed into the shredder. But because she was just a child, she received only a small wage. The family lived in worse poverty than they had in Sanandaj.

During these years, Nazanin's father's health deteriorated to the point where he could no longer work. But he was rarely home. Nazanin had no idea where he went and never asked. Nazanin's mother became more and more bitter.

Hojat left high school in his first year to work as a security guard. When he wasn't working, he was going to dogfights in the fields; sitting in friends' homes smoking the *ghalyan*, a water pipe; looking at pornography from the Karaj black markets and chasing girls.

If Nazanin got in Hojat's way he had no qualms about hitting her, even right in front of his mother or father. Somayeh suffered worse, though, when her father came to Karaj for work and she was ordered by the family, including Nazanin's father, to move back in with him. Ne'mat took a job selling fruit from a cart he wheeled around the neighbourhood. He had become even more mean-spirited, and he took out all his pain on Somayeh. She endured so many traumas to her head that there were days when Nazanin wondered if she was all right or bleeding inside like Leila had. Frequently she would start a conversation only to stop mid-sentence. Nazanin would snap her fingers in front of Somayeh's face to get her attention. When she did, Somayeh couldn't remember what she had been talking about.

Nazanin lost her job at the factory once the company no longer needed her, but she didn't return to school. Her days were spent doing chores. Suddenly Nazanin found herself almost seventeen, her own dreams of becoming a teacher slipping away. Her mother, pregnant once again, had become distant with her, spending any time at home resting for fear that the child would be stillborn like the last.

When the baby was born healthy, Nazanin's father was the only one to celebrate—Maryam was exhausted and weak, for she was no longer a young woman. The baby was a boy, "and I name him Arsalan, which means bravery," her father had beamed. "This boy will make me proud!"

Nazanin looked over at Hojat, who was glaring at his father, his nostrils flared. *Good*, Nazanin thought as her father tickled Arsalan's neck and promised to buy him sweets when he was older and take him to the park on his shoulders. *Hojat will soon see what it feels like to be discarded for someone else.*

The only time Nazanin found beauty in the world was when she sat in Chamran Park, watching the birds and thinking of Leila.

"YOU ARE BAWBAKHT!" her mother screamed at Nazanin as she threw a lukewarm glass of chaee at her daughter's face.

"Why are you like this?" Nazanin yelled back, wiping her face with her sleeve. "Why do you have no life in you anymore?"

"Because it was beaten out of me, like it will be beaten out of you," Nazanin's mother spat back. "Now, please go and don't come back for a while. Go to Somayeh's, somewhere, anywhere but here."

Nazanin rolled up her mat and packed into a plastic bag her only other dress and a blue headscarf. It was late winter, only a few weeks from Nowruz, and Nazanin had asked her mother if the family could celebrate that year, perhaps even jump the fires set up for Chaharshanbeh Suri in the alley with some of the neighbours. Her mother had coughed up blood into her hand and wheezed, then stared at Nazanin. "Look, I am sick," she yelled. "We have no money for me to get help, let alone for anything else."

When she arrived at Somayeh's father's house, the wire gate was open. Nazanin slipped inside and saw that the front door, despite the cold weather, was also wide open.

"Somayeh," she called out as she entered. "Are you home?"

The room was dark. Nazanin turned on the overhead light and heard someone stir, and then whimper, beneath the cushions on the rug. "Somayeh? Is that you?"

Somayeh poked her head out. Her face was flushed and smeared with her lipstick and blush. Lines were drawn across her cheeks with heavy kohl eyeliner.

"What are you doing?" Nazanin asked, dropping her belongings and pulling the cushions away. "You know not to wear makeup around your father. Did he do this to you? Did he draw the marks on your face?"

"He wasn't supposed to be home. Look." Somayeh rolled up her sleeve to show fresh burn marks from heated spoons. "We have to run away."

"Calm down," Nazanin said, taking Somayeh's hand. "You need to clean yourself up first, and then we will decide what to do."

"I am running away today," Somayeh said, ignoring Nazanin. "I met some boys. They told me where they stay when they do not live at home. I know where it is. I have been there. Come with me?" she pleaded, her eyes darting back and forth as she pulled herself up and began stuffing clothes into a plastic bag.

Nazanin went to the kitchen and poured cold water on a cloth. She then held Somayeh still as she washed her face. "We can't run away," she told Somayeh. "You know what they say about girls who run away."

"Where else are we going to go? Back to your house? My father will find me, like last time. Remember? You were there when he nearly broke my arm as punishment. I am not staying here. I am going and you can come with me or stay."

"I can't go home," Nazanin murmured. "My mother is in one of her moods and wants me to stay away for a while."

"What?" Somayeh gasped. "She's never kicked you out before. Where does she think you will go? Why did she do this?"

"All I wanted," Nazanin cried out, "was a little warmth in the house for Nowruz."

"Then come with me," Somayeh said, putting on her manteau and boots.

NAZANIN AND SOMAYEH headed toward the furthest reaches of their neighbourhood, where many of the buildings were rundown and few people walked the streets. Eventually, Somayeh led Nazanin to a three-storey apartment building. All its windows were patched up with large planks of wood and the front door was off its hinges.

Once inside, Somayeh reached behind a pile of rubble and pulled out a lantern and a pack of matches. When the room was lit, Nazanin could see that it—and the entire building, she guessed—was abandoned. There was nothing there except dust.

"How did you know to find that?" Nazanin asked, pointing to the lantern.

"Because I've been here before. What do you think? When my father abuses me, I stay home?"

Somayeh told Nazanin to follow her up the stairs, which were chipped and broken. She then led Nazanin to a room at the back of the third floor. She knocked three times on the rusted tin door and then whispered, "Are you there? Anybody there?" The door opened and a rosy-faced boy with a slim frame and greasy hair looked out. He was wearing jeans and a dark jacket, and a cigarette dangled from his mouth.

"We've been waiting for you," he said, winking, when he saw Somayeh. "Come in."

Somayeh introduced the boys, who were about eighteen, to Nazanin. They sat cross-legged on cheap, worn rugs. A boy who introduced himself as Abbas handed Nazanin some *barbari* bread, which she took but did not eat. She lowered her head and let Somayeh do all the talking. When Somayeh turned the conversation to her father beating her, Nazanin nudged her with her elbow. "Shush," she said. "You can't talk about such things with strangers. Please, Somayeh," she pleaded. "I don't feel comfortable staying here. Can we go home?"

"What home?" Somayeh snapped.

Relenting, Nazanin laid her head down on a dirty cream-coloured cushion, pulled her manteau tightly around her body and closed her eyes.

She awoke in the morning to the chirrup of a swallow sitting on the ledge outside the window. "I'm going home," Nazanin said upon seeing Somayeh.

"I'll come with you," said Somayeh, her cheeks flushed and hair messy.

Just as Nazanin predicted, her mother was full of remorse that her daughter had stayed out all night. She pulled Nazanin into her arms, wailed as if she were at a funeral and apologized. She then gave Nazanin 10,000 toman with which to buy a new headscarf at the bazaar—"For Nowruz."

Nazanin and Somayeh took the minibus to the city's main bazaar and spent the morning walking up and down its aisles. They ran their fingers through the silk and satin fabrics sold to the wealthy women for making dresses. They listened to the permitted religious music at the CD shop and to some Iranian pop music the shopkeeper let them hear at the back. They stopped for cantaloupe juice and then admired the gold necklaces in the glass windows of the jewellers. Nazanin bought a new headscarf for herself and red lipstick and blush for Somayeh to replace what her father had destroyed.

As the noon call to prayer echoed through the caverns of the market, Nazanin said that she wanted to go home. They emerged from the bazaar, passing two young men, maybe five or six years older than Nazanin, who were leaning on their motorbikes and smoking cigarettes. The young men started to tease the girls, whistling and asking them what they were doing for the afternoon. Nazanin and Somayeh ignored them and kept walking. As they made their way to the minibus, Nazanin stopped at a shop where she purchased a kitchen knife, which she tucked away in her purse.

"What is that for?" Somayeh asked.

"For cutting fruit," Nazanin said. "One day, I will buy a bunch of bananas, cut them up and make a banana salad."

As they neared the minibus, Somayeh told Nazanin to stop. "I want to tell you something," she said, hugging her arms around herself and rocking back and forth. "I have a boyfriend," she chirped. "He is so handsome. His name is Hamid."

Somayeh's cheeks were glowing and her light brown eyes sparkled. Even though it was the prettiest and happiest she had ever seen Somayeh, Nazanin felt as if she had been hit hard in the stomach.

"I don't have a good feeling about you having a boyfriend," Nazanin said quietly.

"Let's call him," Somayeh said, ignoring Nazanin's concern. "Let's call my boyfriend."

"I don't think we should." Nazanin tugged on the sleeve of Somayeh's manteau. "Let's just go home."

"No. I want to call him at the pay phone. Come with me. We walked past it."

Nazanin followed Somayeh and watched as she dialed. When Somayeh hung up, she told Nazanin that her boyfriend was on his way. "Please be happy for me," she said. "With Hamid, when we marry, God willing, I will leave my father's home for good, maybe even Karaj. He's going to come now with his friend Roozbeh. Hamid told me he is already at the bazaar, somewhere on the other side."

"I came to Karaj to help look after you!" Nazanin exclaimed as the two stood on the curb, waiting for Hamid. "But we've been through so much, you and I, since we got here. If it wasn't for my mother and me you'd be . . . ," she trailed off. "And now this? I would not have come if I had known I would have to go through all I have for you. And now you are going to run off with a man you just met?"

"And where would you have gone if you had stayed behind?" Somayeh asked, not making eye contact with Nazanin.

Nazanin looked up at the darkening clouds. "I would have stayed with Hana," she whispered into the wind. Somayeh did not hear.

The two shuffled their feet to keep warm, both girls refusing to look at each other.

Hamid and Roozbeh eventually drove up on motorbikes, with a third young man, whom Hamid introduced as his brother.

"Come on," Somayeh said to Nazanin. "Hamid and Roozbeh will take us home."

"On their bikes?" Nazanin shuddered.

"Don't be afraid," Somayeh said.

But instead of going home, the boys drove around Karaj, stopping at a medical clinic, where Hamid's brother got off to meet his mother.

Nazanin started to protest again. "Somayeh, we really have to get home." Somayeh didn't listen and instead hopped back onto Hamid's bike. They all drove around some more.

As they turned the corner into one of the poorer areas of Karaj, the two young men who had been taunting Nazanin and Somayeh earlier at the market appeared on their motorbikes and rode up beside them. They sneered at Nazanin and Somayeh, then took off.

Nazanin shivered. "I really want to go home," she shouted into Roozbeh's ear.

"Okay," he replied. "But I want to have a cigarette first."

The two bikes came to a stop and Nazanin and Somayeh got off to stretch their legs. Roozbeh, still seated on his bike, lit up. Before he had even taken a second drag on his cigarette, the two young men from the market approached them. One came up close to Nazanin. "This is our area. What are you looking for?" he snarled, yanking off her headscarf.

"Get lost, asshole!" Nazanin yelled. The man took a small step back. Nazanin picked up a small rock and threw it at his head. He laughed when it ricocheted off his forehead.

"Roozbeh," Nazanin said, running up to him. He had been calmly watching what was happening. "Get me out of here please."

Roozbeh started his motorbike as Nazanin put her scarf back on, tying it tightly so it wouldn't blow off in the wind. But as she was about to get on the bike, the young man who had accosted her walked over and pulled off her scarf a second time.

Nazanin screamed, and Hamid and Somayeh rushed over. Roozbeh turned off his motorbike just as a third young man riding a bicycle stopped in front of them. He gave high-fives to the two men from the market and then moved toward Nazanin, touching her breast. "I want to take you with me, to an abandoned house," he said.

Nazanin was speechless. She wanted to lash out but her body felt numb. She slowly shook her head in confusion. Her eyes darted from side to side. "Are you following us?" she tried to ask the young men, but no words came out. She managed to take a step back. Tugging on Roozbeh's sleeve, she begged him with what words she could find to take her home.

Hamid and Roozbeh raced off on their bikes, with Somayeh and Nazanin holding on tight. But the other two motorbikes, the third man now sitting on the back of one, followed closely. Hamid and Roozbeh slowed down as they neared a vacant field. One of the pursuers pulled Somayeh off Hamid's bike, and she rolled onto the ground. All the bikes came to a halt, and the three men who were harassing Nazanin and Somayeh got off theirs. Hamid and Roozbeh turned off their engines but remained on their bikes. Somayeh stood up, rubbing her bruised thigh, and started screaming at the young men, "Why are you doing this?"

The man who had been on the bicycle grinned. "I have a place. I want to take you there."

Roozbeh and Hamid both started up their bikes. Nazanin, who had got off to help Somayeh, turned. "What are you doing?" she asked, searching their eyes, but they were blank.

The three men began to push Nazanin and Somayeh into the field. The dried grass crunched beneath Nazanin's shoes as she walked backwards, trying to get away from them. "Help! Help!" she shouted, hoping Hamid and Roozbeh would come to her defence.

Her calls were drowned out by the wind.

Two of the men continued to push Somayeh, but in a direction away from Nazanin, while the man who had been on the bicycle continued to harass Nazanin. "We have an empty house for you," he said, reaching out and touching Nazanin's breast. "We will have some fun. That's what girls like you are good for, no?"

"No," Nazanin murmured, shaking her head. "I'm not that kind of girl."

She looked over and saw Hamid and Roozbeh taking off on their bikes, leaving the girls alone. She looked at the other two men, who were now kneeling by Somayeh. She was lying on the ground face up, her nose bloody and her head turning from side to side. Spittle fell from her mouth. One of the young men pinned down her hands while the other started to take off her pants.

Nazanin no longer saw the man in front of her. Instead, she saw her father's friend, the man who raped her. Mohsen. In her mind's eye, she was no longer in the vacant field but in her old home in Sanandaj.

"Where is your father?"

"He's not home. We're all staying on the other side of Sanandaj."

"Then what are you doing here?"

Just as Mohsen had done, the young man hit Nazanin across the face, causing her to stumble. She caught a glimpse of Somayeh's bare legs as one of the men began to climb on top of her. Nazanin, her hands shaking, reached inside her purse and gripped the kitchen knife she had just bought at the market. She held it out in front of her as the man lunged toward her.

"If you come closer, I will stab you," she cried out in the loudest voice her parched throat could manage.

He lunged forward once more, and the knife penetrated his left arm.

"I swear to God I will hurt you again," she said as he stopped to look at the wound. Then he stepped forward and grabbed her neck, digging his long nails into her skin. Holding the knife in front of her, she felt it go into something at first hard and then surprisingly supple. The young man's body became lifeless, and he slowly slipped to the ground, pulling Nazanin by the hair down with him.

CHAPTER 14

NAZANIN AFSHIN-JAM

March 2005, Vancouver

═══════

I was sitting in my sister's airy kitchen, telling her and Peter enthusiastically about a book my new Internet friend Eric Jerpe had
given me as a gift for my success at Miss World. Eric's book, *The
Return of Scheherazade*, is based on the story of Scheherazade—also
referred to as Shahrzad—the heroine in the famous Persian collec-
tion of fables and folk tales *One Thousand and One Nights*. Eric has
a different interpretation of the original ending. He starts his book
in the present time, when a young man, Romeen, marries a young
woman named Roxana. On their honeymoon, the couple fly from
Tehran to Shiraz, the city of gardens, and then head north by car.

On a deserted stretch of the road, they come across an old man
walking on the embankment. The couple stop and ask the man if he
needs help. He replies in Old Persian, *"Spenta-mainyu,"* which the
couple translate to mean "the spirit of good."

After some discussion, Romeen and Roxana agree to take the
man to where he wants to go, the Mountain of the Sacred Spring.
As they drive, the man reveals his name, Porzand, and that he is
a Zoroastrian magi, or holy man. Porzand and Roxana engage in
a discussion on metaphysics, including the importance of the good
mind and the meaning of perfect strength. While they talk, Romeen
becomes increasingly perturbed. "Religion has failed us," he eventually interrupts. Romeen talks about the hypocrisy he sees in the cur-

rent Islamic Republic of Iran, where traffic cops in Tehran are more interested in arresting women for wearing bright-coloured clothes or loose headscarves than directing traffic in one of the world's most congested cities.

"Things will change for the better," Porzand replies. "Hopefully, there will be enough *spenta-mainyu* to induce the return."

"The return of whom?" Roxana asks.

"Shahrzad, of course," the magi says. "Shahrzad from the *Nights*."

"In *One Thousand and One Nights?*" asks Roxana.

"Yes," Porzand replies.

In the original *One Thousand and One Nights*, King Shahryar discovers that his wife has been unfaithful. Not wanting to be shamed in his next marriage, the king decides he will wed a virgin every day. The night after the nuptials, he kills the bride from the day before and marries another. King Shahryar goes through so many young virgins that eventually there is only one left. Shahrzad is the daughter of the man who has been entrusted to find the king his virgins. Against her father's wishes, Shahrzad agrees to wed the king, knowing it may very well mean her death.

But Shahrzad is clever. On the night of the wedding, she starts a story, which she recounts for many hours until it is time to retire for the evening. The king agrees to put off Shahrzad's death for one day if she agrees to come back the next evening and finish the story. When she returns, however, she does not end the story. She starts a new story instead, and again it is a story she does not have time to finish. Her execution is stayed again, and then again and again. Shahrzad became known as Shahrzad the Storyteller or Shahrzad Gheseh-goo, and her stories include "Ali Baba and the Forty Thieves," "The Seven Voyages of Sinbad the Sailor" and "Aladdin's Lamp." After a thousand and one nights of stories, the king, so enchanted with the storyteller, agrees to let Shahrzad live.

Porzand, the magi, explains that after King Shahryar's death, zealous iconoclasts came to power. In the name of religion, they destroyed many great pieces of art. Shahrzad, who had become a patron of the arts, was targeted for death. A mob tracked her down. But she headed to the Mountain of the Sacred Spring and disappeared into the mountain.

Over the years, many people have seen visions of Shahrzad, who vows to return in her physical body when there is enough *spenta-mainyu* in Persia, the land of Zoroaster's birth, to enable her to cross back over from the spiritual plane to the earthly one. Repeating what has become the mantra of all Zoroastrians, Porzand ends the legend by telling Roxana, "The land of Zoroaster shall brighten the skies with the eternal truths of Asha—the path of good thoughts and good words and good deeds."

My excitement showed as I neared the end of the story I was recounting—my hands were flying about in the air, and I was bouncing up and down in my chair. "This sounds so similar to the Shia belief in the coming of Mahdi, the hidden twelfth imam, who, it is said, will emerge at a time of great destruction on the earth and herald a time of peace and harmony," I told Peter. "This is also similar to the Christian belief of the second coming of Christ, who will bring salvation to the world. But in Eric's book it is a woman! I have always believed that, before any saviour comes, the healing of this world will come through women." I was so pleased I was beaming.

"Like Dr. Catherine Hamlin," I then whispered to myself, thinking of the Australian doctor I had met on a trip with the Miss World organization. Catherine had moved to Ethiopia in 1959 and founded the Addis Ababa Fistula Hospital with her husband in 1979. She spent her career selflessly helping Ethiopian women.

As I had learned during that trip, obstetric fistula occurs in pregnant women as a result of prolonged, obstructed and often unassisted labour. Continuous pressure of the baby's head inside the mother stops blood flow to part of the bladder tissue and sometimes the rectal wall. The babies are often stillborn. The mothers, if they live, tend to have urinary and fecal incontinence, since the affected tissue dies, resulting in a hole between the vagina and the bladder or rectum. Obstetric fistula is rare in most Western countries, for doctors there recognize the problem early on and the patients are treated quickly. Because of a lack of proper medical facilities in much of sub-Saharan Africa, obstetric fistula is a major health issue for women there. It is also a social issue: because of the women's stench, they are often ostracized by their communities and even by their own families.

In Catherine's hospital, the women undergo a simple operation, spend a few weeks in recovery and then are sent home with a brand new dress to symbolize their new life, cured and no longer outcasts. Despite their pain and being stigmatized, the patients I met wore big smiles. And Dr. Hamlin, who could have had a very comfortable life in Australia, remained in Ethiopia even after her husband died, to continue to help the women. I remember watching Catherine, an elderly yet strong woman, as she moved through the hospital gently stroking the patients' face or hand and making sure they were as comfortable as possible.

"So what do you want to do next, Nazanin?" Peter asked, pulling me out of my reverie.

"Whatever I do, I want to keep helping others. Miss World gave me a stronger voice to speak out, and I want to reach even more people on the issues close to my heart. I think I can be an asset, at the least by connecting those in need of help with others who can help them."

"What about music, Nazanin? Nothing reaches people better than music. What about making a record?" he asked.

I tilted my head and eyed him suspiciously. "I agree with you that songs have no borders and they reach the hearts and souls of all who listen. But are you kidding? Me? The girl who can't sing even one little bit? I won't even sing in church because I am embarrassed someone will hear me!"

"Yes," he replied, nodding. "I think anyone can sing and, with a good producer, make a good album."

Peter is a music producer. His top talents have sold albums in countries around the world. He met my sister in 2001 when she was selling a condominium in the building where Peter lived. Peter was heading to a meeting with Bif Naked, one of his star clients. Peter started talking to Naz, and when he discovered she was a realtor, he told her he wanted to buy a new place. It was merely a ruse. Really, he wanted to date her. Bif, who witnessed the exchange of business cards, said chemistry flew between the two the moment their eyes met.

Little did I expect when I stood beside Naz as her bridesmaid that I would become part of her husband's career plans.

"We can start tomorrow, Nazanin," Peter said with a big smile. "We'll go in the studio and we'll see how your voice sounds. Then we will make a record."

Singing was nothing I ever aspired to do, and I harboured no expectations that I would burst onto the music scene, with no prior experience, and sell out stadiums like Madonna. But what did appeal to me about Peter's idea was writing songs and performing. Since I was a child I had penned poetry, as well as performed in theatre throughout high school, before acting in television shows and commercials in university. At first, my writings were about the great heroines of whom I was painting pictures with my mother; later, my poetry was about the boys I had crushes on. I spent my allowance on glitter glue, stickers and fancy scented stationery so the writing would be showcased on prettily decorated pages. So although the singing part of Peter's plan was new to me, writing and performing certainly weren't.

Peter and Riley, his daughter from his first marriage, found me a few voice coaches who agreed to help with my training, including Sarah McLachlan's former coach, Judith Rabinovitch. Then the little album I was making for distribution in Canada turned into a big one, becoming a potential international release.

Many years before my working with Peter on the album, Bif Naked's dog bit online-gaming entrepreneur Calvin Ayre's ankle, resulting in Bif and Calvin striking up a conversation. Later, Calvin remembered his first encounter with Bif and asked Peter if she would sing at his upcoming corporate party. Peter refused the offer, explaining that Bif didn't do corporate parties, birthdays, funerals or weddings. Calvin was persistent and so Peter attempted to dissuade him by asking for a very large fee for what amounted to a thirty-minute acoustic performance. Calvin met the fee, and the performance became the start of the joint venture between Her Royal Majesty's Records, Peter's company, and Calvin's newly formed Bodog Music.

In order to be considered for this chance of worldwide release, I practised more frequently. I spent my days going from one vocal coach to another, learning to breathe, stretch my mouth and vocal chords, and relax. One coach even suggested I do yoga as a way to prepare. At night, I went through my diaries and notebooks searching for inspiration for the lyrics. It was important, Peter said, that the lyrics be an extension of my life experiences. I wanted the lyrics to be from my heart.

"Here is one of my old poems," I said, passing him a glittery piece of paper: *Ma chère, ma chère rose, ouvre-toi pour que je vois ta beauté, ouvre-toi pour que je sente ta splendeur*—My dear, my dear rose, open up so I can see your beauty and smell your splendour.

"Absolutely sucks," Peter replied. "Too cliché. Dig deeper."

"I can't do this," I lamented to Naz a few weeks later. "I want to quit. I can't write."

"Try harder, Nazanin," my sister said. "Instead of looking at your past writings or what people have written you for ideas, why don't you look at photographs from your life? Find your emotion there, in your lived experience. What have you felt passionate about in your life? When did you really feel? Find that, and then write from that place."

So I did. I came across a photograph that had been taken of me a couple of months earlier with the all-time heavyweight boxing champion Evander Holyfield. We were on board "Global Peace One," a Boeing 747SP carrying some 76,000 pounds of food and medical supplies to parts of southern India and Sri Lanka. Global

Peace Initiative had invited us, along with journalists and a group of Christian high school students from Cincinnati, to deliver aid after a tsunami devastated Indonesia and coastal areas in the region. During that trip, I spent time at Charity City, an orphanage in Hyderabad, playing games like duck, duck, goose and soccer with the children. I was touched by the smiles and graciousness of the children and other local people I met, even though they lived in such poverty, particularly those in the slums I visited.

I then dug all the way to Iran, reviewing all the letters and appeals I had received for help, from mothers wanting divorces from their abusive husbands to young women contemplating prostitution just to pay the rent. I finally came up with a verse that would eventually be used in my single, inspired by my own family's plight and escape from Iran.

They were on the march then
In 1978
They filled our minds with hate
They deceived the nation
In the name of religion
And soon it was too late
When the soldiers came
We were on the run
Our lives forever changed
That was no solution
Regressive Revolution
Together we must stand

"Great! Inspirational!" Peter declared. "Now find me some emotion to go with this. Give me some feeling so that anyone listening wants to stand with you."

But after that, I hit writer's block.

One day in the recording studio, Peter asked for a break so he could take a phone call. He left me alone for about twenty minutes. I had brought in a few of my photo albums, as Naz suggested. I flipped one open and found myself staring at a picture of Miguel, one of the most special, intelligent and spiritual friends I have ever had. He mentored me, taught me so much about life, in 2000, the year I got to know him. I called him my guardian angel on earth. He changed my life for the better, and made me a stronger person by encouraging me to follow my dreams.

But when he went into depression and I saw a man who used to be so vivacious, charismatic and alive turn into a dead man walking, I was crushed. I realized then that none of us is invincible and that life can change dramatically from one minute to the next. The man I had so looked up to took his own life.

I could hear my heart pounding. I followed my breath, and as tears started to fall, I found myself singing.

Someday
We will find a way
Someday
Someday
Someday
Someday
The darkness fades

Miguel was from the Philippines and had grown up Catholic, like me; however, he knew the scriptures far better than I ever would. One night over dinner of homemade *kare kare*—Filipino oxtail stew with green beans and peanut sauce, my all-time favourite dish—I opened up to him.

I told him about an incident in church when I was eight years old that moved me so greatly that it affects me to this day. Miguel was the first person I ever told about it outside my immediate family. It occurred just after my father had told me about Iran and his scars. There was nothing different about that Easter Sunday, at least not to begin with. I wore a faux rabbit-fur coat with matching mittens and a poufy velvet and taffeta dress. When I arrived at church with my mother and Naz, I looked around at the long line of pews and at the altar, the two stained-glass windows behind it depicting the Virgin Mary.

"Alleluia, Alleluia, Alleluia . . . *o filii et filiae Rex coelestis, Rex gloriae morte surrexit hodie*," sang the choir.

Father Scott, who had baptized me and conducted my First Communion when I was seven, walked up to the lectern and motioned for the congregation to sit. As he wiped his large, brown-rimmed glasses, I smoothed down my skirt and then reached over to hold my mother's hand.

"Jesus rose today," Father Scott eventually said, his hands outstretched, his loud, deep voice echoing through the long hall, which was full for the Easter service and quiet except for a baby cooing in her mother's lap. "The son of God was sacrificed for us. Jesus died for us so that our sins could be forgiven . . . so that we could live in light . . ."

Just as he said this, an overwhelming sensation took hold of me. Everything around me blurred and I could see only Father Scott. I heard clearly each word of his sermon. Tears filled my eyes. My mother handed me a tissue from her purse. It smelled of leather and her perfume. Mixed with the scents of the incense and the melting candle wax of the church, it comforted me.

When Father Scott finished the sermon, the congregation kneeled in prayer. I tried to steady myself by taking deep breaths. My face stained with tears, I looked up at the church ceiling of white stucco. In my peripheral vision I could see a mural of Jesus and his disciples. Just at that moment, the sun shone through one of the stained-glass windows, the rays falling on my upturned face. I closed my eyes and let the sun bathe me in light.

Ever since that day, I told Miguel, I felt I had inner dialogues with God. I connected and I never let go. Miguel told me that I must have felt the presence of the Holy Spirit.

Miguel had a permanent sparkle in his eye. He taught me that life was about living in the moment, about the people whom I would meet along the way and about the art and joy of sharing. He exemplified this way of life—people he met during the day would almost always be invited out for dinner or back to his apartment for a meal.

But tragically, after a trip back to the Philippines, Miguel took his own life. When I heard this, I recalled the last words he had said to me: "The worst evil in the world isn't how we physically and emotionally hurt each other with our words, fists or unjust laws, but when we crush each other's spirituality. That's when we lose all hope and we die." I learned many years later that his brother, who was Miguel's own mentor and inspiration, had betrayed him in the family business and in friendship.

I was still thinking about Miguel when Peter returned to the recording studio and found me huddled over my notebook, scribbling down lyrics:

Someday
We will find a way
Someday
Someday
Someday
Someday
The darkness fades

"I want these to be in one of my songs," I said to him. "For Iran, for Miguel, for everyone who still dares to dream."

CHAPTER 15

NAZANIN FATEHI

February 27, 2005, Karaj, Iran

———————

Nazanin was cold. She pulled the sleeves of her dress over her hands and kept her chin buried in the collar of her manteau. She lowered her eyes. "Where is Somayeh?" she asked. "Is she all right?"

"The forensic physician is checking her," the interrogator said, shifting his weight in his chair. "Now, tell me what happened after you stabbed the boy."

"I didn't know it was me . . . I mean, I didn't know it was my knife," Nazanin said slowly, tears in her eyes. "After we fell, my mind played tricks on me. 'Did I stab this man? Or did he stab himself? Is this my blood? Or is this his?' My eyes darted from the knife to my hands—from the knife sticking out of his chest to my hands . . ."

"What happened next?"

"I heard his voice, at least in my head. 'We have a house near here. We will pay you whatever you want.' He kept calling me 'slut.' He pulled off my headscarf and was ripping open my manteau as he pushed me backwards. I'm so cold," Nazanin whispered, changing the subject. "Can I take a break to warm up?"

"After," the interrogator said curtly. "When you finish giving your statement."

Nazanin stared at the white plaster wall behind the man. "I want to see my mother," she said after a while.

"We will tell her where you are after you finish telling us what happened," he replied in a voice so gruff that it startled Nazanin.

Nazanin wrapped her arms around herself. "I heard the other men shouting and I looked over," she began. "They were standing waving their arms at me and yelling, 'Slut, slut, you will die for what you have done.'

"I was very afraid for Somayeh, so when the men ran off, I hurried to her side. She was lying on her back, her face was bloody and there were cuts on her lips, cheeks and arms. I got her sitting up, and then I did up the buttons remaining on her shirt and wrapped her torn manteau around her. She was talking nonsense. 'Somayeh!' I said. 'Get a hold of yourself. We have to get out of here. I think I have done something.'

"Is Somayeh all right? Did those men . . . touch her?" Nazanin eyed the interrogator suspiciously.

"You will see Somayeh soon and she can answer all your questions. Now, go on."

Nazanin leaned back in her chair. "I stepped out into the street, in front of a car coming toward us, waving my hands. The car stopped. An older man rolled down the window and started yelling at me, but I interrupted him. I told him I had been attacked in the field and someone was still there hurt, maybe even dying. I told him to call Emergency," Nazanin said. "I don't remember what happened after that," she said in an almost inaudible voice. I felt like I was going to vomit. I felt . . ."

"Get to the story," the interrogator butted in. "I don't care how you felt. Do you remember stabbing the man in the field?"

"No," she said, shaking her head.

"But you told the man in the car you had pulled the knife out," a second interrogator, who had just walked into the room, interjected. "You told the man in the car that you had stabbed someone."

Nazanin gasped and held her hands out in front of her. They were clean. "My hands were bloody. Who washed me?" she asked.

"The nurse. Your face was bloody too. The nurse also combed

your hair and gave you a new headscarf," he said. "Why did you have a knife?" the second interrogator asked.

Nazanin looked at his long black beard. "I bought it at the bazaar. I was afraid," she said.

"Afraid of what?"

"Afraid of what people, what men, might do to me. I knew . . ."

"You knew what?" the first interrogator, whose tone was now kinder, asked, leaning forward.

Tears rolled down Nazanin's cheeks. "I knew what those men were about to do to Somayeh," she said. "I knew what they wanted to do to me."

"So you bought the knife for protection," he said with a scowl. "You planned on using it to hurt someone else."

"No," Nazanin murmured, wiping her eyes with her sleeve. "No."

THE INTERROGATORS TOOK A BREAK, and a guard gave Nazanin a stale piece of bread and some watery beef stew to eat. When the interrogators returned, they sat down in a huff as if they were angry at her, wiping their perspiring brows and butting out their cigarettes in the ashtray on the table.

"My name is Babaii," the first interrogator—the nicer of the two—finally introduced himself. He pointed at the other man. "And this is Mr. Karimi."

"You killed that man," Karimi butted in roughly. Nazanin's knees began to shake. "He died in Shahid Madani Hospital. His name was Yousef Bagheri. What do you say to that?"

Nazanin opened her mouth to say how sorry she was but no words came out. Her head began to spin.

"I feel faint," she eventually said quietly.

"What's that?" Karimi yelled, banging his hand on the table and making Nazanin jump.

"May I have a glass of water?" she asked, swallowing hard. "I don't feel well."

Babaii waved for the guard to get water. "Tell me about Somayeh," he said, picking up some papers that lay on the desk in front of him. "Somayeh told her interrogator she wasn't living at home when the attack took place. Are you and Somayeh runaways?"

"No," Nazanin said, shaking her head. "I am not a runaway, but Somayeh has difficulties at home. Her father beats her."

"She said," Karimi read from one of the papers, "that when you both lived in Sanandaj, her father, Ne'mat, would take heated spoons and burn her arms. Another time, he took an electrical cord with two wires sticking out and gave her an electric shock with it. Somayeh said she started to run away back in Sanandaj by sleeping underneath her neighbour's shed."

"It's true."

"And she moved with you to Karaj?"

"Yes," Nazanin said sadly, thinking of Hana, and how she might be with her now if it weren't for Somayeh. "My father tried to protect Somayeh, but he couldn't."

"Why was her father so mean to her? Was Somayeh a bad girl?" asked Karimi.

"No," Nazanin gasped. "She was innocent, like her mother. She was beautiful," Nazanin said, picturing Somayeh's shining eyes and glowing skin when she told her about Hamid. "Somayeh ran away in Karaj for a while," Nazanin pressed on. "But she had to. She feared for her life when she moved back with her father. We didn't see her for a long time. Finally we found her. She was living in a home for orphans. She had told the staff there that her mother and father were dead."

"Why would she have done that if she wanted to live with her mother all along?" Babaii asked. "She was old enough by then to move out with her. Her mother could have received custody."

"Somayeh wasn't right," Nazanin replied. "Her head was so mixed up, she wasn't thinking straight. My mother pretended she was Somayeh's grandmother and we were able to visit her in the orphanage once a week. We brought her apples, juice, rice and stew and we bathed her—her hair had become tangled from not brushing and she smelled of her own waste. She would sit on the washroom floor while the water was being drawn, rocking back and forth with her thumb in her mouth, like a baby.

"My family eventually took custody of her, and we brought her home for a while. But Somayeh's father convinced her to move back with him, saying he wouldn't hurt her anymore. I knew . . ." Nazanin sobbed, lowering her head. "I knew what those young men were going to do. I knew she wouldn't be able to handle it. I knew . . . I knew . . ."

"You knew what?" Karimi said. He stood up and moved beside Nazanin, leaning in so close that she could feel his warm, stale breath on her cheek.

"Please tell me the truth. I didn't really kill this boy named Yousef? He is fine, right?" she sobbed.

Nazanin spent hours in the airless interrogation room, drinking glass after glass of water and holding herself steady by placing her hands on the table whenever she felt faint. Karimi chain-smoked cigarettes and blew the smoke into Nazanin's face, making her feel even dizzier. She tried to remain calm and answer his questions. But he was loud and blunt and told her that he was Turkish and didn't like the Kurds. "Except, of course, for my friend Babaii here," he said, patting the other interrogator on the back.

"So how did you know about rape? Have you had sex before?" Karimi demanded, slamming his fist on the table again.

Nazanin blinked back her tears.

"Are you a runaway like Somayeh?" Karimi pressed on. "Did those men who came after you expect something because maybe . . . maybe you are a runaway and a prostitute? The nurse says the medical examinations confirm that you are not a virgin. You've been fixed."

Something deep inside Nazanin broke. "No," she yelled, banging her own fist on the table. "Never! I didn't want to go with Somayeh the night before to the abandoned building where we slept. I wanted a good life. I wanted to go to school. To read. To be a teacher and a storyteller . . . I never wanted to move to Karaj." She broke down, thinking again of Hana. "I was raped," she said, tears soaking her cheeks. "I was raped in Sanandaj, and I knew I was about to be raped again by this man you call Yousef. I pulled out the knife to defend myself. I did it to protect Somayeh's chastity. Please, please," she stammered, "don't tell my father."

She raised her hands up to the ceiling. "Khwa, please make them understand and see I am just a child. I want to go home. I didn't mean to hurt anyone. I just want to go home." At that moment, Karimi slapped her hard across the cheek and screamed at her to pull herself together. The force of the blow, which was so strong it drew blood, stunned her so much that she was breathless and began to choke on her saliva.

CHAPTER 16

NAZANIN AFSHIN-JAM

March 2005, Vancouver

―――――――――

As soon as I turned the key in the door of my parents' condominium, I could hear my mother singing Patsy Cline's "Crazy."
I peeked around the wall in the hallway and saw her standing in the
kitchen, hunched over the table, completing the painting she had
started about two weeks earlier, of a family of crows, each crow representing a member of Naz's family. My sister had recently given
birth to her second child. My mother has always respected crows
for being one of the most intelligent creatures and also thought her
grandchildren, like their parents, Naz and Peter, were wise beyond
their years.

"Is that you, Nazanin?" she called out, not looking up. "Give
me a minute and I will make us some tea." She continued singing.
I stifled a giggle. My mother's latest obsession was country music,
which she listened to at deafening volume and sang at the top of her
lungs, as if she herself were a chanteuse.

I slipped off my beige rainjacket and hung it up. I then picked up
my Persian cat, Shahtoosh, whom I had got in Paris during my third
year of university studies at Sciences Po—the same university where
former Iranian prime minister Mohammad Mosaddegh had studied.
I rested the cat on my shoulder like a baby being burped and took
her for a stroll around the condo. I took a long look at the foyer and
living room, full of art and antiques. Over the years, my mother had

accumulated many pieces, so many that I always felt that walking into my parents' place was like walking into a small private museum, complete with Louis XIV console, Russian icons and colourful Asian wooden chests and handcrafted figurines. The hallway was lined with a large, gold enamel–framed mirror and thick, wooden carved frames with religious paintings of Jesus, Mary and angels. Of course, there was a little of Iran everywhere too—multiple Persian rugs and kilims covered the hardwood floors in every room.

My mother switched from country music to Cat Stevens's "Wild World," which she belted out in her thick Persian accent as she pounded her paintbrush into the canvas. I decided to let my mother have her fun, so I moved into my parents' bedroom. The same silk painting of the doves I loved so much as a child hung on the wall. I kneeled to the floor and stared into the eye of the lone dove flying toward the heart.

"Dear God," I started my prayer. "Teach me to use my blessings to help advance humanity. Lead me where you want me to go."

I HAVE ALWAYS PRAYED. For a while, when I was fourteen, I even wanted to be a nun.

"*Seva*," I had written for a class assignment during this period of my life, "is an ancient Persian and Sanskrit word that means 'in service to others,' in which one has no expectation of personal gain. *Seva* is altruistic generosity. Mother Teresa exemplifies *seva* more than any other person I know of."

I hadn't told my plan to anyone for several months. Then one night as we ate cinnamon spiced lamb-shank stew, my father asked me, "Have you decided what you want to do after you're finished your schooling?"

I smiled meekly. "I don't know."

"Come on, Nini," my sister chided. "An astronaut? A surgeon? Prime minister?" My sister pressed and pressed until finally I blurted out, "A nun. I want to be a nun!"

"Nazanin," my mother gasped, standing up quickly and accidentally knocking her plate to the floor. "Please tell me I didn't hear you correctly. You don't want to be a nun!"

I nodded.

"Why?" my father asked in a softer voice.

"Why, Nini?" Naz repeated. "You have the highest grades in your school."

I told my family about *seva* and about Mother Teresa.

"You can do that *seva* thing without being a nun!" Mom exclaimed, finishing her glass of wine and grabbing the bottle for a refill. "What about grandchildren? I want grandchildren!" She banged her chest with her fist. "I don't want you to do this."

I laughed, as I always do when I'm nervous. "This is what I want. Be happy for me."

"Nazanin," my father said. "You can live a life helping others and not become a nun."

"Yes, your father is right," my mother added on her way out to the porch for a cigarette.

When she was out of earshot, my father leaned over. "Don't tell your mother you want to be a nun again until this is what you really, really want. She might have been the one to introduce you to Christianity, but her dream is for you and Naz to get married and have children. Plus," he joked, "she would burst into tears if you walked into the room in a nun's habit. She wants to see you in chic clothes and jewels and find your Prince Charming. She always says you are a princess on the inside and outside, and that you deserve the best."

Later that night, I read some of the stories of the world's greatest women, none of whom were nuns, including Mary Wollstonecraft, Harriet Elizabeth Beecher Stowe and Florence Nightingale. I was inspired by their stories but not completely swayed. I had vowed to commit myself to God and live a life like Mother Teresa. "But, Lord," I prayed that night, "I have wanted children, lots of children, since I was a child myself. Do you want me to have children?" The digital alarm clock showed 11:11. That was my answer.

"I will live a life of service," I told my mother the next morning. "But not as a nun."

I WALKED BACK into the kitchen just as my mother turned on the tap to wash her paintbrush, singing a few more notes.

"You should get Peter to tape you singing sometime," I teased her as she spun around. "The Nashville twang doesn't sound quite the same with your Persian accent."

Holding me tight and kissing my cheek hard she said, "Those country music people have great drama. I like the highs and lows of their lives. These people struggle, love, lose love, cry and make up again—you know, like we Persians. They have passion. They express themselves."

My mother and I both laughed. But then her expression turned melancholy. "What is bothering you, Nazanin?" she asked, tossing her paintbrush into the sink and pulling me toward a kitchen chair. "Tell me. I know something is wrong."

Looking into my mother's gentle brown eyes, I felt the crushing weight in the pit of my stomach that I knew she felt every day when she thought about Iran. I understood, for the first time, why she was so dramatic in her actions and speech, and why she was so attracted to the sorrowful lyrics of country music and the haunting sounds of Handel's *Messiah* and Mozart's *Requiem*. Her soul was hurting, as was that of every Iranian dissident and the majority of Iranians held prisoner of the regime. My mother wanted to love and surrender to love, but a wall blocked her from doing so: the wall of the Islamic Republic of Iran. By virtue of being the daughter of one of the shah's generals and married to my father, she could never return and walk the streets she had as a child, visit her school friends or smell the rose blossoms whose beauty had inspired her as a teenager to become an artist. The love she desperately wanted to return to had become black with hatred and patriarchal traditions.

"It's the songwriting. It is so difficult to write from such an emotional place," I said, choking on my words.

"I know. Miguel's tragedy hurt you greatly," my mother whispered, thinking he was the cause of my melancholy. "But you could not have saved him, Nini, no one could have."

"I just wish there wasn't so much suffering in the world. How do I, a solitary person, make a difference?" I asked.

"One of my favourite quotes is by the Sufi mystic Rumi," my mother said. "'Your task is not to seek love, but merely to seek and find all the barriers within yourself that you have built against it.' That is our only responsibility as humans, to be love and love all, unconditionally. But, Nazanin," my mother said after a pause, "what is it you are really searching for?"

"I've known since I was young that I was being called to do something important in this world. But I just don't know what it is specifically. I don't know my purpose, my calling, why I am here."

"You are very much like your grandfather, Papa jaan," my mother said. "You are so smart, yet so sensitive. It's like . . ." She paused. "It's like you are him."

I'd been told many times by my mother and her sister Sima that I have my grandfather's facial features and his personality. My grandfather, Gholam Reza Ghafouri, whom the family referred to as Papa jaan, died four years before I was born. My only knowledge of him is from the stories that have been told to me over the years and well-worn black-and-white photographs that my mother keeps in photo albums. One of those photographs is of my mother at age three with her parents, taken outside the house that became my only memory of Iran. It was Nowruz and my mother is wearing a form-fitting, light blue long wool coat that flares like a bell at the bottom. My grandfather is bundled up in a long coat and scarf.

"I love your coat," I told my mother when I first saw the photograph, at about age seven. "I want one just like it." She laughed and told me a story about the coat. After the photograph was taken, the family went for a walk. At one point my mother slipped her hand out of her father's and darted across the street. Before Papa jaan could catch her, she had taken off her new coat, which was a Nowruz present, and handed it to a small child who wasn't wearing one. The child said thank you with a dazed expression in her eyes and grabbed onto her mother, who was begging for money and hoping that the celebration of Nowruz would make the passers-by more generous than usual.

"You know, Nazanin, any other father would have been upset that his hard-earned money spent on an expensive new coat for his daughter was given away like that, but Papa jaan, he was proud of me that day. He had morals and wanted to help others too."

Papa jaan was born on a chilly March day in 1908 in Samarkand, now part of Uzbekistan. He came from a modest family, which earned its income by trading Persian carpets, textiles and jewellery with Russia and China on the Silk Road. Like me, Papa jaan did well in every subject he took at school. But law was what he loved most, inspired, my mother tells me, by his sense of justice. He obtained three university degrees: two in law and a third in political science.

Papa jaan was tall, well-built and handsome, with black hair that greyed at the sides as he aged. He had soft, honey-coloured eyes and thick eyebrows, like mine. He wore his military uniform by day, and at night he donned suits tailored for his height and build. He filled my mother's childhood home with music and fine wine and spirit, often organizing gatherings and parties of Iran's brightest and most successful writers, musicians and politicians. Papa jaan was also a sportsman, enjoying any free moment horseback riding, swimming or playing tennis.

Like most men of my grandfather's background, Papa jaan joined the military in his late teens, working his way up to eventually become a brigadier general in the Iranian armed forces. For many years he lived in Mashhad, where *Shahnameh* author Ferdowsi was born, a large city near the border of Afghanistan and Turkmenistan, the latter in my grandfather's day being part of the Soviet Union. My mother and her two sisters, Shahin and Sima, were all born in Mashhad.

My grandfather's rise in the military didn't come without controversy, for he based his entire life on living by his morals. He had no fear telling other people, including the shah, what he believed were the best paths to walk. It all began when, as a brigadier general, my grandfather wrote Shah Mohammad Reza Pahlavi, who was also the *bozorg arteshtaran,* or commander-in-chief of the Iranian armed forces, criticizing him for allowing his subjects to kiss his hand when they greeted him. My grandfather always gave the shah a military salute to show his respect for the shah's role in the military. "But no one," my grandfather had written in a letter to the shah, "should kiss the hand of Iran's king—or anyone else for that matter."

In that same letter, Papa jaan told the shah that some people close to him were not being truthful. These people were merely trying to please the shah and were not telling him what was really happening in the cities and in society at large. They just wanted to be in the shah's favour and feared saying anything to him that would actually make him a better ruler. They were not doing their duty.

My grandfather went on to say that SAVAK, the country's secret police, security and intelligence service, which had been established in 1957 with help from the United States' Central Intelligence Agency, was not well liked. Many people wanted to rise up against it because of the policemen's detention and torture of anyone opposed to the shah's reign. "In many cases," my grandfather had written, "SAVAK has misused its power, and its abuses have caused much dissent aimed not only at them but to you, the great shah. SAVAK has become synonymous with terror and suffocation.

"If we continue to hurt people who are expressing their points of view," Papa jaan had written, "we have become nothing more than a dictatorship, rather than the shining star of modernity in the Middle East."

The shah was not receptive to the comments. It was noted in my grandfather's military file that he was refractory and that he refused to greet the shah in the appropriate manner, by kissing his hand. But those closest to Papa jaan knew he loved the shah. He believed the shah loved his country and wanted to make the country prosperous and the people proud.

The second black mark against my grandfather came when he openly supported Mohammad Mosaddegh, who wanted to democratize the country, hold free elections and nationalize the oil industry, which had been under British control since 1913 through the company that would later become British Petroleum. Mosaddegh became prime minister in 1951 and was well loved for his social reforms, including the creation of a countrywide unemployment insurance program. My grandfather, along with many others in Iran, cheered Mosaddegh on, believing that through him, the shackles of Iran's relationship to Britain would be broken. "Papa jaan used to say," my mother told me, "'I wish the Shah and Mosaddegh could sort out their differences and work together.'"

My grandfather was heartbroken when Mosaddegh was forced to leave politics. Not long after he did, my grandfather stopped working as a military judge because he worried that he might make a mistake in his judgments. "Papa jaan would toss and turn at night, weighted down by these worries," my mother continues. "He didn't want the blood of another man on his hands."

The third and final strike against my grandfather came when he became commander of the military base in Sabzevar, a strategic and important base close to the Soviet Union. A crowd during a military parade in Mashhad carried placards with the photograph of the shah, as was tradition. But it also, without my grandfather's prior knowledge, carried placards with photographs of him, to honour his service to the city of Sabzevar. Almost immediately after that, my grandfather was forced to take early retirement. It was rumoured among his peers in the military that the shah feared another *coup d'état*, this time with the shah being removed from his position and my grandfather exalted, taking on the leadership. "But nothing could be further than the truth, Nazanin," my mother said. "He swore an oath to be loyal to his country and the Iranian constitution. He would never betray or usurp the shah."

My grandfather was shocked and crushed by his forced retirement. "The man who believed in and loved his country, the man who always sought out and practised justice, could not understand why he was put aside in his peak years, when he could be the most help to his country and his nation," my mother said emphatically.

The only thing that could pull my grandfather out of his depression was his volunteer work with Iran's Boy Scouts and the Baghcheh-baan Institution, an organization that worked with deaf and mentally challenged children. He became president of the latter organization, helping raise money for surgeries for the children and for programs to enable them to go to school. "One day, he left early in the morning to go to his volunteer job with Baghcheh-baan," my mother continued in a low voice. "And he never returned. We were told he had a heart attack in his car. This was a man," she said, pounding her fist on the table, "who was in excellent shape and who had just had a perfect checkup with his doctor. We will never know the truth behind his death. But it was very sad for all of us. We never supported that revolution though, Nini," she added, her eyes filled with tears. "The shah did a lot to modernize our country. But that revolution killed all my dreams."

My mother set a steaming cup of chamomile tea in front of me. "When I was nine years old, I virtually lived in Papa jaan's big library, with tall oak bookcases full of literature and encyclopedias, law periodicals and historical books," she told me. "One book I read and reread was the Bible. 'Who is this person who thinks exactly like me?' I asked my father.

"'That is Jesus,' he replied with a big smile on his face, understanding my childish question.

"'I like this man. I want to learn more about him,' I said.

"Papa jaan then told me that Christianity was based on the teachings and life of Jesus and that I could study Christianity too if I liked. 'What are we?' I asked him.

"'We Iranians were forced to take on Islam, but at my core, I believe in Zoroastrian principles. Good thoughts. Good words. Good deeds,' he answered.

"When I told my father during a summer holiday home from studying art in Italy that I had converted to Christianity, he was very happy for me," my mother continued. "He said that he supported my decision because in the end all that matters is the faith we have in God and the faith we keep close in our hearts—not how we get there. You, Nazanin, have faith in God." My mother rapped her fingernails on the kitchen table. "Ask God to guide you where you need to go. Draw on Papa jaan's strength and carry on his legacy of trying to make the world a shining star."

CHAPTER 17

NAZANIN FATEHI

Spring to autumn 2005, Karaj, Iran

―――――――

Nazanin spent more than a week at the police station. During the days, she suffered brutal interrogations that started in the morning and lasted until the evening, and in which she was slapped and punched. At night, she was locked up in the detention centre, but her fear prevented her from sleeping. As a result of her exhaustion, and confusion as to what was happening to her, all Nazanin remembered of the drive from the police station to what would be her temporary new home was the rain dripping down the windows of the police van and blurring the light from the lampposts. Nazanin's nerves had settled now that she was out of the police station and out of reach of Yousef's family, who had camped out in the waiting room hoping to see her and maybe even hurt her. She actually found herself beginning to relax from the motion of the vehicle. Somayeh sat beside her. Though reunited, they said little to one another. Nazanin had no words left in her. She found her body slipping, like the rain droplets, down the cool faux-leather seat, her head eventually falling limp on Somayeh's shoulder.

Somayeh nudged Nazanin with her shoulder and whispered for her to wake up as the van stopped at a tall double-swing gate topped with barbed wire. Two men wearing khaki uniforms with machine guns strapped to their backs opened the gate. The rain had stopped, and Nazanin peered out the window as the vehicle turned into a driveway and came to a halt underneath a canopy in front of an old house.

Nazanin and Somayeh were ordered out of the van, then led by two more guards through the large black front door. In the foyer was a plastic-covered couch, and they were told to sit down. All Nazanin wanted to do was sleep, but the bright fluorescent light kept her awake—for what seemed like hours. Eventually, a short, fat woman wearing a black chador emerged from a nearby room. Nazanin moved to stand up, but the woman motioned with her hands for her to remain seated.

"I know you are both tired," the woman said, clasping her hands together. She introduced herself as Khahar Eslami, and this—Sister Eslami—was how she wanted to be greeted, as it reflected her devotion to the regime. As the guards undid the girls' handcuffs, Khahar Eslami explained that they were at a juvenile detention waiting for their court dates. "I am in charge, at least inside here. Don't worry, this place is more like a home than a scary jail," she said, her sparkling eyes making Nazanin feel safe.

Nazanin and Somayeh followed Khahar Eslami to the main office, which held a large mahogany desk that stretched almost from one side of the room to the other. Three leather couches lined the other walls. Nazanin scanned the titles of the books on the bookshelves. All were in Persian, which she no longer understood, having been out of school for so long. "You like to read?" Khahar Eslami asked. "You can come here any time and borrow books."

Khahar Eslami led Somayeh and Nazanin up a back stairwell, down the second-floor hallway and to a room where two girls sat on the floor sewing. "They will be sleeping in the room with you," she said.

Continuing on their tour, Khahar Eslami opened a door at the far end of the hallway. Inside, a young woman with short curly hair was folding clothes. "This one here," Khahar Eslami said, waving at the young woman. "Until we have enough girls and need space, she gets a room to herself. There are many rules here, which I will go over tomorrow." Khahar Eslami's face and tone of voice suddenly became very serious, almost scaring Nazanin. "Foremost is, don't talk to her unless you have to—like if you need to use the toilet and she is in there, or you both find yourself washing your clothes at the same time."

Khahar Eslami showed Nazanin and Somayeh their room. Four girls were already there and had made their beds on the thick-carpeted floor with blankets from the pile Nazanin spotted in an open cupboard. "There will be eight of you in here," said Khahar Eslami. "Sleep where you like. We serve breakfast at seven, lunch at noon. You will awaken at five for morning prayer, and each take a shower after that, if you want one. You don't have any clothes," she then said, her eyes scanning Nazanin and Somayeh's rumpled manteaus and dresses. "So until your parents come for a visit with supplies, we will find some donated clothes for you to wear. Right now go to the kitchen and eat your dinner. Tomorrow morning, first thing, you also both bathe. You smell terrible."

Somayeh sat down on the floor with the other girls and introduced herself. But when Nazanin sat beside her, Somayeh waved for her to go away. "Sleep over there," she hissed, taking off her headscarf and shaking her long black hair loose. "I'm in this mess because of you. Go away."

Somayeh crossed her legs and looked away. Nazanin wanted to cry. She wanted to hit Somayeh—she wanted Somayeh to feel her pain. Instead, Nazanin slowly turned and began rolling out her blankets. Then she stopped.

"How dare you say that," Nazanin whispered to Somayeh. Somayeh ignored her. "Listen to me," Nazanin shouted. "I'm here because of you!"

"I want you to go over there and leave me alone," Somayeh hissed. "We will talk about this some other time."

BUT NAZANIN AND SOMAYEH didn't speak. In fact, Somayeh did her best to avoid Nazanin. In the warmer weather, Somayeh stayed outside on the back terrace, which was lined with a thick cement wall with barbed wire across the top to prevent the girls from escaping. Somayeh and the other girls did pantomimes, told jokes, and sewed dolls out of pieces of fabric, while Nazanin flipped through the Islamic magazines from Khahar Eslami's office. Whenever Nazanin tried to approach Somayeh, she would turn a cold shoulder and walk away.

Somayeh's nights, though, were plagued with demons. It always began with moaning, which would waken Nazanin. Then Somayeh would start perspiring and, still asleep, fling all the blankets off her quivering body. Finally, she would scream, waking herself and the entire room. The first time she did this, Nazanin, thinking Somayeh must be reliving her ordeal in the field, rushed to Somayeh's side.

"Go away," Somayeh said, spitting in Nazanin's face. "I don't ever want to see you again," she added as she hugged one of the dolls she had made.

ONE AFTERNOON IN EARLY AUTUMN, as Nazanin was coming up the stairs, she met the young woman with whom she had been ordered not to speak coming from the washroom, towelling her short, damp hair. "What have you got there?" the woman asked. Nazanin showed her the cover of the magazine she was carrying.

"It's all propaganda. A government magazine that forces the writers to write what it wants. Good thing you can't read," she said, leaning in close, her eyes shifting from side to side to make sure no one overheard. "My name is Goli and I'm lonely here," she whispered. "No one is allowed to talk with me. Come into my room for a bit."

Nazanin looked back down the stairs. She could hear voices drifting up from the kitchen. She nodded. She too was lonely.

As the two sat beside each other on the floor chewing candied fruit, Goli asked Nazanin about her life and family. Nazanin's mother had visited her twice so far and had brought her a few changes of clothes; her purse, which had been left at the police station; and soap, toothpaste and shampoo.

Goli sighed. "Your mother loves you. She does, even if sometimes she does not show it. It's the oppression of our people."

Nazanin raised her eyebrows and shook her head slowly.

"You don't understand," said Goli. "That's okay. I didn't either until I joined the guerrilla group in the mountains. In this country, if you are rich, you have the opportunity to leave or pay off anyone who gives you trouble. If you are in the middle, you can survive by pretending you believe in what they stand for, which means the women wear their headscarves in public and pray, and the men grow stubble or beards and go to mosque. But if anyone—Fars, Kurdish, Azeri, Arab, Lur, Baluch—want more than what they were born into, to demand their basic human rights in any way . . . well, they're doomed."

"I had a friend in Sanandaj who used to speak like you," Nazanin said, smiling at the memory. "She was older and she taught me to read."

"But you stopped before you really began to learn! You are different from that girl who is in here with you. She is mentally frail, whereas you are strong and sturdy. When she gets out, she'll marry the first boy who proposes to her. He'll abuse her and her children. But you, well, you have a lot of battles ahead of you, but some good could still come to your life. You have the spirit of something . . . of someone . . . strong yet sensitive.

"Did you ever like fashion?" Goli asked.

"One day I cut my hair," Nazanin said, holding up a strand. "I dyed a small section at the front light brown, too, with fabric bleach. My brother Hojat hit me on the head with a mirror. Sometimes when I close my eyes and then open them quickly, I still see the shards of mirror falling around my feet. I suffered so much abuse. But Somayeh has suffered worse."

Nazanin and Goli heard steps outside the door.

"Shush," whispered Goli. "You can't be found in here. Hide in the cupboard."

Nazanin tiptoed across the room. She opened the cupboard door slowly so that the hinges would not creak and crawled inside, hiding herself on the bottom shelf beneath some blankets.

Goli peeked into the hallway and then breathed a sigh of relief. "It's okay," she said, coming over to Nazanin. "It's just one of your roommates."

"But it's early. None of them usually returns to the room until the late afternoon, once their doll making is done. Let me go see what she is doing."

Nazanin poked her head out the door and cautiously looked both ways to make sure no one saw her leaving Goli's room, then quickly stepped out into the hallway and headed to her room.

"What are you doing?" she yelled upon seeing Vida, one of her roommates, rummaging through her things.

"Somayeh said I could have these," Vida said, holding up Nazanin's purse and a cream-coloured flowered dress.

"What else did Somayeh say?" Nazanin asked as she tugged on the items to get them back.

The two girls were soon in a tug-of-war. Vida's face became redder and redder as Nazanin held onto the plastic purse strap in one hand and her dress in the other. Their hair flew wildly around them as they moved each like they were *koshtigeer*—wrestlers—one step forward and two steps back. Nazanin, fearing that the purse handle would break and her dress would tear, suddenly let go—so abruptly that Vida fell backwards, hitting her head against the wall. She slumped to the floor as Nazanin grabbed her things.

Vida cradled her head in her hands for a few seconds. As Nazanin turned her back on the girl to leave the room, Vida jumped on her from behind, pulling her by the hair down to the ground. She got on top of Nazanin's chest and started slapping her face. Nazanin screamed and kicked, and managed to kick Vida to the ground. She had just climbed on top of her when Khahar Eslami, Somayeh, and three other girls, having heard the scuffle, entered the room.

"You have a court hearing tomorrow," Khahar Eslami said to Nazanin as she stood in front of her desk several hours later. Gone were Khahar Eslami's pleasantries. Her eyes were now dark and brooding and her tone of voice cold and monotone.

"You have to believe me," Nazanin pleaded. "Vida was going through my things. She was going to steal my purse and dress. She hit me first. Look." Nazanin turned her head to show Khahar Eslami her cheek, red from the girl's slaps.

"That may be so, but I saw what I saw," said Khahar Eslami. "You were on top of Vida and about to hit her on the face. You have a court hearing tomorrow. After that, it will be decided what your punishment will be."

When Nazanin returned to her room, she found Somayeh sitting on the floor, folding Nazanin's clothes. "Nazanin," she said, snuffling when she saw her. She had been crying. "I am so sorry I have been mean to you. I've just been so scared."

"What are you doing?" Nazanin asked, taking her clothes from Somayeh.

"I wanted to smooth out the creases for you. Nazanin," Somayeh said in a low voice, "you are not going to court tomorrow. They are taking you to prison."

Nazanin stared at Somayeh.

"It's true. I heard Khahar Eslami talking before you went to her office. I am to blame for all of this."

Nazanin knelt down and pulled Somayeh into her arms. "I am so sorry all of this is happening to us . . . but I . . . we . . . are innocent."

"I wasn't raped," Somayeh said, pulling herself from Nazanin's embrace and taking her hands into her own. "You saved me."

CHAPTER 18

NAZANIN FATEHI

Autumn 2005, Rajai Shahr Prison, Karaj, Iran

———

It was morning as Nazanin was driven to Rajai Shahr Prison. She had never spent time in this part of Karaj, with its rundown cement buildings, market stalls, street vendors and beggar woman wearing niqabs. She was astonished by what she saw, her mouth agape. At one point, the police van passed a group of women, many wearing frosty lipstick and baby-blue eyeliner. "The prostitutes," said the burly female guard sitting beside her. "You must know this area." She clucked her tongue against her teeth. "A girl like you!"

Nazanin was too tired and scared to argue.

When they arrived at the prison, a guard removed Nazanin's black headscarf and then wrapped a long, billowy navy blue floral scarf around her head. "You must wear this at all times in the court-yard or walking the halls of the prison," she said in a voice that was surprisingly deep and strong given her petite, delicate frame, which reminded Nazanin of Somayeh.

"What are you in for?" the guard asked, pulling the items out of Nazanin's bags and laying them out on a steel table.

Nazanin, her eyes downcast, slowly told her the crime she had been accused of. "But I am innocent," she said. "I was only defending myself."

"Right," said the guard, now searching the pockets of Nazanin's purse. "You will be staying here for a long time."

Nazanin's body trembled and her face felt hot. "But I am innocent," she repeated. "I was defending my niece and my honour. They will let us out—maybe even tomorrow."

The guard rolled her eyes and laughed. "Mahabad Fatehi, I don't want to hurt you. You'll feel enough pain inside there," she said, pointing to the wall behind her. "But you will probably be here in prison for three or four years, and that will be just while the judges decide what to do with you."

Nazanin bit her lip to stifle a scream.

A SHORT, ROUND WOMAN with hair above her lip and one long black eyebrow introduced herself as Mrs. Mohammadi. "I am in charge here," she said, opening a thick metal door and guiding Nazanin into an office. There she opened another door and told Nazanin to follow her. They walked single file down a corridor lined by prison cells. "This is the wing for women who have committed violent offences," Mrs. Mohammadi said, stopping in front of one of the cells, her voice hard, her hands on her wide hips. Mrs. Mohammadi undid Nazanin's handcuffs. "The door to your cell will be open during the day, starting at about 8 a.m. when the breakfast cart arrives. You will be locked down anytime between ten and midnight. If you're good, we leave the cell doors open all night. If you're bad, we'll lock you up. You don't have to wear your handcuffs on the ward—unless, of course, you've been bad."

As Mrs. Mohammadi turned to speak to another prisoner, Nazanin took in the ward—the papers strewn about on the dark, cold cement floor, the damp laundry hanging on the bars of the cells' doors. A baby sat in the middle of the corridor wearing only a soggy cloth diaper and sucking its thumb. Nazanin took a few steps forward to peer inside the nearest cell. It was lined with three sets of bunk beds, all occupied. Some of the women were sleeping, two were reading, another was lying down playing with a string twined between her fingers.

Mrs. Mohammadi took Nazanin by the elbow and continued down the corridor. "You will sleep at the end here. There are only two of you in the cell, at least for now. A third may come." She left Nazanin standing in the middle of the cell holding the two plastic bags that contained her belongings. Nazanin swallowed hard to hold back her tears.

"So you are the girl," said a voice from the top bunk. Nazanin looked up and into the round, smiling face of a much older woman. Despite her age, the woman quickly threw her legs over the side of the bunk and leapt down to the floor. "I am Azar," she said, placing her right hand on her heart. "You are the girl they are placing with me." She pushed back some grey hair that had slipped out of her bun. "You can call me Madar Azar." She took Nazanin's bags and placed them underneath the bed. She then took Nazanin's hands into her own. "Would you like the bottom bunk? I've made my home on the top, but I can switch if you feel more comfortable up there."

"The bottom is fine," she replied as Madar Azar—Mother Azar—removed Nazanin's headscarf. She sat down on the bed and patted the mattress to indicate for Nazanin to do the same. She then handed Nazanin an apple from the chest pocket of her navy blue cotton dress. As Nazanin ate the apple, Madar Azar told her story.

Madar Azar had been at Rajai Shahr Prison for two and a half years, charged with murdering her husband with a kitchen knife. "But he was trying to kill my granddaughter," she told Nazanin. "That man abused me and my daughters, and when he went to hit little Lily, I just lost it. I took the knife I was using to cut some beef and threw it at his head."

Madar Azar was sixty. She had three grandchildren and she wanted to go home to her village outside Karaj. As she talked, Nazanin looked into her new friend's round brown eyes, the irises of which were circled in gold, and she thought of her own grandmother. The only time she had ever met her paternal grandmother was when she attended the wedding of her father's sister. Her grandmother was kind to her, but Nazanin heard her say under her breath, "If only you were not Maryam's daughter."

Madar Azar's voice broke into Nazanin's thoughts. She was explaining that underneath the vacant bed on the opposite side of the room she had stored her clothes, cookies and fruits. "My family is good to me," she said. "Feel free to help yourself to anything you want to eat.

"I'll be your mother inside here," she continued. "And first off, I have a word of caution. Don't become friends with those prisoners out there." Madar Azar pointed to the other cells. "Some of those women are very dangerous and crazy, but they are smart, cunning like foxes."

AT ONE END of the prison ward were the washrooms and showers. About midafternoon, Madar Azar headed there to take her turn to wash. Nazanin was alone in the cell, sitting cross-legged on her bed, when four inmates walked in.

"We've all heard about you," said a tall young woman with greasy shoulder-length hair.

"I'm the boss here," said a shorter young woman. Her long black hair was tied back with a ribbon, and she was wearing jeans beneath her long black dress. Nazanin felt uneasy and pulled her legs in close.

"I don't want any trouble," she whispered.

"We don't either, which is why you are going to give us your purse," said a third, older woman with dark circles under her eyes and lines creasing her face. She removed Nazanin's belongings from underneath the far bed.

"Please don't," said Nazanin, starting to get up.

"My name is Mandana," said the young woman who had introduced herself as the boss, pushing Nazanin back down onto the bed. "You must listen to me. Every new inmate who comes in here must give us—my group and me—something as a gift. Didn't your mother teach you to bring a gift to your host when you visit someone's home? We want your purse," she said, "and your headscarf."

As Mandana passed the purse around, Nazanin stood up, her legs shaking. For a moment, her mind went back to that day at the school. "Jaash, jaash, jaash . . ." she could hear the children call out. She closed her eyes tight, trying to block out their voices. "Mandana," Nazanin eventually exploded, a strength emerging from inside of her that she didn't know existed. "Who the hell are you?" she cried, partly in Kurdish, partly in Persian. "I am accused of murdering a man twice the size of you. Do you think I am afraid?"

Mandana stepped back. The other women stared at Nazanin, who was breathing heavily. "Nobody stands up to Mandana," whispered the older woman.

Mandana, red-faced, regained her composure and took two steps forward. "I want you to shut up. Let us take your purse and headscarf or I will hit you."

Nazanin stepped toward Mandana. "I will hit you back."

Mandana drew her right arm up as if to hit Nazanin. But instead, she grabbed Nazanin's head and bit her ear. Madar Azar returned to the cell just in time to see the other women retreating, the older one tossing Nazanin's purse and its contents across the bed. Nazanin had fainted to the floor.

When Nazanin woke and opened her eyes she was temporarily blinded by the sun that streamed in through the window and reflected off the whitewashed walls. She was in the prison's medical clinic. Her ear pounded and she reached up to feel a thick bandage. She winced from the pain that ricocheted through her head and down her neck, and called out for help.

A woman shuffled up beside her. Without saying a word, she picked up Nazanin's wrist and felt her pulse. She then checked Nazanin's heartbeat with a stethoscope. Nazanin started to explain about Mandana but the woman put a finger to her lips. "Shush," she said, pointing to the four other beds in the room. All were occupied by patients, two of whom were sleeping with their arms on top of the sheets, revealing wrists wrapped in white bandages.

"Take this," the woman said, handing Nazanin a large orange pill and a half-filled glass of water.

Nazanin reached for the pill and then stopped with a shudder. The pill looked like the one her father had given Hojat's dog, Rocky. Nazanin shook her head and pushed the pill and water away.

"You have to take this," said the woman.

"Are you trying to murder me?" Nazanin asked. "This is the type of pill that killed my brother's dog when it had rabies."

The woman smiled and gently set down the water and pill on the table beside Nazanin's bed. Nazanin relaxed. But then, with great force, the woman grabbed Nazanin's wrists and leaned in close. "You are nothing but a dog. And when the judges hear your case, you will get what is coming to you, like that dog of your brother's. Now, I am telling you," she said, spittle landing on Nazanin's cheek, "you will take that pill, you will swallow it and you will continue to take that pill every day that you are here in prison."

Nazanin's hand shook so much as she lifted the glass to her lips that droplets of water spilled from the glass onto the front of her dress, which was covered in bloodstains. She put the pill under her tongue and slowly swallowed. The woman smiled and took the glass back. "That's a good girl," she said, patting Nazanin's shoulder. "A very good girl." When the nurse was out of sight, Nazanin spat the pill out as far as she could.

FOR A WHILE, life in prison for Nazanin was a routine that time blurred. Nazanin made sure she was never left alone in the cell. When Madar Azar went to the washroom or the shower, so did Nazanin. In the afternoons, Madar Azar and Nazanin walked for hours in a circle in the courtyard to stretch their legs. Whenever they saw the hose unused, they scrambled to claim it, to wash their clothes. And at night, before going to sleep, Nazanin and Madar Azar would slip out of their cell to the only window in the ward and look at the moon.

And every night, Nazanin and many of the other inmates had to line up to take one of the orange pills. The guard administering the pills forced her to swallow it by making her stick out her tongue and showing that it was gone. After Nazanin had taken the pill for the first time, she went into convulsions and started foaming at the mouth. Her body then became rigid, and her head turned to the side. Madar Azar rolled her onto her stomach so she wouldn't choke on her tongue and called for help. The guards took Nazanin to the medical clinic, where she was given an injection of some other drug. When Nazanin had recovered from the fit, Madar Azar told her that her eyes had rolled to the back of her head. "I thought you were going to die," she moaned.

Nazanin continued to have to take the drug nonetheless. Although the violent reaction lessened, her perception of reality tilted. She would wake in the middle of the night and spend hours listening to the crying babies, and to their mothers singing as they tried to soothe them back to sleep. Every now and then she would hear the patter of feet outside her cell and then a banging coming from one of the washrooms. In the early days, Nazanin covered her head with the rough, grey blanket and tried to drown out the sounds by reciting the Yaseen Sura and praying for sleep—which only ever came in the morning now, sometimes just when the breakfast cart was arriving. She would sleep until midday, when she felt little hands playing with her hair.

It was Asal, an angelic child with chestnut-coloured hair worn in uneven pigtails. Asal's mother was convicted of murder and Asal had been born in the prison cell, on the cement floor, into the hands of one of the other prisoners.

Nazanin played Amoo Zanjiir Buf—Uncle Chain Builder—with Asal and told her the story of the three little goats. Nazanin and Asal became close, which softened Nazanin's relationship with Mandana, Asal's mother's close friend in prison. Eventually, Mandana started to wave Nazanin over to join her in the courtyard. Some of the women had stretched a tattered net from one wall to another and used it to play volleyball. And one day, Mandana even asked Nazanin to join her team.

Nazanin began to lose weight, for she could hardly eat the

prison food—barely cooked eggs, hard potatoes and soup that consisted mostly of water. She longed for her mother to come with *shalamin*. But Nazanin's mother didn't show up for a long time. By the time of her first visit, Nazanin was so thin, her face scarred by pimples from the lack of nutrients in her diet, that her mother accused her of doing drugs. About all her mother could do was cry. "I knew I was cursed the day that woman drew the eye on me," she wailed, "but I never imagined a daughter of mine would end up in prison."

EVERY DAY, Nazanin pleaded with Mrs. Mohammadi to be returned to juvenile detention. "I will submit your name," she would reply coldly, "and see if they accept it." But they never did.

And then came days even darker. The drugs were changing the women. At night, those given the medication screamed and yelled. Mandana and her group would gang up and attack one of the younger women, pulling her hair, smashing her teeth and kicking her in the groin. Nazanin never joined in. But the drugs kept her in such an agitated state that she could no longer stay lying in her bed—she had to pace the corridor. Once, she saw Mandana and her friends, including a woman named Katrin, take the lead in beating up a frail new inmate. They had tied her arms behind her with her headscarf and were spitting in her face. The inmate, a young woman named Hanni, writhed on the floor, wailing for the guards.

One morning, Nazanin awoke and, weak from lack of nutritious food, hobbled to the washroom to wash her face, only to find Hanni hanging from the ceiling pipes, her headscarf around her neck. She was half-naked, her skin covered in bruises and cuts. Dried blood caked her torso. When the prison investigated, one official said that she thought Hanni was dead before she was hanged. She had been kicked to death.

"Why do they make us take these drugs?" Nazanin asked Madar Azar as she paced back and forth in their cell. The two had just returned from the courtyard.

"The guards want to calm you down," Madar Azar said.

"But they don't calm us down," Nazanin said, shooing away little Asal, who had run up to her and was pulling on her dress, wanting to play a game. "Why don't you take them?"

"Because I am an old woman. I stay to myself, and I have never caused any problems."

"But I don't cause problems," Nazanin replied.

"To them you do," she said, jerking her head toward the guard's desk. "You've killed a man, you beat up a girl in the juvenile home and Mandana nearly bit your ear off. *Azizam,* my dear," she continued with a sigh, "you have a good heart, but you are young, and you had so many strikes against you. I wish that you were my own daughter and that I could carry your burdens. But I can't."

Nazanin and a few of the other inmates, including Madar Azar, complained to Mrs. Mohammadi that the pills made the inmates hurt each other. Nazanin hoped it would garner her a transfer back to the juvenile home, since she was much younger than most of the other inmates. Instead, the guards became harsher, locking down the cells at ten. If the guards found anyone awake after that, the prisoner would be taken and beaten. The inmates who had been assaulted told stories in the courtyard of what happened in the interrogation room. "A guard named Khadem will hit you with an electrical wire," Mandana whispered to Nazanin. "So as soon as your cell is closed, you close your eyes and don't open them until you hear the breakfast cart in the morning."

But one night, Nazanin was giggling, remembering something Madar Azar had said earlier in the day. Mrs. Mohammadi, hearing Nazanin, snuck into the cell and shined a flashlight into Nazanin's open eyes. "I knew you were a troublemaker," she said, grabbing Nazanin's hair and pulling her down the hall to the interrogation room. Before they entered the room, Mrs. Mohammadi demanded that Nazanin put on her chador and smooth down the creases in the dress she was wearing. "You were supposed to be asleep," Mrs. Mohammadi hissed.

Mrs. Mohammadi remained in the interrogation room even after Khadem walked in. Nazanin was struck by the size of his hands—large, wide and thick. He smacked a whip against the wall. "Take off your chador," he ordered in a deep voice that filled the room.

Nazanin shivered. "I've been told to never do that in front of a man," she said, looking down.

Khadem hit his left hand with the whip. "Take off your chador and your manteau and do as I say," he ordered.

Nazanin began to cry.

"Do it or else I will ask you to get completely naked."

Nazanin did as he said and then laid her body across the metal chair, as instructed. The whip sliced through the air with great force and then across her back, through her thin cotton dress. Nazanin's body burned as she felt her flesh breaking. After enduring about forty lashes, she passed out.

NAZANIN SPENT DAYS lying on her stomach in bed after the beating. When her wounds were healed enough that she could walk, she went to the courtyard to join the others. She had little life left in her. Her fingernails were now brittle and her hair was falling out. Nazanin had seen her prison mates disappear one by one, not because they had been released but from suicide, Mandana told her. Even Mandana's friend Katrin, who put fear into the hearts of everyone she bullied, had hanged herself.

"Remain strong," Madar Azar told Nazanin. "Do whatever you need to do to not give in to the demons in your head."

CHAPTER 19

NAZANIN FATEHI

November 2005 to January 2006, Rajai Shahr Prison, Karaj, Iran

─────────

On a rainy day in November, Nazanin's mother visited her for a second time. She sat in the chair opposite Nazanin in the waiting room and complained that, like when they were back in Sanandaj, the neighbours no longer spoke to her. This time, though, it had nothing to do with Nazanin's father but with Nazanin. Arsalan, now almost one year old, drooled on her mother's shoulder as she lamented, "Everyone knows we have a daughter in prison for murder."

"But I am innocent," Nazanin said quietly. "While I was at the police station, I had to go into a room with Somayeh and the two men who attacked us. I stood before a judge. He was tall, he had glasses and he was nice. He asked me to tell him what happened. When I was done, he said to me, 'You should have cut off his penis, brought it here and put it on my desk. I would have freed you myself.' Dayah," Nazanin whispered. "I am going to be free. This judge believed me."

But Nazanin's mother was no longer listening but instead was complaining about her health ailments, including the trouble she was having breathing and her sore, arthritic hands that prevented her from cleaning properly. Nazanin felt completely alone. As soon as she returned to her cell, she crawled into bed. Her mother didn't visit her again for many months.

"PUT THESE ON," Mrs. Mohammadi said, tossing a pair of brown plastic shoes onto Nazanin's bed. It was an early morning in January. The call to prayer had taken place, but the breakfast cart hadn't yet arrived. Nazanin was confused and tired from lack of sleep because of the drugs.

"You also need your manteau and chador. A guard will come and get you in ten minutes. Be ready," snapped Mrs. Mohammadi as Nazanin rubbed her eyes.

"Where am I going?" she asked when Mrs. Mohammadi turned to leave.

"To court," she replied curtly.

WHEN NAZANIN ENTERED the courtroom, she saw Roozbeh and Hamid. When she passed the two other young men who had attacked her and Somayeh they called her names under their breath. "*Ghatel, jendeh*"—"Murderer, whore."

Nazanin was escorted to a seat at the front of the room beside a slim man who had slicked-back brown hair and was wearing a black suit. He leaned over and introduced himself as her state-appointed lawyer. "I'm handling your case," he said quietly. "You don't have to do anything. Let me do all the talking unless one of the judges asks you to speak." He pointed to five men sitting at a table facing Nazanin. "Those are the judges. If they ask you something, you answer the question."

Nazanin, not wanting to catch the eye of any of the judges, looked down. "What is going on here today?" she whispered to the lawyer.

"It's your court case to decide if you are guilty of murder or not."

Nazanin gasped. "I wasn't told that."

"*Ghatel,*" one of Yousef's friends said a little more loudly.

One of the judges slapped his hand on the table, ordering the room to be quiet. He introduced himself as Ghazi Mohammadi—Judge Mohammadi—the chief judge in the case. He then introduced the other judges, including Judge Rahimi, as well as the court assistant, who was taking notes, and the prosecutor. As Judge Moham-madi explained in Persian the court rules, Nazanin looked around the small, dimly lit room, taking in the dull yellow walls and scuffed floors. Most of the spectator seats were empty. No one from her family was there.

"Does my mother even know I am here today?" she whispered to her lawyer. "And where is Somayeh?"

"I don't know," he replied. "I have sixty cases at my office. I do my best. I wish I could do more."

Judge Mohammadi continued. "We have witnesses in the court-room and the accused. We have the testimonies and the reports of the police and the medical examinations.

"Please call up the first witness," Judge Mohammadi said, motioning to the court prosecutor.

The prosecutor stood up. "Roozbeh Molaei," he called out.

Roozbeh swore on the Qur'an that what he was about to say was the truth. He then answered the judge's questions, starting with his age and education, followed by what he remembered about the incident.

After Roozbeh testified, the attackers were asked to stand up. One was introduced as Salman Parchami, the other as Mahmoud Tekeh. The young men said that they were innocently hanging out the day of the incident. They claimed that they had not chased the girls on motorbikes, nor taunted them at the market. They testified, rather, that the girls had approached them to speak with them but that they had tried to ignore them.

At one point, Salman was asked if one of his friends had pulled off Nazanin's headscarf. "Yes, because we wanted the girls to leave us alone," he answered.

"Is that all you did?" one of the judges questioned.

"Yes."

"Did you say anything to provoke the young women?" Judge Rahimi asked.

"No . . ." Salman said, trailing off. "That girl there," he then continued, pointing to Nazanin, "threw bricks at me."

"What did you do back?"

"We may have thrown something at her, but it was all innocent. You must believe me," he pleaded.

"Did you, Yousef or Mahmoud say or do anything else to make the girls angry?" Judge Mohammadi probed.

"No . . . I mean . . . maybe we said something like 'Come with us to an abandoned house.' But we wanted to frighten them so they would go away. It was not serious. We would never have done such a thing."

"That is a lie," Nazanin said, rising to her feet. "They are all lying."

The judge shouted at Nazanin to sit down and be quiet.

A recess was then called, though everyone remained in the courtroom. The judges huddled together and spoke in hushed tones. After what seemed like forever to Nazanin, Judge Mohammadi cleared his throat and stated dryly, "The mother of the young victim has not appeared at this meeting; however, she has asked this court to sentence Nazanin to death."

He turned to Nazanin. "Do you have anything you want to say?"

Nazanin blinked. She didn't understand. Her lawyer nudged her to stand up. "I . . . I . . . what are you saying?" she managed to get out.

"Do you have anything you want to say in response to the wishes of the deceased's family?" Judge Mohammadi asked again.

The courtroom became quiet, all eyes glued to Nazanin. Her gaze fell to the floor.

"Believe me," she stated in a low steady voice, "I did not intend to kill Yousef. I was just trying to defend myself and my niece, Somayeh."

"What made you stab Yousef?" the judge asked matter-of-factly.

"I . . . I . . ." she stammered and then, in a more controlled voice said, "He had grabbed my breast. I thought he was going to . . . you know . . . the way men do." She paused before continuing. "I am not a bad person. I am a good person. How many times do I have to say that I did this to defend our honour and chastity?"

Judge Mohammadi banged his hand on the table. Nazanin was having a hard time focusing and she caught only a little of what he said next. "Branch 71 of the Criminal Court finds Ms. Mahabad Fatehi, known as Nazanin, guilty of the murder of Yousef Bagheri, son of Ali. We will retreat to a closed section to determine her punishment."

Nazanin, too stunned to speak, sat back down and remained seated as all the judges except Judge Mohammadi left the courtroom. The court assistant called for her to come forward.

"You have to sign that you accept the verdict," he explained as Nazanin stood motionless in front of him. "Your crime is the murder of a twenty-three-year-old boy," he continued. "Your signature indicates you have accepted the conviction. Do you understand?" he asked. Nazanin continued to stare at her brown plastic shoes. "You are signing that the trial was fair and justified."

"Take your index finger," her lawyer said, making Nazanin look, "and place it in this blue ink."

Nazanin's vision blurred. Nazanin could see the court assistant and her lawyer out of the corner of her eyes, but their instructions to her were garbled. Numbly, she followed her lawyer as he showed her where and how to place her inked blue finger on the bottom of the page.

"That is your signature," he said.

"Ms. Fatehi," Judge Mohammadi said in a loud voice, jolting Nazanin from her trance-like state. She had forgotten that he was there. "What happened that made you want to stab Yousef?" he asked again.

"I thought they were going to rape Somayeh. I had to protect her. I am innocent. I am innocent," she repeated over and over as the prison escort dragged her away.

WHEN NAZANIN RETURNED to the prison, she was placed in a different cell. A guard told her that Madar Azar had packed her clothes, toothbrush and purse for her. All of the items had been placed on top of her new bunk bed. This ward, Nazanin was informed, was close to Madar Azar's. "You will see her in the courtyard," the guard said. "But we felt you would be safer here."

Nazanin sat down on the bed. "I was safe where I was," she said in a low voice, pulling out her dresses and undergarments to make sure everything was there.

"But you are guilty now," said the guard. "Who knows what the others will do in the middle of the night to a teenager guilty of killing a man."

When the guard had left, she laid her head down on the pillow, curled up her legs and closed her eyes. Just before they had left the courtroom, the guard had given her a white pill to take. Unlike the orange pill, this medication took Nazanin into a deep sleep—but not so deep that she could escape her dream of the walls. It was the second time the dream had taken hold of her—the first time had been about a month earlier. In the dream, hands were pushing her up against a tall cement wall. When she turned to fight back, no one was there. Then the walls began to move in on her.

Nazanin groaned in her sleep and banged her fists against the wall. "No, no," she screamed. "Get away from me." Someone was holding down her arms and legs. Still asleep, Nazanin began to kick and push against the weight.

"Wake up." Someone was slapping her face. *"Helsa lea khaw,"* said the female voice again in Kurdish. Slowly Nazanin's legs and arms relaxed and she became conscious of her surroundings.

"It's a dream," the young woman holding down Nazanin said. Nazanin looked into the woman's emerald-green eyes. She then turned and saw that three other women were all holding down various parts of her body.

"I am Jwan," said the woman with the emerald eyes. "And this," she said, pointing to the others, "is Sharmin, Kajal and Serwa. We're all Kurdish. Mrs. Mohammadi came here yesterday and told us you would be coming. She said you were going to have a tough day at court and that we should look after you."

"How did she know?"

"Everyone knew," Jwan sighed. "We thought the judges had made their decision before you even entered the courtroom. We figured the family's loss would have outweighed any testimony you, a female, would have given."

"The witnesses lied," murmured Nazanin, sitting up slowly. "Who are you again?"

"We're your new cellmates. We're in prison for various offences," Jwan said. "I stole some food. Kajal robbed the same grocery store. And Serwa and Sharmin stole electronic equipment and resold it on the black market."

Nazanin said nothing, but her eyes darted from one woman to another. Then she sighed, her voice hoarse from her fear and from screaming. She began to cry. The women all crawled in close, stroking her back and hair. "Shush," Jwan whispered soothingly. When Nazanin's tears kept falling, Jwan sang a lullaby, the same lullaby her sister Leila used to sing to her.

"Where did you learn that?" Nazanin snuffled as her crying subsided.

"In Taq Taq, Iraq—that is where I am from. My family moved to Iran as refugees when I was just a baby. We were escaping Saddam Hussein's war against us. All the men from my village were gone, taken by Iraqi forces. Dead. My mother and the other women decided to leave Taq Taq. My mother had heard stories of Kurdish women being taken by the Iraqis to Egypt and other Arab countries and forced to be prostitutes. But she was run over by a pickup truck driven by a Kurdish child, also fleeing Taq Taq, as we headed by foot over the mountains to Iran. I was raised by my older sister, in a refugee camp in Sardasht."

"Where is Aso now?" Nazanin asked.

"She died in the camp from a respiratory disease. When I was big enough, I migrated to the cities—first Mahabad and then Karaj—so I wouldn't have to marry a man thirty years older than me. We all met each other," she said, pointing to Kajal, Serwa and Sharmin, "on the streets and, ever since, we've stayed together. In the warm weather, we survived by doing odd jobs, like delivering groceries or cleaning homes."

"We're older than you," Kajal broke in. "You shouldn't even be in jail . . . and probably wouldn't be if you weren't Kurdish."

"What do you mean?" Nazanin asked.

"Because you never had a chance at a good life," Jwan replied.

"The government may say," Sharmin added, "that the court system here does not discriminate against you because you are Kurdish, but even if that were true, you are poor and you never had much of a chance of achieving any of your dreams . . . just like the rest of us."

A FEW WEEKS LATER, Nazanin found herself awake in the wee hours of the morning, pacing the corridor. At about five o'clock, a middle-aged woman whom Nazanin had never seen before stumbled out of her cell and across Nazanin's path. Nazanin's eyesight was blurry from lack of sleep, and her mind was in a fog. Thinking that the woman wanted to kill her, Nazanin snarled, "You cannot pass me."

"Why?" asked the woman, stopping in her tracks. "I want to use the toilet."

"Because you think I am a runaway. That I sleep with boys to make money. That I am a *jendeh*," she spat.

The woman shook her head. "I've never met you before. You don't know what I think, *azizam*."

But Nazanin's mind was playing tricks on her. At first the woman appeared to be Mohsen, and then one of the judges in the courtroom, laughing at her. Nazanin shook her head wildly, trying to clear her head. As the woman tried to skirt past her, Nazanin lunged. She started to hit the woman and was pounding on her chest just as Mrs. Mohammadi opened the door into the corridor.

Nazanin was sent to solitary confinement in a cell somewhere deep in the basement of Rajai Shahr Prison. She slept on the cold stone floor, with only an itchy, threadbare wool blanket to keep her warm. There was no light except that which streamed in through the cracks in the door. She had no change of clothes, nor was she given water with which to clean herself. Cockroaches crawled on the left-over food the guards refused to take away and which had started to rot. She was enveloped in the odours of her sweat and the urinal in the corner, which was a dugout hole in the ground.

Her meals consisted of warm broth containing a few vegetables and pieces of meat, three times a day. Once after taking a spoonful, she felt something hard and sharp in her mouth and quickly spat it out. When she held it up to the light, she saw that it was a jagged tooth. Nazanin screamed and banged on the door, but no one came. All she heard was laughing: the other prisoners in solitary confinement laughing at her.

Nazanin lived in this cell no bigger than a shed for nearly two months. Her only sanctuary was prayer and the Yaseen Sura. She tried to hang on to Hana's words that even in the darkest days, light will shine. But Nazanin's heart was sinking fast.

Whatever remaining hope she had left her the day a guard came to get her. Nazanin thought she was returning to her cell, but the burly guard hissed, "We have to make one stop first." She scowled as she wrapped a headscarf around Nazanin and handcuffed her.

"Why do I have to wear these?"

"Because you are wanted in the main office."

Nazanin's feet dragged as the guard guided her down the long corridor. Nazanin choked on the stench of vomit, blood and disinfectant. Panic gripped her and her body jerked. She moved to kick the guard in an attempt to run away but stopped herself, knowing that if she did, she would be sent back to solitary confinement.

When they finally reached the door leading to the office, Nazanin felt her legs about to collapse. "I am going to faint," she told the guard. "Can I rest for a bit?"

"No," she said. "They are waiting for you. I think they have something to tell you about your trial."

In the reception area, Nazanin was ordered to sit. She hung her head, feeling the stares of the others in the room. Then the office door swung open and a woman stepped out and waved for Nazanin to approach. As she stood up, Nazanin was conscious of her own smell—her perspiration and foul breath—from being unable to clean herself properly.

Khwa, let this be good news. Let me be free today, Nazanin prayed silently. *Let the judges have decided that I am innocent after all. And that I can go home.*

A woman sitting behind a desk in the office motioned for Nazanin to sit in the vacant chair in front of her. "The court found you guilty. And now I have your sentence," the woman said in a deep, hoarse voice that hinted at years of cigarette smoking. "*Besme ta aala*"—"In the name of God," she began. The woman put on a pair of glasses and began reading from a document. "Ms. Mahabad Fatehi—Nazanin—according to the request of the immediate family of the deceased, the *oliya dam*, you are sentenced to *ghesas*. The issued sentence is given to you, and you may apply for an appeal within forty days of issuance of this sentence."

Nazanin could feel her heart pounding. "What does that mean?" she asked in a weak voice.

"The law of *ghesas* is the law of retribution. It means an eye for an eye—that if you made someone blind, you are blinded . . . if you killed someone, you are killed."

"Pardon?"

"You are sentenced to death by hanging," the woman said. "You need to sign now and wait until your execution date." She slipped the piece of paper toward Nazanin. The guard grabbed Nazanin's right index finger and pressed it against a blue inkpad, then on a line at the bottom of the document.

The woman behind the desk waved for the guard to take Nazanin away. "Tell the next person to come in," she ordered.

Nazanin tilted her head and stared at the woman. "Why are you doing this to me?"

"Because you killed someone," the guard answered. The door to the office swung open and a nurse walked in carrying a needle. "This will calm your nerves," the guard said as the nurse headed toward Nazanin.

"No!" Nazanin screamed, kneeing the guard in the stomach. She then ran behind the desk and knelt in front of the woman who had read out her death sentence.

"*Be Khoda*, I swear to God, I am innocent. It was self-defence," she said in Persian, holding her hands up in front of her as if in prayer. "Please . . . please listen to me. You haven't even asked me any questions. You didn't hear my side of the story. You just gave a decree without—"

The guard slapped Nazanin across her cheek with such force that she fell onto her side. Her headscarf slipped off and her long black hair flew across her face.

"Please do not give me death," she sobbed as saliva ran down her chin. "I have just turned eighteen. I am just a child."

"Get her out of here," the woman behind the desk ordered the guard, who picked Nazanin up around the waist. "Get her out of here!"

CHAPTER 20

NAZANIN AFSHIN-JAM

Late February to April 2006, Vancouver

———

B ack in my condominium, that evening I first heard about Nazanin and after I had made my decision to help her, I managed to
sleep for a couple of hours. I woke to the sound of Etta James's "A
Sunday Kind of Love" on my alarm clock. As Etta sang about wrapping her arms around someone, I wondered aloud who was holding
Nazanin. I imagined her alone in her dark, cold cell.

"God," I whispered. "Guide me. Because I don't know what I am
doing. Help me help Nazanin."

I then remembered that before I had fallen asleep, I had emailed
Vincent to tell him I would do what I could and ask whether he knew
anything more about Nazanin. I rushed to the computer to see if he
had replied. He had. But he knew no more than I did.

Vincent, a translator by profession, wrote that he had learned
about Nazanin from a blog that had reported the story from an Iranian news website. Vincent didn't even know Nazanin's last name.
All he had to add was that he had tried to get this story to certain
French journalists but they had said it wasn't newsworthy enough
because executions in Iran were commonplace. This got my blood
boiling, and I could feel my whole body heat up with anger. To calm
my nerves, I made some chamomile tea.

As I drank the tea, I made a checklist of things to do. My action
plan included first finding out if Nazanin's story was true: Did she

really exist? Did this really happen to her? I'd then need to find out whether anyone else was helping her. And finally, and most importantly, I needed to find her—the name of the prison she was at—and also her family. In general, I needed to learn far more than I already did about Iran's laws, especially those pertaining to women and children.

After sending out an email to all my friends and contacts asking if they had any suggestions of ways to help Nazanin, I figured I should draft a petition to be ready for the worst-case scenario: that Nazanin's story was true. So I searched online to see what I could discover about similar cases. I learned that a woman named Afsaneh Norouzi had been sentenced to death for killing a police officer who had tried to rape her on the tourist island of Kish. Norouzi, a mother of three children, said she was defending herself. While Norouzi waited to be executed, Iran's Supreme Court heard the appeal and ordered a retrial. Some reports credited pressure from abroad, generated by a woman in Germany named Mina Ahadi, for the court's decision. In the subsequent trial, Norouzi was freed. She had spent three years in prison.

I breathed a little easier. *If Afsaneh Norouzi could get off after being accused of killing a policeman, then surely Nazanin has a chance.*

I left many messages at Amnesty International's Vancouver office, with no reply. I then contacted Amnesty International's head office in Ottawa, only to be passed off from one volunteer to another. This back-and-forth went on for weeks. I was hoping, given the issue, that someone there would give me guidelines on how to start a campaign. I realized that for now I was going to have to do this alone.

I SPENT DAYS drafting a petition calling for Nazanin's release. I was also starting to get replies from the email I had sent out. Most discouraged me from getting involved. It was an uphill battle. The Islamic Republic of Iran wouldn't budge. Be safe. A childhood friend, now a lawyer, was the most direct of all. "Nini," she wrote, "you are wasting your time. There is nothing you can do about this."

Then, finally, a Persian filmmaker, TT, who had shot a video on Bam before the earthquake that was shown at the charity events I was involved in, agreed to do what she could. She offered to convene a meeting with two of her friends interested in helping me. One was a woman named Negar Azmudeh, an immigration and human rights lawyer. The other was Dr. Mitra, who was involved in Iranian cultural events in Vancouver.

When I entered Dr. Mitra's home for the meeting, I was running on pure adrenalin from lack of sleep. I was now spending less and less time on my music and more and more time on the Save Nazanin campaign. I was also running on fear. "What if we are too late, and Nazanin is already dead?" were my first words to Negar, who was sitting on the white leather couch.

Negar smiled as I sat down beside her. "Don't worry," she said. "Nazanin may sit in prison for several years before an execution date is even set. Chances are the death sentence was just published in one of the Iranian newspapers, so the worst-case scenario is that you have forty days. Her lawyer has forty days to file an appeal. She won't be hanged before then."

"What if she doesn't have a lawyer? What if he or she doesn't file an appeal?" I asked, my voice and hands jittery.

"Let's hope the lawyer does. Then you will have much more time, especially if the appeal is granted."

"But even if there is no appeal, do you think we have time to launch a proper campaign to help save this girl?" I pressed.

Negar nodded and I sat back, feeling a hint of relief.

After we were all seated at the dinner table, Negar gave us an overview of Iran's discriminatory laws against women and children. After dinner we went into Dr. Mitra's office to brainstorm. By the end of the evening, we had decided we should contact high-profile women, including Queen Rania of Jordan, whose husband I had met, and Benazir Bhutto, whom I had met a year earlier—both of them were involved in human rights issues—and ask if they could help plead for Nazanin's release. We made a list of international human rights organizations and a list of local media we could contact to get the news out into the world. The goal was to get as much press as possible. We all agreed to keep the focus on human rights.

"Whatever you do, don't make this a political campaign," warned Dr. Mitra. "Don't start speaking publicly about how bad the Iranian fundamentalist regime is. Then things could become dangerous for everyone, including Nazanin in Iran."

A FEW WEEKS after my decision, I received confirmation, thanks to inquiries sent out by Negar to Iran's law society, that Nazanin existed and that she was indeed a minor on death row for a crime she committed in self-defence. But no one knew which jail she was in, and I didn't know if she even wanted my help. I hoped that someone would discover her whereabouts soon and inform me, and that what I was doing might help spare her life. The petition I had drafted was nearly polished and ready to be released to the public, but I was still holding it back, feeling the wording wasn't quite right. A gut instinct told me I was missing something. At the top of the petition, I had put the names of the people it was directed to, including regime officials in Iran, the head of the judiciary, Ayatollah Shahroudi, as well as key figures at the United Nations.

I asked Peter if I could take a break from the album to dedicate myself fully to Nazanin's campaign, at least for a while. The same day, Shaun Lawless, a filmmaker who had shot me in some commercials and acting jobs, was over at Peter's office discussing the shoot for my upcoming musc video. I told him I was working on the Save Nazanin petition, and he suggested I contact one of his friends, a prosecution trial lawyer with the International Criminal Court. "Maybe she can give you some advice on the wording of your petition," he said. "Or people you can meet to lobby for her release."

I wrote Shyamala Alagendra, who emailed me back immediately.

"You know, Nazanin," she wrote, "Iran is a state party to the International Covenant on Civil and Political Rights and the Convention on the Rights of the Child. Both of these prohibit the use of the death penalty against people who commit crimes when they are eighteen years of age or younger. Nazanin falls into this category. Iran has broken international law."

"Nazanin is just a child. How can they be so brazen as to sign international treaties and then violate them?" I wrote back.

"It happens all the time," she replied.

After our email exchange, I sat staring out the window at the clouds and at the Pacific Ocean below. I realized why I had taken on the cause, despite so many people telling me not to. There is nothing in this world that stifles progress more than the abuse and oppression of innocent people. The most innocent of all are our children. Oppressed and abused children grow up to be oppressors and abusers themselves, and then we wonder why we have wars, poverty, hatred and corruption. Put simply, the root of all of our problems is power and ego at the expense of the most vulnerable and innocent—the powerless.

I recalled an Aboriginal saying to the effect that, in every action, we must think of the impact it will have on seven generations to come. My thoughts then turned to myself. If I had remained in Iran, maybe I would be exactly where Nazanin is now. My father would have been killed. My mother would have struggled to raise us. I heard my mother's voice in my head, repeating the words of Albert Einstein: "The world is a dangerous place, not because of those who do evil, but because of those who look on and do nothing."

I finished up the petition, adding in the information Alagendra had given me, and then posted it on the PetitionOnline website. A talented website designer in Vancouver named Nima had volunteered his time to design and host a website for the campaign. I also posted the petition there, as well as daily updates on the developments in Nazanin's case. I vowed on the website that I would personally take every signature to the United Nations headquarters in New York.

Within twenty-four hours, the petition was getting signatures.

And within three days, I was receiving email requests, mostly from Persian media outside Iran, requesting interviews. One of the interviews I agreed to hold was with Mostafa Saber, a columnist with a Persian Communist newspaper.

Saber asked me to chronicle what I had done so far to raise awareness of Nazanin's case. I told him and then sighed, saying I really wanted to find the woman involved in Afsaneh Norouzi's case, Mina Ahadi. "I know her well," Saber said. "I will put you in touch with her directly. She's great. She takes this work personally, as her husband was murdered by the regime in Iran just after the revolution for his left-leaning beliefs and activities."

The first thing I noticed when I finally spoke to Mina was the warmth in her voice. Her tone was both inviting and confident. After just a few words, I felt I could trust her. She told me she had heard about the case—though she didn't know Nazanin's last name either—but she had seen my petition online and that was why she had not got involved. "I felt relief that someone was championing the cause," she said.

Mina talked about her work. In addition to taking on individual women's cases, lobbying for their release and for fairer trials and laws, she was also instrumental in forming an anti-stoning campaign, which involved petitioning the Iranian government to stop this barbaric practice. When a woman is stoned, she is wrapped from head to toe in a white shroud and buried up to her neck. People, mostly men, then throw stones at her until all that can be seen is blood seeping through the fabric. Men and women in Iran are subjected to this kind of punishment for adultery.

"You have such knowledge," I told Mina. "Can we work on Nazanin's case together?" She agreed to be my partner. She said she would help coordinate meetings with key politicians in the European Union and at the United Nations.

"I will also talk with the families of the inmates with whom I am working. They visit the prisons weekly. They will ask the women inside the prison if they know of Nazanin. Nazanin is young. If she is in any of the prisons where I have clients, they will know about her. Everyone knows about the young ones. Within two weeks, we should be able to find her," Mina said confidently.

CHAPTER 21

NAZANIN FATEHI

March to April 2006, Rajai Shahr Prison, Karaj, Iran

Nazanin was moved yet again to another cell, this one housing an older woman named Fatemeh, who reminded Nazanin of Madar Azar, with her age, soft facial features, round physique and gentle mannerisms. Like Madar Azar, Fatemeh brushed Nazanin's hair and rocked her in her warm embrace when she was hurting, which was almost all the time since receiving the news that she was going to die. Sleep offered no reprieve. Her nights were plagued by the recurring nightmare, which always ended with the walls moving in on her.

One day as Nazanin lay on the ground, her prayers half finished, Fatemeh whispered to her, "My grandmother once told me to stop seeing with the eyes of my mind, and listen to the voice of my heart. Try to do that, *azizam*." She peeled an orange and placed half on Nazanin's bed.

Nazanin, her dry and split hair sticking to the tears on her face, looked up and shook her head. "What heart? I have no hope anymore. None. I am a dead person."

"So am I," said Fatemeh, sitting cross-legged on the floor beside Nazanin. "I have been sentenced to death too. And what did I do? I was divorced, which was the first strike against me. The man with whom I was living, my husband under a temporary marriage, was addicted to taryak. He was high on drugs and half-naked, screaming at my daughter—who was only fifteen—and pushing her to the bed when I walked in," Fatemeh lamented. "We started fighting and he said to me, 'Don't worry, your portion won't be reduced. You'll get your share.' I was so afraid for my daughter, I slipped off my head-scarf and strangled him."

"We are both now dead for protecting people we loved," Nazanin said, sitting up and crossing her legs.

"But I am fighting my sentence, Nazanin," Fatemeh said in a strong voice. "I vow to do what I can to get out of here and find my freedom again. I still feel my heart; it is beating and it loves, and those terrible guards and this horrible prison will not take that from me. My heart knows it is pure, it feels freedom, it feels me holding my daughters in my arms again."

But Nazanin had lost all feeling. In the middle of the night, she lifted up the corner of her bed and unscrewed the bed leg. She then tried to jab the screw sticking out of the leg top into her stomach. When it would not break the skin, she rubbed, then pounded, the screw into the veiny part of her wrists.

When Fatemeh awoke, she found Nazanin lying on the bed with her arms splayed out, soaking in blood. But she was still breathing. Nazanin spent two weeks in the hospital, and then at the prison clinic, most of the time lying lifeless, her wrists covered in bandages, just like those of the women she had seen when Mandana had bitten her ear.

When Nazanin rejoined Fatemeh in the cell, she was so high on sedatives that she moved very slowly, though it felt to her as though her feet were barely touching the ground, and spoke so quietly that Fatemeh couldn't make out what she was saying.

"You know, Nazanin, I wanted to tell you that there are people on the outside of Iran helping some of us women in prison here," Fatemeh said as she tucked Nazanin into bed one afternoon. "I myself am working with a woman in Germany named Mina. She is raising awareness of my case and trying to get foreign governments to pressure Iran to stay my execution. Do you want me to speak to her about you?"

Nazanin groaned, closed her eyes and rolled over.

Fatemeh didn't leave Nazanin's side for more than a week. She sat on the bed and told her children's stories. Nazanin's eyelids fluttered every so often to indicate she was still in the land of the living, if barely. She was unable to think of anything—her mind was blank. But then her fingers would brush up against her bandages and she would be reminded of her future. It was then that she would break down and cry.

Two weeks after returning to her cell from the recovery at the clinic, when Fatemeh had left to speak to another inmate, Nazanin snuck to the washroom and tried to hang herself with her chador. She tied the flowered fabric to one of the steel pipes and wrapped the other end around her neck. She stood on a chair and, when she was ready, kicked it out from under her. Fatemeh entered the washroom just in time to save her.

"You have to stop this, child," Fatemeh sobbed as she rocked Nazanin in her arms. "I know it is so horrible inside here, but we have each other. We do! And you have to have faith there is a reason for all of this—something good will come."

"But what about those horrible things they say they do to girls like me before they kill us?" Nazanin sobbed, burying her head in Fatemeh's chest.

"Like what?"

"I heard the guards rape young girls like me, so we will be impure and unable to enter paradise."

"Oh, *azizam*," Fatemeh said, rubbing Nazanin's back. "Don't listen to them. They won't . . . they won't. It has happened, but it is rare. It is not Islamic—though nothing about this regime is Islamic. Even if you do die—and I want to believe there is still hope—God will take you to paradise. Be like this heroine I heard about when I was a little girl. My mother told me of a girl in France named Jeanne d'Arc, who, legend has it, followed God's voice and saved her country. But then her countrymen turned her over to the English, who labelled her a witch and burned her at the stake. But 600 years have passed since she walked the earth, and she is now revered as one of the most important women in history. Perhaps the greater meaning of Jeanne's life is to inspire us and generations of women to come to follow our hearts no matter what obstacles stand in our way. There is meaning in your life, Nazanin, and you live that life until your last breath. Don't give up before then."

"MAHABAD FATEHI," the voice on the loudspeaker echoed throughout the ward. "Mahabad Fatehi."

Nazanin quickly leapt out of bed and slipped on her headscarf. Whenever an inmate's name was called, she had to check in at the main office, head covered. Usually it meant the inmate had a visitor.

"Maybe my mother has come," Nazanin, nearly smiling, said to Fatemeh.

"Whatever the reason, it will be good this time, watch."

"I'll ask her for money to buy cucumber and feta cheese sandwiches for us." Nazanin said, beaming as she followed the guard down the corridor.

"In here," the guard said to Nazanin, stopping suddenly at a door.

Nazanin was puzzled. "This isn't where I meet my mother," she said.

"Your mother isn't here," the guard replied harshly. "It's your lawyer."

"My lawyer?" Nazanin gasped. "The one from the trial?"

"I'm not sure," the guard said, pointing. "He claims he is your lawyer and he wants to see you." The guard opened the door and pushed Nazanin into the room.

Nazanin sat down slowly on the metal chair set opposite the man, who was impatiently tapping the table with a pen and the ground with one of his feet. He rifled through some papers in front of him before introducing himself as Mohammad Mostafaei.

"I'm a lawyer," he said brusquely. "And my group, the Network of Volunteer Lawyers, heard about your case and, well, here I am."

Nazanin, her eyes lowered, said nothing.

"I was here visiting other inmates, as my law group takes on cases that involve human rights violations and there are some women whose files we might take on. I thought I would visit you while I am here," he continued.

Nazanin said nothing. She was groggy from the sedatives the guards were giving her so she wouldn't attempt suicide again. She was also leery of this man—of any man who had to do with the court.

"I don't think we will take on your case," he admitted. "But I wanted to meet you. It's just . . ."

"Why?" Nazanin asked, startled. Her cheeks flushed and her brow was now perspiring. "Do you think I am guilty, like everyone else does?"

Mostafaei stopped tapping his pen and his foot became still. Nazanin could hear his laboured breathing. Without looking up, she saw him withdraw a handkerchief from his suit pocket and wipe his brow. "I'm sorry," he said. "I was expecting someone else when I agreed to meet with you."

"Who?"

"You are just different," he said in a much softer voice. "What we . . . my group . . . had heard about you led us to believe you were hardened, gruff and violent."

"Oh," Nazanin sighed.

"Can you tell me about your case?" he asked, leaning forward. "Please, I want to know."

Nazanin tried as best she could to give an account of the crime and the court proceedings, and Mostafaei took notes. But her head tingled and her eyelids were heavy. All she wanted to do was rest her head on the table and sleep. Remembering was hard work.

"Did you give any testimony in court?" Mostafaei asked at one point.

"No."

"None at all!" he exclaimed.

"Well . . . a little bit, but I wasn't asked the same questions the boys were," she said, tears falling down her cheeks. Nazanin was sure she could hear Mostafaei's heart beating. "The judges listened only to the witnesses. You are a lawyer," she then said in the strongest voice she could muster. "I am just a stupid, poor girl. But I know what is right and what is wrong. How can those judges sentence me to execution when I didn't even say anything? The boys lied." Her shoulders slumped as her head tilted to the side. "They lied, and now I am a dead person."

"When I first heard about your case," Mostafaei said, "I believed you were a runaway, someone who, while not deserving such a sentence, might not be able to be reached emotionally so that any of us can help you. Do you understand?"

Nazanin shook her head.

"It doesn't matter," Mostafaei said, waving a hand in the air. "The important thing is that I look at you now, with your doe-like eyes and innocent face, and you are me," he said, smiling weakly. "When I was thirteen, I was living on the streets, holding down two jobs. There are only two differences between you and me: I am Persian and a man and so had opportunities—and though I had to work harder than many other men to take advantage of these opportunities, I still had them. You are poor, a girl and Kurdish and have no such opportunities. I will take on your case.

"I don't have your file, but your other lawyer, I am sure, has filed an appeal," he continued. "If that appeal is successful, I and my colleagues from the Network of Volunteer Lawyers will defend you from there. You won't have to pay us, and we will mount a case, offer testimony and make sure the judges hear your side of the story."

NAZANIN WOKE the next morning to the scent of camphor. For a moment she thought she'd been transported to Hana's home. But then the sound of a baby crying in another cell and two women bickering in the washroom reminded her of where she was. "You need some healthy food," said Fatemeh, holding a container of rice and beef stew. "I have more good news for you," she then said. Nazanin sat up.

"You had fallen asleep before I returned last night from visiting my daughters. We stayed together for a long time, talking. I miss them. But never mind that," Fatemeh said, coming over to Nazanin. She ran her finger down her face, forcing Nazanin to close her eyes. "That woman in Germany that I told you about, the woman named Mina, sent a message out to all the family members of the women she is working with in prison. I never told this Mina about your case, but Mina is trying to find you!"

Nazanin gasped and quickly sat up.

"Word has got out of Iran that you, just a child, have been sentenced to death. Mina is working with an Iranian woman living far away in Canada who has the same name as you."

"Mahabad?" Nazanin asked quizzically.

"No, silly girl. Nazanin. Her name is Nazanin too, and she and Mina are helping you."

"How?"

"I don't know yet, but I think they are going to do what Mina did for Afsaneh Norouzi, and get the international community to put pressure on Iran to set you free. Nazanin, they need photographs of you."

"I have a photograph at home. It was taken a few years ago," she said enthusiastically. "My father was calm and loving that day. He had all the children and my mother stand together and a neighbour take the photograph. That was the day when he told me how unhappy he was with his life."

"What did he say, Nazanin?" Fatemeh asked, taking Nazanin's hands in hers.

"He said he saw terrible things in the war that he could never forgive or forget. He took Hojat and me aside in the evening and told us that he had, just by indirectly being involved in the war, supported the killing of people, his own people, Kurds. He never would be able to get past that. He tried to block the memories out but they haunted him in his dreams. 'I am a broken man,' he wailed. 'I have done so much bad.'"

"Can you get a message to your mother?" Fatemeh asked. "Tell her to come to the prison. Do you have your mother's phone number?"

"We don't have a telephone. In an emergency, our next-door neighbour, a Turkish woman, she would let us use her phone, but I don't remember the number."

"But the prison will have it on file, for someone called your mother to tell them you were here initially." Fatemeh was now kneeling on the floor spooning stew into a bowl, which she handed to Nazanin. "Tell Mrs. Mohammadi that you need to see your mother, that you have something important to tell her before you die. I suspect once your mother hears the news that people outside Iran believe your story, she'll want to help any way she can too."

"Why do you think that?" Nazanin asked, wide-eyed.

"Because I am a mother too, and mothers always know. Your father is controlling your mother, but deep down she knows the truth. And yes, your father is unhappy. Only unhappy people inflict such sadness and hurt on others. But it is no excuse. He may have been in pain, but he put that pain on all of you. Your family is not cursed. They are unfortunate because of their poverty and being Kurdish under a regime that feels very threatened by minorities. But your mother still could have raised all of you in a home with love and kindness, not abuse and bad words. Your mother will have a chance to feel relief, that her intuition about you being innocent was right, and she will now have ammunition to fire back at your father and say, 'I believe in Nazanin!'"

"You think too much of my mother," said Nazanin.

"My daughters have given me questions from Mina and Nazanin to ask you," Fatemeh continued. "I will write down the answers and give them to them when they return at the end of the week."

"What kind of questions?"

"Details of the crime, the court that convicted you and . . ." Fatemeh trailed off.

"And what?" Nazanin probed.

"And your life story. People must realize," she added, "that you are not just a number in prison. You are a human being, a daughter, a girl, a person with dreams and feelings, emotions and sensitivities."

CHAPTER 22

NAZANIN FATEHI

April to May 2006, Rajai Shahr Prison, Karaj, Iran

———

Fatemeh sat on the bed with her legs outstretched, while Jwan leaned backwards on a chair, her arms draped over the back. Fatemeh had asked Jwan to be present when Nazanin told her story, in case there were things she needed to explain about her life in Kurdish. While Nazanin spoke Persian, her vocabulary wasn't much greater than that of an average twelve-year-old.

Nazanin answered simple questions first.

"Your favourite movie?" Fatemeh asked.

"Anything Iranian, like they play in the prison," she said, referring to the evenings the women were allowed to go to the recreation room and watch Iranian films, all of which had been screened by the state to make sure they contained no derogatory statements about the Iranian government or any women not following Islamic dress code.

"Favourite music?" Fatemeh asked next.

"The famous singers Shadmehr Aghili and Ali Tafreshi, and other Persian pop music."

"What did you like to do most, as a child?" Jwan asked.

"I liked it when I rode a donkey. I want to learn to horseback ride," she replied dreamily.

"What do you want to be when you get out of prison?"

Tears filled Nazanin's eyes as she stared first at Fatemeh and then

Jwan. "I always wanted to read, to become a storyteller. I want to be a teacher."

Tears flowed down the cheeks of the two other women as Nazanin then told them about Yousef's darting eyes and his long fingers that pushed her backwards.

"How did you know what these boys wanted to do to you?" Jwan asked.

"I just had a feeling," she replied, waving the question off.

"What kind of feeling?" Fatemeh pressed.

Nazanin blushed. Part of her felt shame. She frequently chastised herself for not having done things differently that day. *If I had just not opened the door. If I had just gone back to Aylar's house after Hana's. If I had just run away.*

Nazanin looked into Fatemeh's soft brown eyes. Her rosy cheeks reminded her of Hana's. She caught a whiff of the rose soap that Fatemeh used on both her body and hair. "Fatemeh, I was touched before," Nazanin whispered.

Fatemeh and Jwan leaned in close and listened as Nazanin told them about Mohsen. "At night," Nazanin said in a low voice, "I can feel his dirty, clammy hands on me. I relive parts of that day over and over again. Sometimes I even ask myself, would I even be here if it hadn't happened?"

"Ah, sweetie, *azizam*," Fatemeh cried, pulling Nazanin into her arms. "You poor thing. All of us wish we had done some things differently in our lives. It can tear at us until we have no soul left. You have to let it go. It can't be changed, you did nothing wrong and you need to find some meaning in it, as painful as the experience was."

OVER THE NEXT FEW DAYS, Nazanin told Fatemeh and Jwan her life story. Jwan, Fatemeh and Nazanin would speak from the time the breakfast cart finished its rounds until early afternoon, when they took a break to walk the courtyard arm in arm. Then the day came when Fatemeh's daughters arrived.

When Fatemeh returned from her visit with them, she confirmed that the Canadian Nazanin had sent out a petition seeking Nazanin Fatehi's immediate release. After she explained what a petition was, Fatemeh said enthusiastically, "I even wrote down some of the wording for you." She smoothed out a crumpled piece of paper she had tucked in her bra so the guards wouldn't see and began reading aloud.

> Urgent action is needed to help save a young life whose only crime was an attempt to defend herself. Nazanin and many like her are caught between two undesirable options. On one hand, Iranian Penal Code severely limits the possibility of using "self-defence" as a legitimate defence to aggression. On the other hand, if Nazanin had allowed the rape to take place, she could still be imprisoned, flogged or stoned for having sex outside marriage unless four male witnesses to the actual rape would testify on her behalf.

"I hope it works," Nazanin said. "I hope Khwa can perform a little magic and get me out of here."

"You've opened your heart, *azizam*!" Fatemeh clapped. "There is magic, but it is in there," she said, pointing to Nazanin's heart.

A FEW WEEKS LATER, however, the magic seemed to have disappeared. The almost endless drone of the Islamic music being played over the loudspeaker in the prison subsided as Nazanin's name was called out. She grabbed her rubber shoes and floral headscarf, expecting to be taken to see a visitor. "Maybe it's Mr. Mostafaei," she said to Fatemeh.

"Get your things together," Mrs. Mohammadi told Nazanin when Nazanin appeared at the door to the guards' office.

"Why?" Nazanin asked, her body instantly gripped with fear.

"Because you're moving," Mrs. Mohammadi replied matter-of-factly as she pushed her way past Nazanin and headed toward the cells. Nazanin stared after her, watching Mrs. Mohammadi's chador flare out behind her.

"I don't understand," she said, turning to the guard in the office, who was filing some paperwork.

"What is to understand?" the guard replied, giving Nazanin a piercing look. "Your file has been transferred to Tehran. You are moving to Evin Prison. You're leaving Rajai Shahr Prison."

"What is this about?" Nazanin cried.

The guard stared at Nazanin, who had turned ghost white and urinated on herself. "What is wrong with you, stupid girl?" she asked, watching the puddle grow on the floor.

"I don't want to die," she said, kneeling in the urine and holding her hands together as if in prayer. "Please. Please! What about my appeal? The petition?"

The guard huffed. "You have to speak to someone else about that. You have a death sentence. Your file has been sent to Tehran, and you are being moved to Evin. It's as simple as that. The orders came down from up above," she said, pointing upward. "It is God's will."

Just as when Mandana and her gang were rifling through her things when she first arrived at Rajai Shahr Prison, something deep within Nazanin was unleashed. "How dare you," she screamed, jumping up and pointing a finger at the guard. "Khwa, Khoda, Allah or whatever you want to call Him is shamed by such words. Nothing that this state stands for, including you, is godly or holy. It is all a demon."

The guard walked toward Nazanin and swiftly hit her across the cheek. Nazanin fell to the ground. "If you weren't being moved to Evin Prison, you'd be in solitary for comments like that. You would be taken away from all these nice older women who protect you. Go back to your cell," she ordered. Nazanin got up slowly, holding her throbbing cheek.

"Pack your things," the guard said.

The bars of the prison cells seemed to grow around her and the corridor stretched longer as Nazanin walked back to her cell. She felt numb. Like she had the day back in Sanandaj that the children called her jaash. She could see herself, as if part of her body were standing at the other end of the corridor, watching. Then she saw Fatemeh exit their cell for the washroom.

Mrs. Mohammadi was talking to the woman who delivered the food cart. Mrs. Mohammadi laughed at something the woman said. Nazanin took off her headscarf and threw it on the ground. When she reached the cart, full of steaming glasses of tea, she pushed it over with all her might. She picked up the samovar from the floor and threw it at the ceiling, where it shattered two of the fluorescent light bulbs. She stood and watched glass scatter along the cement floor, the hallway now dim, lit only by one remaining light bulb.

The other inmates came rushing out from their cells at the noise. Their eyes moved from Nazanin, her dress stained with her own urine, her face white and clammy from fear, to the shards of glass on the ground.

Mrs. Mohammadi's eyes narrowed.

"Are you going to execute me now?" Nazanin said to her forcefully.

"I don't want to hear anything more from you," Mrs. Mohammadi replied, her hand in the air about to strike. "When you are done cleaning yourself, you're going to spend the night in solitary."

A GUARD PUSHED NAZANIN inside the small solitary confinement cell and threw the handful of clothes she had brought with her on the ground. As soon as Nazanin heard the door lock and the footsteps of the guard disappear down the hallway, she pulled out the chador she had hidden among her things. She ran the rough polyester fabric through her hands and thought of Hana, of Leila, of the mountains where she rode the donkey. She closed her eyes and then lifted the chador over her head so that her entire face and hair were covered. She then felt for the end of the chador and began wrapping it around her neck, again and again.

Nazanin felt the fabric growing tight around her face. She was starting to see stars, and her breathing became more difficult. Her body slumped. When she was nearly unconscious, she suddenly felt a presence in the room with her. It was Leila, wearing a beautiful white Kurdish dress, spinning like a Sufi dervish with one hand up in the air, the other hand down. Nazanin could hear the tinkling of the gold coins sewn into the fabric. "Sleep, sleep, my pretty-eyed daughter. *Lai lai lai lai kizholei chaw kazhalm . . . Lai*," Leila sang in her soft, sweet voice.

I'm coming, Leila, Nazanin said silently.

Leila stopped singing and dancing and walked toward Nazanin. "But it is not your time—"

"What are you doing, you whore?" the hoarse voice of a guard croaked. Nazanin felt hands grasp the chador, pulling it loose from her neck. She wanted to kick and fight back, but her body wouldn't move. She felt the rough hands untwisting the chador. Suddenly, Nazanin saw a light streaming in through the doorway. She lay on the floor and coughed.

The guard yelled for someone to fetch water as she grabbed Nazanin's wrist and felt for a pulse. She let out a sigh of relief. "You'll live," she said. "And your breathing and pulse are strong enough that you don't need to go to the clinic. You can still stay here for the night and thirty more."

When Nazanin finished drinking the glass of water, the guard took back the glass, along with all of Nazanin's belongings, leaving her with only the thin, clean cotton dress she was wearing and a wool blanket. "You can't be trusted," she said as she slammed the door shut.

Nazanin spent the night shivering within the thin blanket, which she had rolled herself in so that she wasn't lying right on the cold cement floor. She could see her breath in the air. The cells echoed with the moans and cries of other inmates. Nazanin wondered whether she was already dead and in *jahanam*—hell.

CHAPTER 23

NAZANIN AFSHIN-JAM

April to July 2006, Vancouver, New York, Ottawa

———

Mina and I discovered it was the Iranian newspaper *Etemaad* that had first published the report of Nazanin's death sentence. Mina also learned that an appeal had been filed: Nazanin's state-appointed lawyer had done his job. We wrote out some questions to have someone ask Nazanin, when and if we found her.

Ever since becoming Miss Canada and having done well on the international stage, I had been meeting people wherever I travelled. I had thousands of names in my email address book. I had sent the petition link to every one of those people, encouraging them to sign. Everything was running smoothly: I had thousands of signatures on the petition within no time. But then I started to get emails I had not anticipated.

"I'm getting death threats now," I said to my father one day. I had dropped by their place for lunch.

"Keep your voice down or your mother will hear! What are they saying?"

"'It will only take one slash across your face and you are done,' I whispered. "Another said. 'A sniper will take you away.'"

Just then my mother entered the room. "What's going on? Why are you whispering?" she asked, raising an eyebrow in question.

"Nothing, Mom. Just, some people are bugging me on the Internet. They are telling me to stop my activities."

"Of course," she said, placing her hands on her heart. "Did you think these mullahs in Iran would embrace you doing this? The more signatures you get on that petition of yours, the bigger threat you become for Iran. Are you sure, Nini, that this is what you want? I love you so much. I don't want anything to happen to you."

I nodded.

"Well, there is never any use in trying to sway you once you've made up your mind. I'll support you in anything you do, as I have always done. However, promise me that if this becomes dangerous, you will stop your activities. I vow to God to make a $200 offering to an animal shelter to protect you throughout this campaign," she then said.

"Are you giving it to VAFA Animal Shelter in Iran?" I asked.

My mother's eyes grew wide. "I didn't know they had shelters for animals in Iran, Nini. They don't treat animals there the way we do in the West. Certainly, there are no doggie spas or gourmet dog food. In Tehran, people are fined for walking their dogs on the street. But when it is to its benefit, the state pays top dollar to import dogs like German shepherds for security to sniff out explosives and drugs and to unleash on anti-government protesters. Under this regime, the mullahs call the dogs *najess*, when they are themselves the dirty ones."

ON A BRIGHT SUNNY APRIL MORNING, at about seven o'clock, the phone rang. It was Mina calling to say that Zahra, the daughter of a woman named Fatemeh whom she was helping, had contacted her. Nazanin was in one of the most notoriously rough prisons for women in all of Iran, Rajai Shahr, in the same cell as Fatemeh, who was watching over her.

"And Zahra even has some of the answers to our questions!" Mina said optimistically. "We now have more information for the press. We just need to contact Nazanin's mother for a photograph."

"Well, that should be easy." I sighed with relief.

"Maybe not," replied Mina. "Fatemeh's daughter told me in our last conversation that Nazanin's mother has not visited her much since she was convicted. She says no one from her family was present at her trial."

"When will the Supreme Court review the appeal?" I asked, changing the subject.

"Soon," she said. "Very soon. We have to hurry, Nazanin. We need to make sure the Supreme Court of Iran feels the international pressure to order a retrial."

Mina said she would email a copy of the interview Fatemeh had done with Nazanin. What I didn't know at the time is that Fatemeh had given Zahra only part of that interview to smuggle out of the prison. So that the guards wouldn't catch Zahra walking out of prison with all the paper Fatemeh had written on, she instead discreetly passed on only the basic facts needed for a newspaper article. I would have to wait a long time to hear Nazanin's life story and understand fully how she really ended up in prison.

A few days later, Mina called to say she had been given the Fatehis' neighbour's telephone number and had organized a conference call with the neighbour and Nazanin's mother for the very next day. The neighbour spoke Turkish, which I recognized because my own mother spoke the language to her mother and siblings when she didn't want Naz and me to understand what they were saying. Mina, who spoke Persian, Turkish and Kurdish, asked the neighbour to fetch Maryam.

I greeted Maryam in Persian and then Mina spoke to her in Kurdish, explaining that we were human rights activists trying to help Nazanin and, to do so most effectively, we needed a recent photograph of her.

"Do you know anyone with a computer who can scan the photo and send it to us via email?" Mina asked.

Maryam went silent. "*Ma besavad hasteem,*" she eventually said in Persian, meaning "We're uneducated." Mina then told Maryam that we would send someone to her house to borrow the photos and scan them for her.

Mina and I remained on the line after Maryam hung up. "Is there a problem?" I asked timidly, sensing Mina's concern.

"Well, when I first asked the neighbour if she felt comfortable speaking with me because of my political activist background, she said she wasn't sure, so I worry that we will not continue to be able to have access to Maryam."

"Then why did she do it this time?"

"She agreed when I offered to pay her some money."

"So is that how it works in Iran?" I moaned.

Mina laughed. "It's how it works everywhere, my dear. And Nazanin's mother, that's how it works for her too. I offered to pay Maryam some money to allow us to borrow the photographs. You are so innocent—you have a lot to learn!"

"How come Maryam hasn't visited Nazanin much in prison?" I asked. Since I do not understand Kurdish, I wasn't sure what Mina and Maryam had said during their conversation.

"Maryam said that she can't afford the bus fare and that she is very busy caring for her other children," Mina explained. "She indicated there are a lot of problems at her home. Her husband has been in and out of the hospital for surgeries for his kidneys. At first she said she wanted money for Nazanin so she could buy her some new clothes and so that Nazanin could buy food at the prison store. But then she said she needed money to help the other children."

I hadn't thought about money or that we would need any. I was focusing on building awareness. But now my thoughts turned to generating some income, for if the Supreme Court did grant a new trial, I would want to hire Iran's top human rights lawyer to take on Nazanin's case, and I suspected that would cost a great deal of money. Mina and I discussed possibilities and she recommended Abdolsamad Khorramshahi, whom Mina said was competent and committed to these types of cases. We contacted him to see if he might take on Nazanin's case, and he said he would do it but would need a retainer of $5,000.

Peter's company sent out a press release on the case to media—

both Persian and mainstream—across North America and Europe. I appeared on CTV, where I emphasized to the public that "this is not just a case of an Iranian woman; this is a case of humanity."

Negar Azmudeh was also interviewed, and she spoke about how women are treated like second-class citizens under Iran's penal code, based on sharia law. Had a man killed Nazanin, she said, likely he would not receive a death sentence, even if the action was done with intent to kill. "Because the value of his life would be twice as much as Nazanin's, a female," Negar explained.

Amnesty International also became quite helpful in advancing the campaign. Amnesty International's headquarters in London issued press releases not only condemning Iran for how it handled Nazanin's case but also pointing out that in that year alone, eight minors had been executed there. In its press releases on Nazanin, Amnesty International referenced the case of sixteen-year-old Atefeh Rajabi Sahaaleh, hanged in public in the city of Neka in 2004. During her trial, the judge assassinated the girl's character. When he sentenced her to death for crimes against chastity, she yelled in a fit of anguish and ripped off her headscarf. For what he considered a disrespectful action, the judge promised to personally slip the noose around her neck at her execution. According to some reports, when the crane lifted, he said to a dying Sahaaleh, "This will teach you to not disobey."

Shortly after Sahaaleh's hanging, the judge was arrested. It had come to light that he himself had sexually assaulted Sahaaleh and, during her interrogations involving whether she had had sex out of wedlock, had tortured her.

Word of the campaign spread across the United States, initially via CNN, and across Europe via the BBC, and suddenly the story of Nazanin and other children on death row in Iran was everywhere. Even Mina couldn't believe the attention it was receiving. "It's not just her plight that is interesting the press," she admitted during one of our phone conversations. "It's you too."

The story appeared in top publications, including the *Telegraph* and *London Times*. I also had interviews with popular talk show hosts, including Sir David Frost in London and the Persian equivalent of Larry King, Ahmad Baharloo at *Voice of America* Persian TV.

And I did my rounds at Fox News with Glenn Beck, Sean Hannity and Alan Colmes, and Bill O'Reilly. Some people wondered why I would go on shows where the hosts clearly knew little about Iran or the Middle East, or appeared to not care to learn. My reply was that I had no fear doing interviews with anyone as long as the message was getting across to audiences worldwide. If a segment of people watching O'Reilly's show, for instance, were of the opinion that Middle Easterners were terrorists and that Iran should be bombed, then I could use the public platform to offer a more balanced perspective, in the hope of showing that there were many innocent people wrongly persecuted under the Iranian regime, including Nazanin. O'Reilly asked me why Iran had gone so downhill. "You are Iranian, and you are okay," he said, insinuating that most Iranians were not okay.

I explained that human rights in Iran had deteriorated since Ayatollah Khomeini's theocracy. "Religion is used as an excuse to control the people," I said, then suggesting that the solution was to support and empower civil society within Iran so that it could rise up.

O'Reilly challenged me, saying that "it is tough in a police state." I countered by citing examples where people power and non-violent civil resistance had toppled dictatorships and authoritarian regimes—the Otpor movement in Serbia, the Orange Revolution in Ukraine and the Rose Revolution in Georgia. "I know it is going to happen in Iran too," I concluded. "As the lyrics I wrote in my song say, 'Someday we'll find a way.'" O'Reilly was as nice to me as I have heard he is with any guest, even though he interrupted often and wouldn't let me finish my sentences. Actually, this turned out to be the case in many of the interviews I had in the United States. It seemed to me that the US media wanted to get through the interview fast and just get sound bites or peppy quotes. This threw me off—the British and Canadian media listened to my answers and asked direct questions based on my responses. The European media interviewed me in much the same way but also often broadcast or printed sexy modelling photographs of me alongside the pieces.

Particularly with the Europeans, it seemed to me that Mina was right: Nazanin Fatehi's case was getting press because they found it interesting that a former Miss World runner-up was involved. "It seems that all the beauty queens answer their questions by saying they want to save the world, but you are really doing it," the German interviewer for *Spiegel Online* told me.

This unsettled me. In my naivety, I believed every media outlet would want to carry the news of a teenager on death row in Iran because the sentence itself was such a violation of our basic rights as humans. I struggled with the fact that some journalists seemed more interested in me than in the issue, but ultimately I was so driven to free Nazanin that I shook off the negative emotions and simply said to myself, *Whatever it takes!*

Friends and old colleagues whom I had not heard from in years resurfaced. A few years earlier, for instance, Professor Andy Knight, from the University of Alberta, had organized a UN conference on children and war at which I was a participant. Professor Knight and his Iranian wife are Baha'i and have a daughter also named Nazanin. He now contacted me, then sent out a mass email to all his contacts requesting that they help in any way they could. One of those contacts was Lloyd Axworthy, a former Canadian foreign affairs minister and professor at the University of British Columbia. I had taken his class on human security in my final year of university, and he had also spoken at the UN conference. Now president of the University of Winnipeg, Axworthy sent a press release out to all the universities in Canada urging them to encourage their students to sign the petition and voice their discontent in any way they could.

While I was making speeches from one coast of North America to the other, calling for Nazanin's release, Mina was giving similar talks in Europe. Some of these speeches involved the women she was directly helping in Iranian prisons, including Shahla Jahed. Jahed, I learned, had been convicted in 2004 of killing Laleh Saharkhizan, the wife of the famous football player Nasser Mohammadkhani. At the time of the murder, Jahed was his temporary wife—in Iran, a married or single man and an unmarried woman are permitted to have a "temporary marriage," or *sigheh*, for various reasons. The duration of these marriages can range from one minute to forever and is determined at the onset of the agreement. My mother is convinced that such laws were put in place as a way to legalize prostitution and sex outside marriage, particularly for the mullahs who interpret sharia law to their own benefit.

News outlets across Iran published and broadcast stories on Jahed because she herself was a fairly well-known television personality. Mina had launched a campaign similar to the one we had launched together for Nazanin. However, Mina was finding it difficult to get media attention in Europe for Jahed and her other cases. As I came to discover, human rights violations in Iran weren't at the forefront of Europe's dealings with Iran. Many European Union nations were trading with Iran, primarily for oil, but also for other commodities. And it was alleged that the Iranian government was using the telecommunications technology it was buying from the West to spy on its own people.

It seemed to me that many countries, those in Europe among them, said that they were concerned with Iran's human rights violations and the death penalty being imposed on innocent people, including children. But in reality, economic self-interest appeared to come first. It all came down to profit. Nonetheless, we persevered.

Then one day my optimism disappeared. As soon as I picked up the telephone I could hear the distress in Mina's voice. "Nazanin is being moved to Evin Prison," she said in a sombre, defeated tone. "I know because her file has been sent to Tehran, which almost always means they are about to execute the person. We didn't move fast enough."

"Or we moved too fast," I gasped.

We both became quiet, for the latter seemed most likely. Mina and I had deliberately not approached the US government requesting that it lobby Iran to set Nazanin free. American pressure, we felt, might make Iranian authorities execute Nazanin sooner rather than later. It would be the regime's way of saying that it doesn't bow to anyone. But while the United States had been left out of our campaign, other international politicians and high-ranking diplomats were involved.

"I've gone too far." I started sobbing.

Mina tried to calm me and said to not lose hope. "Let's get more information before jumping to any conclusions," she urged.

When I told James the news, he said that he had been afraid of this. "You have to be prepared for the best- and worst-case scenarios. If Nazanin ends up being executed, you cannot shoulder the blame. I am afraid for your psychological health," he said, putting a comforting arm around me. "You have to look after yourself or else you won't be good to anyone. I miss you. I feel like you are hardly here anymore, even when you are by my side. This campaign has completely consumed you."

James, who was my rock and constantly looking out for my best interests—never mind being a great financial support during the campaign—was right. I'd been working on the campaign from morning until night, and I barely paid attention to anything else. My friends became used to my declining their invitations to go out and, eventually, they stopped calling me altogether.

On the odd night that I did accept an invitation to a friend's birthday or a dinner, I would try to celebrate, but I didn't enjoy my time. Try as I might, my mind inevitably ended up back on the campaign and I always left the event early. I felt an overwhelming sense of guilt: guilt that I was doing the wrong thing by taking on Nazanin Fatehi's cause; guilt that I led a privileged life compared with hers; guilt that she was where she was; guilt that I was letting everyone, including my loved ones, down. Sometimes I curled up in the fetal position and just cried and cried. When James saw me like this, he would remind me of the saying that had moved me so much when I was in China: "Be not afraid of growing slowly. Be afraid of standing still."

Despite James's comforting words, after Mina's unsettling phone call I couldn't sleep for many nights. My mind was in a state of turmoil, filled with thoughts that I had sent Nazanin to a premature death. In the mornings I would throw up—mostly water, for I wasn't eating. For the next little while, I spent my days focusing on the campaign so intently that I forgot all about nourishing myself, unless James or my family put a plate of food down in front of me.

I decided I was going to be as optimistic as I could, despite the overwhelming grief I felt over the news of Nazanin's file being sent to Tehran, which might mean we were too late. I sent a letter to Kofi Annan, at the time the secretary-general of the United Nations, requesting an appointment with him in order to deliver the petition, which within three months had received over 130,000 signatures.

I prayed, as my mother recommended, and, like magic, little miracles started to occur. What I found when I surrendered to a higher power was that the people I needed most appeared when I needed them.

Liberal MP Belinda Stronach and Amir Rouhani, the Iranian-Canadian assistant to Conservative MP Royal Galipeau, had each contacted me personally after seeing me talking about Nazanin on CTV and lent their support. "I can set up a press conference," said Stronach.

I told Rouhani about the offer, and he thought it was a good idea but cautioned me to have it in a neutral place. "My advice to you," he said, "is focus on human rights and be non-partisan. Have your news conference somewhere that no party can claim the issue for its own. Welcome to Parliament Hill," he said wryly. Everything, like in beauty pageants, is about politics.

So I did just that. On a balmy June day, I arrived in Ottawa for meetings with various members of Parliament, including Dan McTeague. McTeague offered me advice on campaigning that he had picked up while petitioning for the release of William Sampson, a Canadian who had been wrongly accused, imprisoned and tortured in Saudi Arabia. Following the meetings I gave a news conference in the foyer of the House of Commons. Representatives from all four main political parties were present—Stronach, Galipeau, a representative of Alexa McDonough for the New Democratic Party and Caroline St-Hilaire for the Bloc Québécois. "I've never seen this before," Rouhani confided to me afterward. "All of the parties stood united in one cause. That is unprecedented since I've been on Parliament Hill."

Stronach said she wanted to do more. She recommended people for me to contact, including Michaëlle Jean, the governor general of Canada, who could speak about the case in diplomatic circles. I told her about the lawyer and his need for a retainer to take on the case, and she immediately agreed to cover his fees.

Everywhere I went, an angel seemed to appear to help me, including Stronach's friend Senator Rod Zimmer, who tried to open a Canadian trust fund in Nazanin's name. Campaigns cost money, after all, and my family and I were paying for much of it out of our own pockets, including the costs of air travel, money sent to Iran to help Nazanin and her family, and even phone calls, which to Iran are pricey. However, the institution Zimmer was dealing with, one of the country's top banks, delayed activating the trust, saying there were administrative glitches—until he marched down to the main office in Ottawa and demanded an explanation. It turned out that the bank was under restrictions in how it dealt with accounts related to Iran. Many of the cheque donations I received were not cashed because of this delay, and by the time the trust was open, the cheques had expired.

However, almost at the same time the trust fund was opened in July, Abdolsamad Khorramshahi contacted me to tell me not to send any money. Nazanin Fatehi and her case had garnered too much media attention in Iran and around the world. He feared for his own safety and that judges might rule against his other clients as punishment if he took on Nazanin's cause. I was left without a lawyer and started to panic, not knowing how much time we had left.

CHAPTER 24

NAZANIN FATEHI

June 2006, Rajai Shahr Prison, Karaj, Iran

―――――――――

Nazanin fell in step behind the guard escorting her back to her cell from solitary confinement. Her feet dragged and felt heavy, as if she were wearing the oversized slippers her mother had worn when her feet had swelled while pregnant. Her arms didn't sway, her head kept falling to the side and, every so often, a muscle in her leg or arm twitched.

The greyness of the prison struck her hard. There was little light other than that from the dull fluorescent tubes that hung from the ceilings. She tried covering her ears to block out the clacking of the guard's boots on the hard floor but her arms felt too lifeless and heavy to lift.

Once back in her cell, Nazanin stared at Fatemeh, who held her arms out to embrace her. But Nazanin turned away. She felt undeserving of the gesture, preferring to be alone in her sunken state. Her fate had been sealed. She dropped her things onto the bed. Fatemeh, understanding that Nazanin wanted to be alone, left.

Nazanin rummaged through her belongings, looking for anything sharp with which she could harm herself. Coming up empty-handed, she headed to the washroom. As she rounded the corner to the shower stalls, she bumped into four young women she had never spoken to before and whom in fact she tried to avoid for fear they would harm her. They were sprawled on the floor, tattooing themselves with needles that family members had smuggled in for them and blue ink they drained from ballpoint pens purchased at the prison store.

"So Fatemeh's little plaything has come to join us," one of the women purred when she saw Nazanin. The woman didn't get up. Her movements were slow, like a waking cat, still sedated from the orange pills the guards had passed out the evening before.

"You can do whatever you want with me," Nazanin said, closing her eyes and lifting her arms up over her head. "I want to die anyway. So kill me, before the guards do."

"Silly girl," said the woman. The others laughed. "We don't want to kill you, we want you to be our friend, except Fatemeh and those Kurdish troublemakers you hang out with won't let you near us."

"They're not troublemakers," Nazanin said, sitting down on the floor beside the women.

"Right," said the woman, rolling her eyes. "I guess they told you the story of how they keep getting thrown in prison for shoplifting. Such an innocent girl you are, *azizam*. They live in the mountains and come into Tehran to spy on the regime. Are you one of them? Can we trust you with our secrets?"

"Can I have a tattoo?" Nazanin said. Now, if they tried to kill her, she welcomed the attack, for it would end her suffering on earth.

"I thought you were too good for such things. I am impressed," the woman replied, three ballpoint pens in one hand and the needle she had just used to tattoo another woman in the other. "What do you want me to do, a design? Some words?"

Nazanin watched as the woman drained the ink into the needle and held it up to the light.

"I want a sun and the shape of the moon on each of my hands," Nazanin said.

Nazanin clenched her teeth in pain as she felt the needle dig its way into her skin. She closed her eyes and leaned back against the wall. She could hear the other women collecting their things and shuffling about. Soon Nazanin could sense that it was just her and the tattooer left. When Nazanin finally opened her eyes, she saw that her hands were covered in blood mixed with ink.

"Don't worry," said the woman as she wrapped damp, blood-soiled cloths around Nazanin's hands. "The blood will wash away and you will see your tattoos."

The woman then leapt up and left. Nazanin was alone. She listened to the water dripping from the taps. She looked at the floor littered with ballpoint pens, blood, and blue and black ink. Then she saw that the woman had forgotten one of the needles. Nazanin picked it up. She drained the ink of a ballpoint pen into the stem of the needle like the woman had done and began writing on her right arm, gripping the needle between her teeth, as her left hand was too sore. *"Bawbakht"* she wanted to write. But she had only the strength to write the first three letters: *Baw*.

FATEMEH BEGAN TO CRY when she saw Nazanin's bloodied hands and arm. "How could you do this!" she exclaimed, as she guided Nazanin to the bed and had her lie down. Fatemeh patted the tattoo wounds with a damp cloth and then wrapped Nazanin's arms in a headscarf she had torn into strips.

"Nazanin, I have news," Fatemeh said. "Mrs. Mohammadi reached your mother. Both your mother and father are coming to see you today."

"Oh no," Nazanin gasped. "I look terrible," she said, holding up her arms. "My father will believe I am a bad girl when he sees these tattoos."

"Come on, we have a few hours," Fatemeh said. "You can wash from head to toe and then put on the best dress we can find on the ward."

"What is the worst thing that has ever happened to you?" Nazanin asked out of the blue.

"Being separated from my children," Fatemeh replied. "That

day I found myself in prison was the worst day of my life. I think of my daughters every day." Fatemeh sat down on the bed.

"No," Fatemeh continued after a pause. "The worst day of my life was moving in with that drug addict of a man who tried to rape my daughter.

As Fatemeh sobbed, Nazanin rocked her and whispered in her ear. "Someone once told me that when it is darkest, we can see the brightest light. Tell me about your brightest stars."

"My children—and meeting you," Fatemeh said, choking on her tears. "You have become my daughter too, and my life protecting you in Rajai Shahr has been so good for me. My service was for you, so you can know how to be an angel to someone else one day. Promise me, Nazanin, promise me that when you get out of prison, if you ever see a woman in need, you will help her in whatever way you can. Help her for me and for all the angels that have touched your life."

"Like Somayeh?" Nazanin asked, smiling weakly.

"Like you did for Somayeh. And don't you worry, *azizam*. If that woman is also like Somayeh and doesn't appreciate your help, one day she might. But every waking hour, the greater forces of this universe will know and love you, for through your service to another person, you are being a messenger of God and that, my sweet dear, is the purpose of living."

"I am going to Evin to meet my death," Nazanin said. "I won't have much time left to help others."

NAZANIN SAT ACROSS from her parents, her eyes lowered, the ends of her headscarf wrapped around her hands to conceal the bandages over her tattoos. She was wearing a clean brown dress of Jwan's and her manteau.

Habib's hair was now dyed a bright copper colour, his cheeks sunken and his skin even more yellow than when she had last seen him a year earlier. His front teeth were chipped. Maryam had gained weight. Her face was tanned and shiny. She complained of pain in her lungs and breathed heavily. Nazanin's siblings, all except for Hojat, were also there, sitting quietly beside their parents.

"Everyone in Iran knows about you," Habib began.

"Everyone in the world does too," Maryam added, her voice raspy. "And everyone believes you."

"But you don't," Nazanin said, looking down.

"I do too," Habib said slowly. "I am ashamed that I thought more about our family honour than you. I am not a good father."

Nazanin sheepishly looked up into first her mother's and then her father's eyes. "You only believe me now that everyone else does," she said slowly.

"No," Maryam broke down and wailed, banging her fleshy arms on the table between them.

Habib shook his head. "No. No, that is not true," he said, his voice pleading for Nazanin to trust him.

"My file has been sent to Tehran. I am being sent to Evin Prison," Nazanin said matter-of-factly. "I am being sent there to be executed. That's what they do. They send the girls away when they want to kill them. In the early hours of the morning, the guards will come and get me. I will stay for a day in a small room, with a copy of the Qur'an. I will be told to read it, despite it being in Arabic, and repent all my sins so I may enter paradise."

"Nazanin, it is not too late," Maryam moaned. "You have so many people on your side. These women in Canada and Germany who called me after getting the number from your friend's daughter Zahra, they have told me about other women like you, sentenced to death, who have been freed. You'll be one of them. I know it. I feel it in my bones."

As her mother continued to wail, Nazanin shushed for her to be quiet. "All I want is for you to keep coming to see me," she said to her father. Nazanin reached across the table and took her mother's hand. Maryam's eyes grew wide when she saw Nazanin's bandages, but Nazanin no longer cared. "If I die," Nazanin said, "I want to be buried next to Leila." She then reached into her dress and pulled out some pieces of paper, which she divided between her parents and siblings, saying, "Each of you, hide these papers on you somewhere so the guards won't see them on your way out." Nazanin reached across the table to again hold her mother's hand. "I had a friend in Sanandaj—Hana. Do you remember her?"

"I do," Maryam said.

"Go to her and give her all the pieces of paper I have just given you. She taught me to read, and she taught me to believe in stories."

"What is written on this?" Habib asked, opening up one of the pieces of crinkled paper.

"It is my story," Nazanin said softly, encouraging her father to close the paper and not read it. "I've given some of this to Fatemeh to give to her daughter. But this is all of my story. Hana must read it first, and then she can decide what to do with it."

The guard motioned that the visiting time was up: Nazanin's parents and siblings had to leave. As they got up, Nazanin banged her head against the table and starting moaning. "Don't leave. Don't leave me. Please don't leave me," she at first mumbled and then screamed.

Maryam turned with tears in her eyes and started to go to her daughter. But the guard blocked her and ordered her to leave immediately.

CHAPTER 25

NAZANIN AFSHIN-JAM

June to December 2006, Vancouver, New York, Geneva

⸻

"Nazanin, are you sitting down?" Mina asked during one of our by then daily conversations in late June. I could hear the enthusiasm in her voice and gripped the kitchen chair as I asked her to continue.

"I just got off the telephone to Iran. The Iranian head of judiciary announced this morning that Nazanin's execution has been stayed. The newspaper *Hamshahri* reported that the Supreme Court ordered a retrial."

"Is she free?" I gasped.

"No, but Nazanin, this is because of our efforts. All the pressure—it worked. She is still moving to Evin, but it is not for an execution. And I have more news. I found new lawyers for Nazanin. Shadi Sadr, a well-known feminist and lawyer with the Network of Volunteer Lawyers in Tehran, and another young lawyer who works with her. His name is Mohammad Mostafaei. He met with Nazanin at Rajai Shahr Prison a while ago. He's already told Nazanin that he would take on her case if she got a retrial, which she just has. Both Sadr and Mostafaei will represent Nazanin in the next trial. Keep up the pressure, Nazanin. Iran may be silenced on its human rights abuses against children—for the very first time."

Nazanin may have got a retrial but she was still at risk of execution, for the judges at the second trial could easily decide on that same fate. There was still much more I needed to do to secure her release.

My hand shook as I held the letter from the French government. In a matter of only a few months, after my many interviews and letters to various diplomats and members of Parliament, numerous countries in the Western world had pledged their support for Nazanin. The translation of the letter from France echoed what so many others had also said: In close cooperation with the other member countries of the European Union, the French government was monitoring very closely Nazanin's situation, as well as the general situation about the death penalty in Iran. The European Union had already and would again ask for clemency for Nazanin from the Iranian authorities. Vincent had also received an official response in support of Nazanin Fatehi and the campaign from the president of Senegal, Abdoulaye Wade, whom he had written.

My first conversation with Shadi Sadr took me aback.

"Why are you doing this campaign?" she inquired dryly after asking me a series of probing questions designed, it seemed to me, to test my motives for taking on the case.

I suspected I knew why she'd done this. An Iranian-American woman claiming to be a defender of human rights was writing blogs under various pseudonyms in an attempt to discredit me and my efforts, saying that I was just a "stupid beauty queen" who was helping Nazanin Fatehi for my own fame and fortune. This woman contacted certain human rights activists, trying to befriend them and urging them not to work with me. These human rights activists eventually contacted me and told me what was going on.

By the end of my first conversation with Sadr, I wasn't sure what she thought of me, but I did trust that she would do the best she could to help Nazanin. Mostafaei, on the other hand, was so welcoming I wanted to melt, especially given all the stress I had been holding inside me. He told me he had visited Nazanin in prison now two times and reported that she was in good spirits. She was growing more and more optimistic of her chance of freedom knowing that some of the most powerful countries in the world were behind her. "But Nazanin is not doing well in prison," he told me. "She has been in some fights. She's been in solitary confinement."

Mostafaei updated me on the case, explaining that the Supreme Court had ordered a retrial but that it didn't have to explain why. It did stipulate that it wanted all the witnesses from the first trial to reappear. "The witnesses have all moved, Nazanin. And not only do they no longer live at the addresses we have for them, but their cell-phone numbers have changed. I have to find them."

"Is that normal to move like that . . . to simply disappear?"

"No. But these are not upstanding young men," Mostafaei told me. I could hear the despair in his voice. "They are rough, and they get into many fights in their neighbourhood. I think they lied. Having gone through the court documents, things don't read right. I have a suspicion they were all friends—and that they had a coordinated plan to carry out mischief and get the two girls inside the abandoned house."

"Then why did the judges believe them so readily?"

"Because it is Iran: sometimes officials put false information into files, add things, make up interviews, to support cases. And besides, a man's life and testimony are worth twice as much as a woman's."

SHADI SADR HAD VISITED Nazanin's family and planned to discuss in her presentation to the court the lack of support for runaway girls in Iran and the stigma society places on them. She told Mostafaei she planned to focus on the sexual abuse Nazanin had suffered prior to the attack in the field and the fact that she was trying to protect her fourteen-year-old niece from the same fate. "One of the judges from the first trial had said that Nazanin couldn't use protecting her honour as a reason for self-defence. His exact words were: 'A girl like her cannot defend herself with the defence of honour because, given the medical records indicating she was not a virgin, she has no chastity and nothing to protect . . . You cannot defend your honour when your honour has already been taken away.'" Even for Sadr, who had seen and heard it all and had built an armour around her emotions, the court's decision was shocking.

A month later, Mostafaei called to tell me that Nazanin was becoming increasingly nervous. "She knows that if the retrial fails, her death is imminent," he said. "I tried to reassure her that she has a chance of being set free. I found the witnesses by pounding the pavement and going door to door asking neighbours and relatives about the young men's whereabouts until I finally found them. I am determined to see Nazanin walk out of that prison—not carried out wrapped in a burial shroud."

After the Ottawa press conference, I flew with Mina to New York City. Mina's friend at the United Nations, Sylvia Hordosch, had arranged for us to talk with Rachel Mayanja, the UN secretary-general's special adviser on gender issues and advancement of women. I was excited but nervous as I went through Security at the UN office across the street from the main complex. I smoothed down my beige pantsuit and waited as the guards checked my purse. They then asked me what was in the canvas suitcase I was towing. "It's full of a printed petition," I said proudly. "We are giving it to the special adviser on gender issues and advancement of women. It is signed by nearly 200,000 people, all asking that a young woman, sentenced to death in Iran, be released from prison."

The guards let us proceed to Mayanja's office. Just before we reached the elevators, Mina pulled me aside. "Nazanin, I think this is one of the most important campaigns ever in Iranian history," she said quietly as UN personnel walked past us. "I've been pushing for years to get the European Union, the United Nations and the media to acknowledge the stoning of women in Iran and the oppression of women under current Iranian laws, but the response has never been quite like this. In Nazanin's case, we are seeing action, unprecedented action. We are playing chess with the government of Iran. And this meeting, if successful, is like moving a rook close to their queen."

I had no doubt that Mayanja would help us. She was from

Uganda, a nation that has seen a great deal of oppression of women and girls. But as soon as I met her, I sensed the meeting wouldn't go as I had predicted. Her handshake was weak and, after directing Mina and me to take a seat on the beige leather couch, she said, "Leave your suitcase at the door."

"It is the petition," I replied enthusiastically.

"It's okay. Leave it at the door," she repeated.

I was distraught. I had had the online petition printed out, having promised the signatories that I would hand-deliver it to the United Nations.

Mina and I sat down across from Mayanja, and I recounted Nazanin's story and told her about the petition. I breathed a sigh of relief when Mayanja commended us on our efforts. But then she looked me in the eye and said that there was nothing she could do. She stood up to indicate that the meeting was over.

"But I promised the people who signed that I would hand-deliver the petition," I pleaded.

Mayanja shook her head and told me again that her office couldn't help us, and to try instead with the Office of the High Commissioner for Human Rights.

"Why?" I implored. "We've been here for only five minutes. Of all people, I would have thought you would understand and help. You are, after all, the special adviser on gender issues and advancement of women."

"Sorry," Mayanja said, making her way to the door to show us out.

Back out in the hallway, I slumped onto the couch beside Sylvia, who had been waiting for our meeting to finish, and began to cry. Mina tried to console me, saying that Mayanja's response was not the end of the world, but I was fraught with emotion rooted in my desperate desire to see Nazanin free. I felt overwhelmed by fatigue, having spent my days from about 7 a.m., when I would call Mina, to well past midnight campaigning for Nazanin's release. I had flown in from Vancouver, and Mina from Cologne, her flight sponsored by James. *What now? This was the top place to go.*

Sylvia brought me a glass of water and tissues, while Mina and I sat side by side on the couch, my suitcase at my feet. At one point I started hyperventilating, and I felt like I was going to be sick to my stomach. I was hunched over, my head down, when I heard a female voice say, "I'll call my friend in the Office of the High Commissioner for Human Rights."

I steadied my shaking hands and legs and waited as the woman made the phone call from an office down the hallway. When she returned, she was beaming. "Go now," said the woman, whose name I never learned. "My friends are waiting for you."

MINA AND I SCURRIED across the busy Manhattan street and approached the security desk at the main United Nations building. Once we were through the X-ray machines, we ran past the displays and the tourists taking photographs to the elevator, barely taking in the panoramic view of the city's famous architecture as we went up. At the Office of the UN's High Commissioner for Human Rights, Goro Onojima, a human rights officer with warm, slim hands, took mine into his own. Craig Mokhiber, the deputy director of the office, was also there to greet us. After being ushered into Mokhiber's large office, I told the story of Nazanin's crime, imprisonment and sentence, and I sighed with relief when I saw the look of concern on their faces.

"We'll do what we can to help," Onojima said, startling me.

"You are being truthful with me?" I asked, tilting my head to the side, skeptical after my meeting with Mayanja. "The petition won't go in the garbage?"

"No," said Mokhiber. "We will send it all to the main office in Switzerland, to Louise Arbour, the high commissioner for human rights."

After our meeting finished, Sylvia escorted us out and wished us luck. "You know," Mina said, "it is very important that two Iranians from two different generations, with two vastly different perspectives on Iran, have united."

IN JULY I WAS BACK on a plane, this time on my way to Switzerland to verify that the boxes of petition signatures had indeed been delivered to the United Nations and that action was being taken. Louise Arbour had agreed to see me. The meeting had been arranged by Payam Akhavan, an Iranian-Canadian international human rights lawyer who had worked at The Hague as first legal adviser to the Prosecutor's Office during Slobodan Milosevic's trial at the International Criminal Tribunal for the former Yugoslavia; Arbour had been chief prosecutor. When I met him for the first time at the Forum of Young Global Leaders, which was being held in Vancouver, Akhavan had also introduced me to Irshad Manji, the founder of the Moral Courage Project. In another of the ser-endipitous events that constantly occurred throughout the campaign, Manji invited me to address her audience at the launch for her book *The Trouble with Islam Today: A Muslim's Call for Reform in Her Faith*.

I had been a bit nervous addressing the crowd in my hometown. I was even more nervous in Switzerland on my way to meet Arbour, a fellow Canadian and one of the most powerful women in the world. I was expecting, as I sat in a deserted restaurant in Geneva waiting for her, to meet a stoic woman with piercing eyes who could bring war criminals to their knees with just a few cutting questions. I was pleasantly surprised when a petite woman trotted in, shook my hand vigorously as she gave me a bright smile and then proceeded to make small talk with Akhavan about family life. Then, turning to the business at hand, she spoke about some of her cases. Both Arbour and Akhavan spoke so eloquently and with such enthusiasm and optimism that I became inspired. For the next hour over lunch we discussed the state of Iran's penal system, world politics and human rights.

Arbour confirmed that the boxes of petition had arrived at her office and that she was writing letters and corresponding with senior politicians and lawmakers in Iran. "I cannot go into detail," she said, "but you should know that action is being taken on Nazanin Fatehi's case and that our office is doing all it can to get an execution reprieve—and help with the overall improvement of human rights in Iran."

MEANWHILE, BACK IN IRAN, Fatemeh was continuing to slip her daughter Zahra pieces of paper with messages from Nazanin to me and Mina. In one of these letters, she wrote, "Do not help just this Nazanin, help all Nazanins." She then asked that we help not only her but all the women in prison, including Kobra Rahmanpour.

Rahmanpour was only twenty-two and, when I received Nazanin's plea, had only ten days before she was scheduled to be executed. Rahmanpour had been convicted of killing her mother-in-law. But she, like Nazanin, always claimed the action was done in self-defence. Because of her family's extreme poverty, Rahmanpour had been forced to marry a man forty-three years older than her. When she moved into his home, he beat her. One time, he was arrested for physically and sexually assaulting her but was set free shortly afterward. Her husband's mother was physically abusive too. On the day Rahmanpour killed her, her mother-in-law had been trying to attack her with a kitchen knife. A medical examiner testified at Rahmanpour's trial that her hand wounds indicated that she was grabbing the knife from her mother-in-law. Nonetheless, she was found guilty.

I spoke at a rally for Rahmanpour in September in North Vancouver, organized by Women's Liberation–Iran. It was one of several rallies held across North America, including protests in London, New York and Los Angeles, the latter attended by Nazanin Boniadi, an Iranian-American Hollywood actress.

It was my first appearance at a public rally and I was disappointed that the couple of dozen people who trickled their way in and out were mostly non-Persians. I expected, given that the event had been advertised by the press, that the Vancouver Iranian community, which numbers in the tens of thousands, would come out in force.

"Where is everybody?" I asked two of the organizers.

"Once Iranians move to the West, it seems like they forget, or they purposely try to block out, the pains of the past," one replied.

"Many get so wrapped up in their consumer-driven lives here that they seem to concentrate more on what Louis Vuitton or Gucci wants to sell them next rather than on helping those still struggling in their homeland," the other exclaimed. "The West makes them too comfortable in their new surroundings."

In my speech, a knot still in my throat from my surprise at so few Iranians out raising awareness of the plight of Rahmanpour and other women on death row in Iran, I said, "We can no longer turn a blind eye to human rights violations. If we do, that in itself is a crime against humanity."

"I feel that the only way we can solve our problems in Iran is through the younger generation, who, hopefully, can be reached before they become tainted with their parents' ideologies and political and party alignments," I said to my father during the rally. He was there with my entire family, including my two-year-old niece, who wore a placard twice the size of her small frame with "Free KOBRA" written on the front. "The youth and their energy and activism both in Iran and in the diaspora abroad are the future," I said, looking at her.

"I agree," my father replied. "You know, Nini, 70 percent of Iran's population is under the age of thirty. The youth are more than the future. They are also the present."

A couple weeks later, I was the keynote speaker at another rally, this one in Berlin and organized by Amnesty International against child executions. Most of the participants were Germans, rather than members of the large Iranian community that is found in Germany. I was becoming more and more disheartened, particularly with the Iranian dissident communities, as I began to see that all the groups were fighting against each other and not directly against the common enemy: the regime in Iran.

Another incident involving someone who I believe should have been offering unconditional support to free Nazanin occurred around the same time. This woman, who has her own human rights organization, contacted me in an attempt to discourage me from having any form of relationship with Mina, and wanting me to work with her instead. She said that Mina's political ties with the Worker-communist Party of Iran would taint my efforts.

"I don't care what political faction people are with," I told the woman, "as long as they have the common goal of advancing humanity."

Not long after that, the woman sent a friend of hers in Iran to speak to Nazanin's mother, relaying the same message she had given to me but this time urging Maryam to cut off ties not just with Mina but with me also. Fortunately, Mina and I had formed close ties with the Fatehi family. Maryam almost reiterated what I had told the woman: "It doesn't matter what anyone believes politically if their heart is good and they want to help."

I was quickly learning that the horrible stories I had read in newspapers of the backstabbing that goes on in Fortune 500 companies, all in the pursuit of accolades and money, also occurs among human rights groups and charities. At one point, I thought of Bam, my conversation with Stephan Hachemi and my realization that maybe he was right. What I was now experiencing—the unprofessionalism and dishonesty among people and within groups I expected to be genuine and philanthropic—stunned me and left me feeling defeated.

What saddened me most was that these groups and individuals had lost sight of the real goal, what was probably their motivation for getting involved in this kind of work in the first place. Now what I was seeing was just plain ego: a need to be recognized, to be the first to send a petition to raise awareness of a human rights issue or to deliver aid, to be called a saviour, to collect the most money.

To make matters worse, one day a couple of Iranian youths leapt out of a BMW and accosted me as I walked down a Vancouver street. In a thick Persian accent, one said to me, "It's good you are concentrating on helping human rights, but do you have to expose it to the world and bring shame on our country? You should keep it to yourself instead of airing the dirty laundry to the world." I suspected they were the sons of regime supporters, new immigrants to Canada, many of whom had invested heavily in several Western countries the money they had taken from Iran's public coffers.

I was also getting emails from Islamists, and people confronted me after talks, criticizing me for focusing solely on execution and children in Iran. "What about the children in Palestine?" some of the most vocal critics asked. The attacks became so aggressive that I started to respond with, "What about the child soldiers in Africa? The children trafficked for sex and forced labour in India? What about the Taliban pouring acid on the faces of young schoolgirls in Afghanistan? What about the persecution of Uighurs and Falun Gong practitioners in China? I can't take on every issue. I wish I could. I wish I could help everyone, but I am only one person. I encourage you to start your own NGO and speak publicly on the issues that concern you most."

A few times I sat alone in the dark of my room in the middle of the night and debated quitting. I wondered if I was doing more harm than good by being involved in Nazanin's case. And was I strong enough to bear the assaults? I would think of Nazanin, and Mina's calls to say she had been in solitary confinement or that someone in her cell wing had committed suicide. I would reread Nazanin's words, her selfless urging for me to help not just her but others also.

In these dark moments, I also thought of the people who were supporting me and the campaign, always the first to jump to write a letter or contact a newspaper, many of whom had no prior experience in human rights campaigning. Other than my family and James, four people stood out the most: Kristian Hvesser, David Etebari, Vincent, and Donna Greene. Kristian, in Scandinavia, had launched a website that posted updates on Nazanin's case and the campaign. David, in Los Angeles, had among other things created and maintained a myspace page for Nazanin. Vincent, in Paris, had written to politicians and journalists and helped with translations. And Donna, in Australia, was spreading the word through other social networking sites around the world. Social networking sites had a profound impact in spreading awareness especially among youth. Hundreds of people had used Nazanin Fatehi's photo as their profile picture on their myspace pages for an entire month. Some had written poems, drawn pictures of her and left encouraging messages on her page, anticipating that one day she herself would be able to read the messages. The Iranian-American rap group Persian Princes composed a song, with lyrics in both Persian and English, called "Nazanin." All the support was very encouraging.

But then I thought of the protestors outside the United Nations offices in Tehran who came out the day after our rally in Vancouver to demand that the executions of several female prisoners, including Rahmanpour and Nazanin, be permanently stayed and that the inmates receive fair trials. Ten of these protestors were detained by police.

One night when I was feeling really low, I thought of my mother and her Rumi quote: "Your task is not to seek love, but merely to seek and find all the barriers within yourself that you have built against it."

Okay, I said to myself, *I'll tear down all these doubts I have, my sensitivities about being attacked. I will carry on, for Nazanin.*

One thing I knew from my experience both as a model and in dealing with the press throughout Nazanin's campaign is that a photograph tells a thousand words . . . and a motion picture is worth a million. Mina and I felt we needed to show the world in video who Nazanin was and what she faced both in prison and, as a girl, living in Iran. The rule of law under the Islamic regime of Iran is nothing like that in Western countries. Judges are allowed to rule on *elm-e ghazi*, which translates to "divine knowledge of the judge." Simply put, a judge is not even obliged to open a case file to sentence someone to prison or condemn him or her to death. If the judge has the "feeling" that God is telling him that the person before him is guilty, then that person is considered guilty.

In Iran, only men are allowed to become judges; women are

considered to be too irrational, emotional and unfit to make the difficult decisions that need to be made. Also, not all judges there have the same legal training as judges elsewhere. They simply need to be fluent in Islamic laws and teachings—some of which date back a thousand years. Some judges in Iran are completely illiterate and therefore cannot even read court documents. It is thus not surprising that these mullahs and religious zealots in Iran do not recognize international laws.

It is true that Iran had signed and ratified the United Nations' International Covenant on Civil and Political Rights, as well as the Convention on the Rights of the Child, which forbids the execution of children for crimes committed under the age of eighteen. However, many judges in Iran claim that the Universal Declaration of Human Rights is not "universal" but a creation of the West only. Rather, their sharia laws are based on their misguided interpretations of the Qur'an. One of the most glaring misinterpretations is that boys are considered adults at age fifteen and girls at age nine, and thus responsible, even punishable by death, for their actions under the country's criminal code. This contradicts its civil law, which sets the legal age for voting and acquiring a passport or driver's licence at eighteen for both males and females.

Furthermore, under Iran's sharia law, a female life is worth only half the life of a male. This means that Nazanin's testimony at court was worth only half of that of a male witness. Had the situation been reversed, had Yousef stabbed Nazanin and she had died, he likely would have not have received a death sentence because he would have been considered to have taken only half a life.

Had Nazanin allowed the rape to take place, she could have still been charged with "acts incompatible with chastity" and been given one hundred lashes. Had Nazanin been married, she would have been charged with adultery and sentenced to death by stoning.

I wanted to show through Nazanin's own life story how all of this plays out in the life of an innocent girl. And as so often happened in the campaign, almost immediately after I told my family and James my plan of making a documentary film, another angel appeared, this time in the guise of a passionate Iranian-Canadian named Hossein Martin Fazeli. At one point during my interview with him for a Persian newspaper called *Shahrvand BC*, I said I wanted to make a documentary film.

"I'll help you," he had replied. "I am an independent film director."

"It's nearing Christmas," I had said. "We have only a month to make the film, which, with the holidays approaching, means we will have to work eighteen-hour days every day of the week."

"I'm in," he had said matter-of-factly. "Actually, I wanted to interview you hoping to have the opportunity to talk about this, as I would like to do a film on Nazanin with you."

Fazeli and I sat down with Peter and explained our idea. With my sister's constant pleas to Peter throughout the campaign to help in any way he could, he could not refuse. She had advocated on my behalf my entire life and she wasn't going to fall short here, either. I would hear her talking, for instance, around Peter's office about Nazanin Fatehi, to whoever would listen. At one point, Peter said to me, "This is a great cause, I support you, but you realize that my biggest motivation for helping you is to make Naz happy." And so, thanks to my sister's persistence, Peter convinced Calvin Ayre to fund the documentary, which we considered the last piece of the campaign before Nazanin's big trial. Peter, with Calvin's blessing, had mobilized the Bodog Music offices in Vancouver, Toronto, London, Berlin and New York to issue my press releases for the Save Nazanin campaign, and when I visited these cities for a rally or speech, they would organize media and help in any way they could with organizing the events.

Over the next week, we auditioned actors to re-enact certain scenes from Nazanin's life, including the attempted rape. One of Fazeli's co-workers managed to find and hire a crew in Iran to interview Nazanin's mother and other family members. During their visit, Nazanin happened to call the Turkish neighbour's house, looking for her mother. Their conversation was caught on tape, over the speakerphone. Nazanin cried, pleaded her innocence and asked why no one believed her. She said she missed her family and wanted to go home.

When I heard the tape, my body chilled. It was the first time I had heard her voice. It was young, soft and desperate.

Not long after our film was completed, I heard that women and human rights activists in Iran had launched a campaign called One Million Signatures for the Repeal of Discriminatory Laws. The goal was to get one million people to sign the petition demanding changes to laws like that which saw Nazanin sentenced to death. Protests calling for the release of Nazanin, Fatemeh, Kobra Rahmanpour, Shahla Jahed and others began to take place in Tehran. Many of the protestors were imprisoned. But as soon as they were released, they were back out on the streets demanding change.

Their courage and dedication inspired me at a time when I desperately needed to be inspired. I have always believed that it will not be one person who will change the world but many, infused with the spirit of Christ, Mahatma Gandhi, Joan of Arc, Nelson Mandela, Aung San Suu Kyi, Wangari Maathai, Catherine Hamlin—and all the men and women, of both the modern day and the past, who have helped improve the dignity and honour of humanity. As Margaret Mead said, "Never doubt that a small group of thoughtful, committed citizens can change the world. Indeed, it is the only thing that ever has."

CHAPTER 26

NAZANIN FATEHI

September 2006 to January 2007, Tehran, Iran

———

Nazanin languished in Rajai Shahr Prison for many months believing she would move to Evin for her execution. It was only on the day she moved, in mid-September, that she was given the news that this was not the case. "You're being moved to Evin because they need you to sew," Mrs. Mohammadi told Nazanin, who was sitting on the bed, folding her clothes and packing them in black plastic bags. "You are not being executed, at least not yet," she continued in a monotone voice. "You need something to do, something to put your mind on. Every second minute you are trying to kill yourself, so we'll put you to work instead."

Nazanin spent much of her first week at Evin hiding in her bed, too fearful to emerge in case she met the prison's version of Mandana or Katrin waiting to initiate her in a hazing ritual. But Evin seemed, from the start, very different for Nazanin. The prisoners, for one, kept to themselves. Several of the cots in her cell were never occupied by the same woman for more than two nights in a row. Nazanin soon discovered that many of the prisoners in Evin were drug addicts, thrown behind bars to come off drugs. Some of the women were prostitutes.

On the eighth day, Nazanin dragged herself out of bed shortly after the breakfast cart made its rounds. She shuffled her feet to the guards' office and banged the door with her fist, which was now healed from its tattooing wounds. A guard opened the door.

"I was brought from Rajai Shahr Prison to sew," Nazanin said. "When do I start?"

"Someone will come and get you when they are ready for you," the guard answered, slamming the door in Nazanin's face.

Nazanin turned slowly and saw that several inmates from other cells were standing close by and looking at her. Nazanin didn't move but her eyes darted from side to side as she tried to identify the lead woman, the one who was about to punch her in the face or take her clothes. One woman with dark, wavy, shoulder-length hair stepped forward. Her delicate movements reminded Nazanin of Leila. The woman stopped in front of Nazanin and started clapping, ever so quietly at first and then louder. The other women joined in.

Nazanin, thinking it was a trick, held her breath.

The woman sensed her fear and stopped. "Don't be frightened, *azizam*. We all know who you are."

Nazanin looked into the woman's gentle brown eyes and blushed. "I'm Shahla Jahed," she said, giving Nazanin a hug. "Mina is helping me too."

Nazanin didn't realize until that moment how much tension she had been holding inside her. She broke down and cried as Shahla led her back to her cell. "I miss Fatemeh," Nazanin sobbed. Shahla got her a glass of water and smoothed down her crumpled dress. "I was so afraid I was going to get beaten up when I moved here."

"You don't have to worry in Evin," Shahla replied. "No one is going to hurt you. Rajai Shahr is the bad prison, full of murderers and insane women the guards drug every night. The women in Evin are mostly harmless. There are many political prisoners here, and many hurting souls, like you, who have been hit hard by this regime that values their worth in terms of their chastity."

Nazanin smiled meekly. "I've heard about you too," she said, wiping her face dry of her tears.

"Isn't it sad that, to the world, Iran's most famous women are famous because they face the death penalty," Shahla said, laughing. "Instead of the country showcasing our incredibly talented and smart women in the sciences, arts and literature!" She started to sing the Iranian national anthem, then stopped and said, "*Azizam*, I will watch out for you while you are here."

Other inmates joined Shahla, sitting around Nazanin on her bed in a semicircle. They told her what they had read about her in the newspapers before being thrown in prison. Nazanin asked Shahla if she thought her death sentence would be overturned. Shahla opened her mouth to say yes, but Nazanin's innocent eyes made her stop. "Nazanin," Shahla said sombrely, "I cannot guarantee anything. Lots of people all over the world know about you, are writing about you and are petitioning for your release. But the Iranian regime listens to no one. You may end up right back here after this is all over."

A FEW DAYS LATER, a guard took Nazanin to a large room lined with desks on which sat sewing machines. She was told to sit in front of one and handed black fabric to sew into a dress. "But I don't know how to sew," Nazanin said, looking into the bloodshot eyes of the guard.

"Then why are you here?" demanded another woman, who wore the prison-issued floral headscarf and a black manteau.

"I assumed I would be taught how to sew when they brought me from Rajai Shahr to do work here. I didn't volunteer to come here—"

"I'm in charge of all the prisoners working here," said the woman in the headscarf. "But I am not here to teach. You will learn as you go. And they'll make sure that you don't step out of line," she said, pointing to the guards standing watch at the sides of the room.

Nazanin slipped into her chair and studied the woman sitting next to her. The woman's back was so hunched that her face nearly rested on the sewing machine. Wisps of grey hair spilled out from beneath her headscarf. But the elderly prisoner's fingers were nimble and she ran the machine like an expert.

When the woman caught Nazanin staring at her, she smiled.

"Do what I do," she whispered, putting her right foot on a pedal on the floor and holding a piece of fabric under the needle. The older woman then held up two pieces of fabric she wanted Nazanin to sew together and showed her where to place the fabric under the needle and how to work the pedal. The two worked like this for several hours. Every time Nazanin finished sewing a line, the woman showed her where to start next—until Nazanin's machine seized. The fabric rolled up into a tiny ball and black thread spilled out from the machine.

"On the side of the machine—that wheel there," her new friend pointed, "turn it in the opposite direction and try to get the fabric out."

Nazanin did what she was told and tugged gently at the fabric, but she didn't see that the needle was stuck in it. The needle broke, half of it remaining in the machine, the other half falling onto the table. "I've broken the needle," she whispered.

"Don't worry," the old woman said. "What's the value of a needle?"

"No," said the female prisoner who had claimed she was in charge. Nazanin jumped at the sound of her foreboding voice booming behind her. "This girl doesn't know what she is doing," the woman called out to the guards, who moved toward Nazanin. "She cannot work here." The woman pulled Nazanin to standing by the collar of her manteau. Nazanin fumbled with her headscarf, which had fallen loose, and then looked the woman in the eye.

"Please," she begged. "Give me another chance. I didn't leave Rajai Shahr to come here not to work."

"You are just a stupid girl," she growled. "Stupid girl."

Nazanin looked down, her face drawn, feeling as if her body were sinking into the tiles of the linoleum floor.

The woman turned away from Nazanin and started talking to one of the guards. Nazanin felt anger bubbling up inside her. Her face became hot and her hands clammy. She reached down and grabbed a wooden ruler, used for measuring fabric, and whipped it across the room.

The guards immediately moved toward Nazanin as the woman spun around and punched her in the eye. Nazanin hit her back and then crumpled to the ground. One of the guards picked her up and took her to solitary confinement, where she stayed for a few days.

But those days were worse than any she had spent at Rajai Shahr Prison. Not only did the insects crawl all over her as she lay in the darkened cell, with only a thin blanket to keep her warm, but there were also mice. When Nazanin was awake, they sensed her movements and did not come near. When she was asleep was a different matter. One time she woke to find a dead mouse underneath her. She had squished it in her sleep. Nazanin screamed and jumped up. A guard came but when she saw what had upset Nazanin, she told her not to worry. "Just throw it over with your leftover food," she said.

"Please, I am scared," Nazanin pleaded. "Give me a new blanket. The one I have has dead mouse in it." The guard said she would look into it. But she never came back.

"God," Nazanin whispered that night. "What did I do to deserve this? You know I am innocent, why am I in prison? Why do I have to suffer like this?"

A WEEK LATER, Nazanin, her eye still black from the punch she had taken, sat across from Mostafaei in one of the rooms reserved for prisoners' meetings with their lawyers. She kept her head lowered as Mostafaei swept his hand through his thick, dark hair and then studied her closely.

"What happened?" he eventually asked, his voice forceful. "You don't look good."

Nazanin explained that she had been transferred to Evin to work. "But I don't know how. And they won't teach me. I just lost it," she said, shaking her head but still not looking up.

"Okay," Mostafaei sighed. "Just try to stay out of trouble from now on, until we have a date for your retrial."

"I live in a cell now with angry women coming off drugs, who smoke these horrible-smelling cigarettes one after the other. My hair smells. My body is rotting from lack of food. And then there is my mind. I hear things . . . I see things . . . I feel I am going crazy," she said slowly.

"Remember what I said: I was once like you," Mostafaei said, leaning in and stretching his hands as close to Nazanin as he could without touching her. "I lived on the streets and was beaten and robbed. I too heard voices: every bad name I was ever called I would hear again and again in those moments at night when I was half-awake at night."

Nazanin looked up at the lawyer's delicate hands.

"I was saved because I had hope," he continued. "I fought my way to go to school, then university and then to become a lawyer. I fought those demons in my head, which were worse than anything people were telling me because those demons told me I couldn't succeed. But I fought, by working hard, both emotionally and physically, and I pulled myself up. Do you want out of here, Nazanin?" he asked in a loud voice that made Nazanin jump.

"Yes."

"Then believe. Fight those voices and images in your head. Hold on to the memories of whatever beauty has ever touched your life, even if it was just for a moment, and believe that you will have that again."

ON JANUARY 10, Nazanin was quiet as she sat in the back seat of the vehicle heading toward the courthouse. She closed her eyes and prayed to Khwa. *Please don't let me be hurt today. Let all be well.* They turned the corner into the courthouse grounds. There were film cameras outside and journalists snapping photographs. A woman pushed her face up against the vehicle's window. She grinned when she saw Nazanin and started shouting to those behind her, "She's here! She's here!"

The guard pushed Nazanin back away from the window and told

her not to look. But Nazanin refused to listen. She leaned forward again on her seat and stared at all the people there to support her.

Nazanin was taken into a room at the back of the courthouse and told to wait. She sat on a stiff metal chair, her hands cuffed in front of her. She watched the big clock on the wall. An hour passed, then another. Mostafaei and Sadr eventually emerged from another room, carrying bulging briefcases. Their faces were red. "There are too many people for the courtroom," Sadr explained, sitting down beside Nazanin. She wiped her glasses with a tissue and sighed. "They're making room in the auditorium. I hope we start soon, as it's getting late in the day. I don't want to have the trial postponed to another date."

While they were waiting to be taken to the auditorium, Sadr told Nazanin that Somayeh would not be in court—Nazanin had been hoping that she would show up. But Somayeh, Sadr told her, had disappeared after having spent three months in the juvenile home. No one, not even Nazanin's mother, knew where she had gone.

Nazanin could barely breathe. The fear that the trial wouldn't take place and that she would be taken to her death instead made her feel sick to her stomach. Sadr assured her that her fears were unfounded. But Nazanin's head pounded and pain shot from her right temple down her arms and into her back.

After about half an hour, a thin man with a bushy black beard walked through the door. "It's time," he said to Mostafaei. "The trial is about to begin."

Nazanin followed the guard down the corridor that led to a set of double doors and then into a large auditorium, with seats placed in a curve that stretched from one side of the room to the other. Almost all the seats were taken. As she moved to the front of the room people whispered "Good luck!" to her. She lowered her head even further, so that her chin was nearly touching her chest. Then she heard a woman's voice say, "We are with you," and she breathed a little easier.

Nazanin sat beside Sadr. Feeling Sadr so close, Nazanin gained the confidence to turn her head slowly to the side to take a look at the people in the auditorium. Her eyes rested on her mother, sitting beside Arsalan, and beside him, her father. "You came," she mouthed the words. "You came!"

Nazanin's gaze then moved slowly to the judges. They were sitting on a stage behind a long wooden desk flanked by orange curtains. Nazanin's pulse quickened when she caught a glimpse of the chief judge's cold, dark eyes. It was a different chief judge from her earlier trial. This one was old, his grey beard almost white, and wore a robe and black turban.

NAZANIN KEPT HER HEAD LOWERED throughout the judge's explanation of the charges laid against her and even once Mostafaei stood at the podium and stated Nazanin's position.

"Mahabad Fatehi, known as Nazanin, is a girl who, at age seventeen, defended herself and her niece in Karaj," he said in his deep, strong voice that always struck Nazanin as odd given his gentle, kind face. "In doing so, Nazanin Fatehi killed a young man. We will present evidence that Nazanin was defending her honour and chastity."

Hamid, Roozbeh, Mahmoud and Salman were all present and announced as witnesses. One of the men then introduced himself as Judge Tardast and asked Mahmoud to stand. After swearing on the Qur'an that what he was about to say was the truth, Mahmoud recounted almost the same testimony as in the first trial, including that he, Salman and Yousef were not provoking the girls but were instead trying to frighten them so that they would go away. Nazanin's heart beat wildly, and she felt a huge weight forming in her stomach. Nothing was different at this new trial. She found herself sinking into her chair.

She didn't move a muscle until about halfway through Salman's testimony, when she—and the other judges, who had appeared uninterested in Mahmoud's testimony—leaned forward.

"Did you know Roozbeh and Hamid?" Judge Soleymani Nia was asking.

"I do not know," Salman said. His face was red and his forehead was dripping with sweat.

"I will repeat the question," the judge said impatiently. "Did you know Roozbeh and Hamid before the incident?"

"We knew each other a bit." A collective gasp filled the courtroom, for this was the first acknowledgment that all the young men were connected.

"Did you ask Hamid and Roozbeh and the girls to come with you to an abandoned building?"

"I do not know," he said.

"You have raised controversial remarks in this trial court, and you pretend to not remember anything, and I do not think this is the case," Judge Eftekhari said.

"Believe me, if I remember anything, I will mention it," Salman replied coldly.

"In your various statements you have mentioned that Mahmoud said something that caused conflict between you and the two girls. What was that sentence?" the judge asked.

"I do not know. I do not remember," Salman said.

"I will repeat the sentence that Mahmoud said and that started the argument: 'I went to see Roozbeh that day; when he heard about the girls, I said to Roozbeh, "If the girls are willing to come along to a house, we can go together."' Is that right?"

"Yes," Salman said sheepishly as many people in the courtroom shook their heads. "Mahmoud's fight started with the two girls then," Salman added, almost as an afterthought.

"In your other testimony, you said you didn't do anything to anger the girls. Do you not think inviting them to an abandoned house would anger them?"

"Yes," Salman said in a quiet voice. "I admit we had intentions."

It was then Roozbeh's turn to testify. He corroborated Salman's testimony. "Before we met the girls at the market, Mahmoud approached me," Roozbeh explained. "He said he had an unoccupied house and we could go there if we wanted to. I told him that

Somayeh and Nazanin were not that type of people. But he and his friends were not convinced and kept repeating the proposal to Nazanin when they saw her."

"And what was that proposal?" one of the judges asked.

"'We have an empty house'—that's what Yousef said to Nazanin."

"What else?" the judge probed.

"'We'll have some fun. That's what Kurdish girls like you are good for.'"

"Why didn't you do anything to stop it?" Judge Kouh Kamarei asked.

"I do not know," Roozbeh sighed, shaking his head. "Maybe I was scared."

"When Yousef suggested to Nazanin to go to the abandoned house, did she accept?" Judge Kouh Kamarei asked.

"No. She got in a fight with Yousef. She wanted him to stop harassing her. He wouldn't."

"Why did you run away and leave the girls alone to fend for themselves when you knew they were in danger?" Judge Tardast asked.

"I was scared." Roozbeh lowered his head. "I was scared."

Nazanin was called to the stand. She stood up on shaking legs, pulled her chador tightly around herself and began telling the judges her story—the same one since day one. "It started at 9 a.m. when my mother gave me money to go shopping at the market for Nowruz," she said in the most confident voice she could muster, a voice she managed to maintain throughout her recounting of events.

"They were on top of Somayeh," she ended her statement. "I thought they were going to rape her."

"Your father has raised the case that you and Somayeh ran away from home and that he did not recognize you two girls as his daughter and grandchild. Is this true?" asked Judge Abdollahi.

"My father is present here at this trial," Nazanin said, swallowing hard, her throat dry. She wanted desperately to believe that this claim was not true.

Nazanin's father stood and addressed the judges. "It is important that this information be cleared for the sake of my family."

"But these claims that she was a runaway are in her file," Judge Abdollahi countered.

"Then you need to look and see who made such allegations," her father replied. "I never said such things to anyone."

WHEN IT WAS HER TURN to take the stand, Nazanin's mother, who had been teary through most of Nazanin's testimony, spoke about how unfair it was that her daughter had had to sign her own death sentence in prison by stamping her inked finger on a line of a document written in Persian. "Nazanin has no education. She doesn't understand anything. She is just a child," Maryam wailed, falling to the ground. Nazanin's father rushed to her side and pulled her up. Her crying was so loud that a guard told her to leave the room until she had calmed down.

Sadr talked about the risks young women like Nazanin face in Iran because of abuse in the home and lack of services in the community for families in distress and for girls who need refuge. She addressed the stigma of being a runaway girl: being automatically labelled a prostitute, and how, if she had been sexually assaulted by Yousef, she was dead anyway in the eyes of society.

Mostafaei then went to the podium to address the judges again. "In the first trial in Court Branch 71, the judges rejected Nazanin's defence, saying she had no honour to defend because she was a runaway. I only became aware of this when I took on the file. But the reality is that, at the time of the incident, she was a juvenile. She was seventeen and she was defending her honour and trying to protect her fourteen-year-old niece." He then brought into evidence that Iran is a party to international conventions governing the fair treatment of juveniles, including not sentencing to death people who had committed crimes as a child.

"You cannot find any woman facing violent attack who will not react," said Mostafaei, "and with all her strength fight back to protect herself and her body. Nazanin didn't have any intention other than defending herself and her niece. She didn't even try to kill, but her defensive reaction resulted in his death. Because of this reason, I ask the court to consider these factors before reaching its verdict."

NAZANIN WAS TAKEN BACK to her cell at Evin. Sadr had told her before she left the courtroom that she felt they were successful but that they wouldn't know the judges' decision for many days.

A couple of days later, Nazanin awoke to cheering and Shahla jumping on top of her to say that the papers were full of the judges' comments. "Reporters asked the judges after everyone had left what they were going to do," Shahla told Nazanin. "They all said innocent . . . of premeditated murder. The judges believed you. Your actions were done in self-defence."

Nazanin shook her head slowly, then looked up into Shahla's sparkling eyes. "So there is hope for all of you too?" she asked. "We'll all go home one day?"

Shahla nodded. "Yes, I hope so. We'll all go home one day."

ABOUT TEN DAYS AFTER HER TRIAL, Nazanin received the official news that the papers had already reported: the court had exonerated her of murder. The judges had ruled she acted in self-defence and she could go free. However, in the court documents that were released, the judges also ruled that she used disproportionate force to defend herself and she had to pay *diyeh*, or blood money, to receive a pardon from Yousef's family. Because she had killed a Muslim man, she had to pay more than she would have had he been non-Muslim. She would also have to pay additional fees because the killing took place during the month of Muharram, one of four holy months of the year in the Islamic calendar, during which fighting is strictly prohibited.

For Nazanin to gain her freedom she had to give Yousef's family the equivalent of US$45,000.

Sadr and Mostafaei filed an appeal for payment of the blood money, arguing that since the judges had ruled her actions were self-defence, she should not have to pay anything. But the appeal could take as long as six months to be heard. When Nazanin heard this, tears started to stream down her cheeks.

"So I have to stay here?" she asked Sadr when she visited her in Evin Prison.

"Yes."

A few days later, Mostafaei met with Nazanin. He had received permission from the court to let her out of prison on bail. The bail was the same amount as the blood money, and if the court ruled that she had to pay Yousef's family *diyeh*, the bail would cover it. Nazanin then learned that the entire $45,000 had been raised by her namesake, Nazanin Afshin-Jam in Canada, who had been campaigning for her release. Some $35,000 had been raised, with a lot of effort, through online donations, mostly from the West; the final $10,000 was topped off by Canadian member of Parliament Belinda Stronach.

"You can leave," Mostafaei told Nazanin. "You are free!"

That night, dozens of people, including Mostafaei and Sadr, Nazanin's family and supporters, and camera crews and print journalists, stood waiting outside Evin Prison, some holding bouquets of flowers and gifts. But Nazanin never came out.

CHAPTER 27

NAZANIN AFSHIN-JAM
AND NAZANIN FATEHI

January 31, 2007, Vancouver and Tehran, Iran

—————

"She is coming out now!" Mina squealed over the telephone. "She is coming out now."

I wanted to believe it. But there had been so many ups and downs over the past few months that I was leery. The last letdown was a few days before Nazanin was supposed to be released, when Mostafaei had discovered that there were outstanding payments that had not been made from another trial. Nazanin had been found guilty of having broken some fluorescent light bulbs at Rajai Shahr Prison the day she found out she was given the death sentence. Mostafaei and a generous Iranian-American businessman named Jafar raised the money to pay the damages the judge had ordered, which amounted to about $5,000.

"Are you sure she will be released this time?" I asked Mina, who was in Germany, alternately speaking to me on one line and to a client's daughter, who was standing outside Evin Prison, on another.

"I just got the phone call from Shahla. She used one of the guards' cellphones. Nazanin is coming out right now."

"Does Shahla know for certain?" I asked cautiously. It was early morning in Vancouver, so it would be evening in Tehran. I assumed that they didn't release prisoners at night.

"The guard just came and got Nazanin," Mina said. "Nazanin

had her things and was saying goodbye to all the prisoners. She is coming out right now."

Much of the same crowd that had gathered outside Evin Prison the first time they thought she would be released was there again, shivering in the damp, cold January air. Nazanin's mother held a khaki ski jacket for Nazanin. It was the second time in her life that Nazanin would receive a new coat. Her siblings were also all there to welcome her back to freedom and take her home. Shahla and Parastoo were the most excited, holding each other's hands, closing their eyes and praying that this would indeed be the day they would be reunited with their sister.

It felt like a year since I had last taken a deep breath, exhaled and relaxed. I said, "Thank you, Lord. Thank you for answering my prayers." A tear slipped down my cheek as I imagined Nazanin's first taste of freedom after nearly two years in prison. "Are cameras there to capture the moment? I want to see her face," I told Mina.

"Yes, a few cameras. Not as many as when we thought she was coming out before. But enough that the world will see this victory. The regime has been brought to its knees."

"How does Shahla get to use one of the guards' phones?" I asked. "I thought they didn't let the prisoners use phones except for once a week for a few minutes?"

Mina laughed. "The prisoners all like Shahla because she connects them with others like me outside Iran, who can lobby on behalf of their cases. But the guards like her because she is famous, having been linked to the footballer Nasser Mohammadkhani. She gets what she wants."

"I hope Shahla gets a fair trial," I said.

"And Fatemeh," Mina said hopefully. "Don't forget Fatemeh and all the other women still sitting behind bars."

IN TEHRAN, EVIN PRISON'S MAIN GATE opened no wider than the distance between Nazanin's two shoulders. The lights of the

TV cameras focused in on the crack. The crowd became quiet and Nazanin's mother, for the first time since she was a child, held her breath and said a prayer she had heard Nazanin recite many times. *And the sun—it runs to a fixed resting place; that is the ordaining of the All-mighty, the All-knowing—And the moon—We have determined it by stations, till it returns like an aged palm bough. It behooves not the sun to overtake the moon, neither does the night outstrip the day, each swimming in a sky.*

Wearing a black headscarf and black dress, Nazanin emerged. She was moving slowly from the trauma she had endured, but her eyes danced in the camera light.

Her mother, smiling from ear to ear, ran toward Nazanin and wrapped the warm jacket around her, kissing her face multiple times.

"You told me once that a *doanoos* had predicted that your tattoo would be seen all over the world. I think this is now," Nazanin whispered as the cameras filmed their embrace.

"I made a wish while you were in prison," her mother sobbed. "I wished that if you got your freedom, we would once and for all be done with this horrible curse and that *doanoos*."

"We will no longer be *bawbakht*?" Nazanin asked.

"No more *bawbakht*," her mother cried, squeezing Nazanin tightly in her arms.

When her mother finally let go, Nazanin stared up into the starlit indigo night sky and recited the Yaseen Sura. "I am free, Khwa," she then whispered. "You heard me, Khwa. You answered my prayers. I am free!"

Nazanin Afshin-Jam

———————

Nazanin Fatehi's release on January 31, 2007, was one of the happiest days of my life. She told me that the suffocating feeling of having a noose around her neck had finally lifted. She was reunited with her family, and for many months afterward, her family, neighbours and strangers in the larger Iranian community treated her like a star. She and her family received flowers, bags of rice, fruits and desserts to celebrate her new-found freedom and the victory over the Iranian regime's draconian use of sharia law. Nazanin was hopeful after her release. She said it was like being reborn, where she had a new chance at life. She wanted to go to school, get an education and become a lawyer so she could help others like her.

The first conversation I ever had with her—over the telephone, of course, as I would never be permitted to enter Iran—was on the day of her release. We spoke Persian and she talked about how happy she was. She was thankful for everything I had done, but I explained that there were many people all over the world, including the 350,000 who signed the petition, who had played a part in securing her freedom.

We spoke frequently after that and, when we became comfortable with each other, we both recounted the struggles we had endured during the year our lives wound around each other. Slowly, Nazanin began to confide in me stories about prison and of her present life and her past. Over time, though, our conversations became less regular. For one, Nazanin was settling into a new life. And I had other families with children on death row contacting me, pleading for help. I realized that my journey with Nazanin was just the beginning. There were many others who desperately needed help, not only in Iran but in the four other Islamic countries—Saudi Arabia, Yemen, Sudan and Nigeria—whose penal codes also incorporate a strict interpretation of sharia law, which, among other things, condemns minors to execution for activities such as sex outside marriage, homosexuality, drug trafficking and apostasy.

Nazanin Fatehi's campaign had inspired me to continue doing what I did for Nazanin for others, by assembling the major players who had dedicated much of their time and talents to the Save Nazanin campaign: Kristian Hvesser, David Etebari, Donna Greene and, of course, Vincent, with whom I had kept in touch since he sent that initial email to me about Nazanin's death sentence.

For a while, Nazanin's name was on the lips of many in Iran. But the press attention slowly faded. And while others may have forgotten about her, I could never forget her soft voice as she recounted to me, during hours upon hours of phone conversations, stories that made me smile and then made me cry. I would hang up thinking, *How could one person have suffered so much in such a short life?*

I tried to help her as much as I could, sending money from time to time for a cellphone so we could keep in touch, and for clothes and other items she needed and wanted. Mohammad Mostafaei did the same by helping set her up in a new home and providing her with household items, including a television. Unfortunately, we could not sustain her on our own. She needed counselling, schooling and eventually a job.

People in Europe, the United States and Canada had offered to house and feed her, and help pay for her education. "I want to come to Canada to be near you and go to school," Nazanin told me. I thought that perhaps emigration to a country with a political system not so judgmental of her past and where she could be assisted in escaping the cycle of poverty her family had fallen into might not be such a bad idea. I spoke with members of Canada's Parliament to see if she could immigrate to Canada, especially since she had been threatened several times by members of Yousef's family, who said they would seek their revenge. The office of Canadian citizenship and immigration said she would be a strong candidate to be accepted. Yet, after months of encouragement to get her *shenasnameh*—her ID card—updated with a photo so that she could apply for an Iranian passport, she still had not.

I don't know whether, subconsciously, Nazanin wasn't ready to leave her homeland and family, or whether there were other obstacles. One day her excuse was that she could not read to fill out the required paperwork, so I hired someone to help her fill out the documents. The next day it was that she had a doctor's appointment and couldn't make it. The many excuses made me eventually realize that she was not ready.

I strongly encouraged Nazanin to go to the Omid-e-Mehr centre in Tehran, run by an organization that helps self-empower, educate and train young disadvantaged women ages fifteen to twenty-five. I later contacted the centre's founder, Marjaneh Halati, who informed me that Nazanin had been at the centre for less than two days. When I asked Nazanin why she hadn't told me, and she replied that she had missed her family and wanted to be with them, so had left. My father and I spent hours trying to convince her that the centre would open up opportunities for her and that she should give it another try. She agreed to try again. But she never showed. When I asked her about this, she said her mother was sick and she needed to take care of her and the family.

In the last year that we spoke, we talked about writing a book together to help raise awareness of the plight of other children on death row. "I have suffered so much," she told me, "and my story needs to be told. I want the whole world to know."

Around the time of this conversation, Susan McClelland, an award-winning magazine and book writer, contacted me to write an article about a young couple I had helped to acquire asylum in Canada. They had been imprisoned while taking part in the student uprisings in Tehran in 1999 and had been punished for wearing a Christian cross and being in possession of a Bible. After their release, they went into hiding, fearing further persecution for their religious beliefs. Finally, fearing death at the hands of the Iranian regime if they remained, they managed to get out of Iran—on foot over the treacherous mountains of Kurdistan—only to be imprisoned in Turkey for illegally entering the country.

I felt comfortable with Susan. She is sensitive and compassionate and non-partisan, similar to me, with the same fire I have in my belly to do something about the rampant human rights abuses in the world. She is deeply spiritual and, also like me, wanted to be a nun when she was younger. *She gets it*, I thought. I wanted her to help me write this book. So I asked Susan to artistically express the repressive nature of Iran's regime on women and children.

I was, however, increasingly losing contact with Nazanin. She had been complaining that she had gotten so used to the pills in prison that she could barely fall asleep on her own, and that when she did finally fall asleep, she had nightmares about Yousef and Mohsen. She was growing more and more afraid for her physical safety, saying at one point that she thought her phone was tapped. A few times, Nazanin's male cousin answered her phone, saying curtly, "Nazanin is out." One day we managed to talk for about ten minutes, during which time she told me excitedly that she had fallen in love and hoped to be married to the man one day. A little while after that, Nazanin called my home, leaving a message saying she was in desperate need of money. She had never called me before—it was always I who initiated contact. But I could not get hold of her in return.

Months passed, and I still could not find her. I tried contacting her through several channels. I got in touch with Iran's most active Kurdish political parties, which have connections with the community. They could not find her. I offered reward money for anyone who could locate her family—none of them could be found.

I hope she is now married and living happily, with peace in her life. But my questions lead me to believe otherwise. Where is her family? Why would they move without telling anyone? Why does her aunt's phone number, which I used every now and again to reach Nazanin, no longer work? Did the regime threaten Nazanin and her family? Did Yousef's family do something tragic? Did Nazanin run off and get married without permission from her family? I hope one day I will have the answers. I am her concerned older sister and pray that she is safe, cared for and loved.

Needless to say, while I have searched for her, I have also worked on fulfilling her wish for this story to be told. I provided Susan with weeks of recorded interviews with Nazanin. She took my interviews, which were a skeleton of the story, and then worked closely with members of the Kurdish and Iranian communities in Toronto and flew to Iraqi Kurdistan—she would not have been granted an entry visa for Iran given her connection to me and this book—to recreate Nazanin's life story and make it as reflective as possible of the young girl's struggles.

Although the characters in this book are based on real people in Nazanin's life, some of the names have been changed to protect their identity. As well, because we were not able to work directly with Nazanin during her case, nor with many other people portrayed in this book, some of their physical characteristics and personality traits are either accentuated or created, and some of the scenes, though based on actual events in Nazanin's life, are in part created from close research and from discussions Susan and I had with informed members of the Kurdish community as to what Nazanin's life may have been like.

Research for the book was further complicated due to incomplete and contradictory court documents pertaining to the hearings and trials, which is not uncommon in Iran. Among other things, timelines are not consistent and official court files and unofficial interviews in the press provide different versions and perspectives of what witnesses told the court. For literary purposes we also combined certain hearings and trials into one, including Nazanin's retrial in August 2006 and the final trial in January 2007.

Since becoming involved with Nazanin's case, I have dedicated much of my life to stopping child executions. To this day, I continue to lobby international governments, non-governmental organizations and individuals to put pressure on Iran and other offending countries to commute the sentences and ban the execution of children, defined by the United Nations as being persons under the age of eighteen. Under sharia law, on which Iran's penal code is based, girls are considered adults at nine, and boys at fifteen, and so they are held criminally responsible for their actions at these ages. This is in violation of several international conventions that the country is a party to, including the International Covenant on Civil and Political Rights and the Convention on the Rights of the Child. At the time of writing, 160 children were estimated to be on death row in Iran.

Since Nazanin's release, I have been inspired to see many people around me, from high school students to whom I had presented the story to members of my family, become involved in campaigns that inspire them—including a walkathon to raise money for women impacted by the conflict in northern Uganda. My sister, Naz, raised a million dollars to help rehabilitation centres for bears in Asia that had spent their lives in small prison cells no bigger than the width of their body, their bile painfully extracted drip by drip by catheters for use in traditional Chinese medicines.

NAZANIN FATEHI'S LIFE was spared. But other juveniles did not have similar fates.

Books could and should be written on each and every child who has been killed by the state of Iran. People need to hear their stories, listen to their voices and honour their souls so that the dead are remembered. Delara Darabi, for example, was executed on May 1, 2009, at a prison in Rasht, Iran. At just seventeen years old, she was convicted of murdering her father's female cousin. Darabi originally confessed to the murder, even though evidence showed she could not have committed the crime. She later admitted that her boyfriend, Amir Hossein

Sotoudeh, was responsible for the murder. He had told Darabi that he would face execution if convicted but, because she was under eighteen, her life would be spared. Before she died, Darabi retracted her statement, and Sotoudeh received a ten-year prison term for his crime.

Makwan Moloudzadeh was executed December 5, 2007, at Kermanshah Central Prison. His alleged crime? Homosexuality. He was accused of committing anal rape with other young boys when he was thirteen years old. All of the witnesses who alleged that Moloudzadeh had attacked them retracted their pre-trial statements during the trial and admitted that what took place was consensual.

On July 19, 2005, Mahmoud Asgari and Ayaz Marhoni, both Iranian teenagers, were hanged in Edalat (Justice) Square in Mashhad, northeastern Iran, for the same offence.

Mohammad Mousavi, a juvenile on death row whose mother had been promised that her son would be released if she would not disclose the death sentence to the media, was executed nonetheless on April 22, 2007, in Shiraz. She only learned of her son's death two weeks afterwards.

While most of the estimated fifty children who have been executed in Iran since 1990 were convicted of murder, the testimonies and evidence against them and their own statements are spotty and almost always inconclusive. But paramount is that all the individuals were under the age of eighteen at the time of their alleged crimes. And, if anything, the incidents were school or street fights gone wrong and not done with premeditation. My hearts are also with the families who have lost their loved ones. Antediluvian laws combined with a regime that has intensified its domestic socioeconomic problems have put many children at risk, as Nazanin was. Troubled youth should not be executed; they should be rehabilitated.

Executions were rampant in Iran during the 1980s, and particularly in 1988. Tens of thousands of people, including children, who were perceived to be a threat to the new Islamic regime were executed. Other individuals whose stories stand out include sixteen-year-old Mona Mahmudnizhad, who along with nine other Baha'i women, was executed in June 1983. Her crime? Teaching Baha'i children's classes. Because her youth and conspicuous innocence became a symbol of the group of Baha'is in prison, she was lashed on the soles of her feet with a cable and forced to walk on bleeding feet. On the day of the execution she asked to be the last in line to be executed so she could pray for the others. All she had to do to avoid execution was denounce her faith, but she refused, and instead, when it was her turn, she kissed the rope and put it herself around her neck.

And last but not least, Dina Parnabi, an Iranian high school student accused of smuggling forbidden literature and criticizing the regime in conversations with schoolmates, was hanged on July 10, 1984, in Tehran. Afterward, her body was stripped and taken to a medical school for dissection.

In 2008, I was approached by two of Canada's political parties to be a candidate in the election expected that year. I chose not to, for a few reasons. Foremost, I wanted to focus on my human rights work. I also couldn't see myself representing any of the political parties and supporting positions or platforms on issues I didn't agree with 100 percent. I've always been non-partisan. I support one party for how it addresses some issues; I support another party on other issues. With this decision made—after a long deliberation, for I did realize being a member of Parliament would give me a platform for the human rights work—I wrote a detailed report in 2009 aimed at policy makers titled *From Cradle to Coffin: A Report on Child Executions in Iran* with Tahirih Danesh. To view the report, visit http://fpc.org.uk/fsblob/1063.pdf.

The women mentioned in the book who cared for Nazanin in prison also met their untimely deaths at the hands of the regime. Fatemeh Haghighat-Pajouh, Nazanin's cellmate and mother of two who had been sentenced to death for having killed her husband when he attempted to rape her daughter, was executed on November 26, 2008. Shahla Jahed, Nazanin's fellow prisoner, was executed on December 1, 2010, at Evin Prison.

In the summer of 2010, Mohammad Mostafaei, who had become one of Tehran's most recognized human rights lawyers, defending numerous children and women for crimes that would be seen as misdemeanours in the West, was forced to flee into exile after he was harassed and his wife and brother-in-law were held in prison as ransom until he presented himself at the jail. Many foreign observers have wrongly speculated that Mostafaei had to leave because of the international publicity that was shone on the case of Sakineh Mohammadi Ashtiani, initially sentenced to death by stoning for adultery, and later sentenced to death by hanging for alleged complicity in her husband's murder. (Ashtiani now has a stay of execution, thanks in no small part to the international campaigns, including one initiated by Heather Reisman, CEO of Indigo Books and Music, and supported by, among many others, Louise Dennys, publisher and editor at Random House Canada, and Laureen Harper, wife of the prime minister of Canada.) Rather, Mostafaei had to leave Iran after he had taken on political cases. Susan and I met Mostafaei—to get details of Nazanin's trial and prison life—along with his wife, Fereshteh, and daughter, who all now live in Norway, from where Mostafaei continues the fight.

Nazanin's other lawyer, Shadi Sadr, fled Iran after being beaten by Iranian plainclothes volunteer militia, called the Basij, and after serving several prison terms for her activism. Sadr has received numerous awards for her human rights work and for her bravery, and she too continues her human rights activities abroad.

Lawyer Shahram Tahi, a legal adviser to Nazanin Fatehi's family, who had been particularly helpful during her retrial, emailed me for the first time in July 2011. Shortly afterward, he began to receive suspicious phone calls that led him to believe he was under surveillance by the regime. Fearing for his safety, he fled to Canada, seeking asylum as a refugee.

Mina Ahadi continues to fight fervently for Iranian rights as head of the International Committee against Executions and the International Committee against Stoning, and as principal founder of the German Central Council of Ex-Muslims.

Despite the challenges and what seems to be a never-ending uphill battle to end child executions, I continue my fight. I have come to the realization, however, that in order to make significant and lasting change in Iran, whereby its citizens have a chance at exercising their human rights and freedoms, this regime must go. I am in the process of forming an organization called United People of Iran, which will be the first attempt of a larger United People project, through which disenfranchised citizens living under repressive rule can join together to help bring freedom and democracy to their countries. Given that the United Nations' membership includes undemocratic nation-states whose authoritarian leaders do not represent the voices of the people, an alternative global institution needs to be established either in place of, or running parallel to, the United Nations. To whom does someone like Nazanin turn when her government has sanctioned her death, despite Iran being signatory to international conventions forbidding it? To whom do the Iranian people turn when their leaders, Ayatollah Khomeini and his puppet, Mahmoud Ahmadinejad, do not represent their voices? Instead of a United Nations, at this point in history we are in need of a "United People." We must create a body that acts as a voice for the voiceless.

Through Nazanin's campaign, I learned many life lessons that will stay with me forever. I count my blessings and thank God every day for allowing me to live in a safe, peaceful, free and democratic country where the rule of law and constitution are based on human rights. I am thankful for having been born in a loving and caring family. I am grateful that through this campaign I truly learned the power of the individual and even more so the strength of good people coming together, striving to do good and making positive changes in this world. I am thankful that I can share this story so that others may be inspired to start their own campaigns or fight for justice in their own way. Drop by drop we can create an ocean of change to put out the fires of injustice in this world.

One promising outcome is that, in February 2012, Iranian officials announced that the country's new penal code put an end to child executions. Sadly, in reality, it's not that simple. A careful examination of the relevant clauses reveals that child executions for drug trafficking have been abolished, but that for murder cases it still remains at the judges' discretion whether a juvenile should face capital punishment. Also, the age of criminal responsibility has not been changed. But at least Iranian authorities are moving in the right direction. We can only keep up the pressure in the hope that they do more.

I am also thankful that through this campaign I met my husband, Canadian member of Parliament from Nova Scotia, Peter MacKay. In 2007, when some children were facing imminent execution, Peter, then minister of foreign affairs, condemned Iran for its human rights violations and pressured state officials to grant these children stays of execution. He intervened personally on some of the cases with his counterpart in Iran. I believe Peter was instrumental in helping to save the lives of some of these children.

Together Peter and I hope to start a family and through our children continue to spread love, compassion and a sense of civic responsibility to give back to this world that has given us so much.

The process of writing this book allowed me to reflect upon Nazanin Fatehi's difficult life, the vulnerable position she was in that led to death row, and the steps I can take to help other women and children in desperate circumstances, both in North America and abroad. *The Tale of Two Nazanins* has thus inspired me to help children and women in distress by supporting and funding educational, counselling, shelter and legal programs, in an attempt to help break the cycles of poverty and abuse that put many at risk. I would also like to develop empowerment and leadership programs for girls and young women, so they can be exposed to great female role models who inspire and guide them to reach their own full potential. I am committing half of my royalties from sales of this book to these initiatives, to honour the story of Nazanin Fatehi. More information on these future plans can be found at www.nazanin.ca.

ACKNOWLEDGEMENTS

This book would not have been possible without the generous assistance of Andy Faas, sponsor for travel and research;
Fabien Baussart, travel sponsor; Soraya Fallah, Kurdish subject matter expert and researcher; Amil Imani, Iranian researcher and fact
checker; Afshin Afshin-Jam, fact checker; Dave Duke and Allan
Marron, lawyers; and Khalid Aboulela.

And for their invaluable guidance and wisdom, thank you to
Noreldin Waisy, freelance journalist, London and Iraqi Kurdistan;
human rights activist Mina Ahadi; Bootan Tahseen, director of the
Bas-news company, Iraqi Kurdistan; Jaleh Afshin-Jam; Fereydoon
Rahmani, chair of the Greater Toronto Kurdish House; Tarq Karezy,
author and journalist, Iraqi Kurdistan; Lily Pourzand; Mehrak
Mehrvar; Ava Homa; Mohammad Mostafaei and Fereshteh Halimi,
Norway; Jaffer Sheyholislami, Carleton University; Yadi Nar and
Babak Yazdi; Shahram Tahi; Mohammad Reza Barjesteh; James
Smith, AEGIS Trust, United Kingdom; Robert Harris, University
of Oxford; and Dr. Izzeldin Abuelaish and Amir Hassanpour,
University of Toronto. Thank you to Rob Collins, Victoria Hughes
and Joyce McGuiney of Blake, Cassels & Graydon LLP and to Janet
Cottrelle of RBC Dominion Securities Inc. for their assistance with
establishing a charity to help women and children in distress. We
would also like to thank our publisher, HarperCollins—in particular, Jim Gifford, Iris Tupholme, David Kent, Leo MacDonald, Neil
Erickson, Noelle Zitzer, Kelly Hope, Rob Firing and Sonya Koson.
Thanks, as well, to copy editor Judy Phillips and proofreader Sarah

Wight. And to Eric Jerpe—may he rest in peace, and may his vision of a better world come to fruition.

Thank you to the following people for putting a remarkable amount of time and energy into helping Nazanin Fatehi: Mina Ahadi; Mohammad Mostafaei; Shadi Sadr; Shahram Tahi; Belinda Stronach; Rod Zimmer; Kristian Hvesser; David Etebari; Nima from MasterDev; Afshin Afshin-Jam; James Schouw; Peter, Naz and Riley Karroll; and Ali Adab. Thank you for your specific roles in advancing the Save Nazanin campaign: Vincent M., Negar Azmudeh, Nahid Riazi, Lloyd Axworthy, Payam Akhavan, Persian Princes, Andy Knight, Emma Bonino, Nazanin Fatehi's neighbour in Karaj and Hands Off Cain.

We would also like to thank many other people who have helped in different ways:

People who initially stepped up to the plate: TT, Dr. Mitra, and Babak.

United Nations personnel, including Louise Arbour, Sylvia Hordosch, Shyamala Alagendra, Fannie Lafontaine, Craig Mokhiber, Goro Onojima and Abiodum Williams.

Canadian parliamentarians, including Royal Galipeau, Dan McTeague, Alexa McDonough, Caroline St-Hilaire, Jason Kenney and Peter MacKay; and designated officials Amir Rouhani, Maria McClintock and Mark Entwistle.

Amnesty International, including Ruth Juettner, Anabel Bermejo, Senta Piringer, Kate Willingham, Cheryl Hotchkiss, Pat Maguire, John Tackaberry and Drewery Dyke.

Dedicated journalists and activists: Mitra Khalatbari; Asieh Amini; Darius Kadivar; Potkin Azarmehr; Kawa Ahangari; KRSI's Alireza Morovati, Pari Abasalti and Farrokh Javid; Mostafa Saber; Iman Foroutan; Ahmad Baharloo; Behnood Mokri; Cyrus Marvasti; Minoo; Beryl Wajsman; Asieh Namdar; Nasrine Sotoudeh; Marjaneh Halati; Abdolsamad Khorramshahi; Kathryn Lopez; Nafsika Karagiannidi; Manocher Masori; Pia and Jamshid Atiabi; Reza Pardisan; Saeed Movahed; Jean-Pierre Montanay; Eric Fournier; Zari Asli; Abass

Mohamadi; Farah Pahlavi; Fahimeh Sadeghi; Irshad Manji; Roya Teimouri; Nazanin Boniadi; Shabnam Assadollahi; Maryam Aghvami; Jian Ghomeshi and many others.

The documentary team, including Hossein Fazeli, M.-N., Naros, Calvin Ayre, Nima S., Miguel Hernandez, Sarah Bergeest and Kirk Karasin.

Lawyers without Borders, which generously offered assistance with former governor-general Michaëlle Jean's inquiry, in particular Poupak Bahamin, Ann-Julie Auclair, Atoosa Mahdavian and Pierre Brun.

Thank you for your contacts and help: Seena Rejal, (BA)2K, Goli Ameri, Fariborz Maseeh, Jamshid Ghajar, Raoul Juneja, Kal Suurkask, Shabnam Rezaei, Shaun Lawless and James McAllister.

And others for your generous support, including Jason Gordon, Miljenko Horvat, Simon Zandkarimi, Farid Rezazadeh, Renate Geering, Naeim Asady, Steven Goitia, Steve Summers, Aasem Sulehria and Hamed Sepehri.

Thank you to all those who requested not to be named and the 350,000-plus people who signed the Save Nazanin petition or have written letters to the UN, Iranian officials, local media, parliamentarians and blogs.

Thank you to the Stop Child Executions volunteers who came afterward and spent months and years forming the organization, including co-founder David Etebari, D.W. Duke, Kristian Hvesser and Donna Greene; and subsequent volunteers, including Aubrey Harris, Afshin Afshin-Jam, Behnaz Shahriari, Aida Khanoom, Hannah Bahmanpour, Lucy Blitz, Mel, Dave Rea, Mojgan G., Inna Lazareva and Tahirih Danesh.

May God bless you all.